Date Due

FEB 27 1986

DATE DUE

PRINTED IN CANADA

JOHN L. GREENWAY

THE GOLDEN HORNS

MYTHIC IMAGINATION AND THE NORDIC PAST

THE UNIVERSITY OF GEORGIA PRESS
ATHENS

Library of Congress Catalog Card Number: 74–30676
International Standard Book Number: 0–8203–0384–4

The University of Georgia Press, Athens 30602

Set in 11 on 13 point Times Roman type
Printed in the United States of America

CONTENTS

❖

INTRODUCTION

In 1802 two golden drinking horns, one inscribed with runes, mysteriously disappeared from the Royal Art Museum in Copenhagen. After a marathon conversation with Henrik Steffens, who had returned to Denmark bringing with him the new gospel of transcendental idealism, the young poet Adam Oehlenschläger awoke from his Ossianic slumbers and in 1803 published the poem whose title is also the title of this study. Oehlenschläger depicts a generation of befuddled seventeenth-century antiquarians sensing the lost drama of the days "when it shone from the North, / When heaven was on earth." Insensitive drudges, the scholars "fumble in fog" and pray for insight: "Give a glimpse back!" The Norse gods, "with star-flashing eyes," answer the plea with a gift of the first golden horn.

Mere empiricists are not to be the finders, however; it is to be a lass with lily-white hands, absorbed in love (at the time, love was considered to be the feminine equivalent of masculine genius). As she extracts the horn from the earth, rolling thunder announces the importance of the act. But not even innocence can bring back the golden age, for modern materialism sees the horn only as treasure. A century passes.

In his lectures Steffens maintained that the poetic apprehension of reality is never quite extinguished. For the "seldom few" who understood the gods' gift, "who sense the High / In Nature's eye," the gods will once more give man a hint of his slumbering origins. This time, though, the finder of the horn is to be a "Son of Nature" (i.e., a plowboy), and once again sympathetic imagery underscores the higher significance of the action. Honor these signs from eternity, say the gods, "for fate is capricious; / Perhaps soon they will vanish." Man has a chance, however, to synthesize the two great mythologies, the northern and the southern: "With Jesus' blood fill them, / As blood in the sacred grove." Here, presumably, is the opportunity to reconcile a fate-dominated myth (paganism) with one governed by Providence (Christianity), for the gods' acts have been providential, and it is man who must respond.

But man does not. Digging and measuring, philistines "see only the gleam, / And not the light above." One with a "sated, prying eye" stole the horns in 1803; at the time of the poem's composition, Oehlenschläger did not know that the horns had been melted down for their gold. To the poet, animated by Steffens's dictum to "see history as a whole," the causality is divine: "What they gave, they then rescinded. / Divinity disappeared for evermore."

Though Oehlenschläger's poem came as a revelation to a literary generation, his nostalgia for an era of Nordic heroism had ample precedent. From the time of the editing of Tacitus' *Germania* in the fifteenth century, poets and scholars alike had fondled a vision of heroic, freedom-loving Teutonic ancestors. It is with the why and how of this vision we are concerned in the subsequent pages.

As an introduction to the methodology of *The Golden Horns,* I would like to suggest an initial answer to the "why" of the nostalgia. No culture can exist without an emotional understanding of its origins. The stories of these origins have several functions: first, they give security, in that the stories of the founders depict the genesis of beliefs of the present and verify them. In historical or oracular form they describe and give images to the inceptions of truths a culture holds to be self-evident: that is, moral facts believed axiomatic. Second, these stories of origins bestow a truth upon the beliefs of the group by attributing them to a power outside human will, either divine or secular. Whether the source be divine fiat or historical process, the effect is the same: actions and values are preserved from relativism.

Furthermore, a deterioration of faith in the veracity of these images of genesis produces a "failure of nerve," an emotional isolation which rationality cannot help, for the function of origins is emotional not rational. I will later argue that this deterioration is inevitable, but at this point we can see the dual impact of Oehlenschläger's poem. At a time when catastrophic political events combined with a widespread disenchantment with Enlightenment empiricism, producing just such a failure of nerve, "The Golden Horns" gave the Scandinavian romantic movement its expressive key in announcing that the horns' disappearance was symbolic of a higher order at work. At the same time the poem and the collection in which it appeared (*Poems 1803*) provided an emotionally satisfying and intellectually plausible alembic for revivifying the dormant Nordic spirit.

The sanctity of moral assertion depends in part upon a belief in origins which is not historical, at least not in an empirical sense. It is here we encounter how the Nordic past was so tenaciously established and reestablished as the origin of trans-Alpine civilization. It is here we simultaneously encounter the term *myth*. The necessity for origins is not a rational one, and rational inquiry often engages in "de-mythologizing" formerly self-evident truths. Yet in the American mind, for instance, the West is more real as myth than it is as history. The images of Wyatt Earp and the O.K. Corral will continue to have a cultural reality as a definitive establishment of the relationship between law and bandit, good and evil. Empirically minded historians may "expose" this event as being "merely" mythical ("myth" here taken in the Enlightenment sense of falsehood), but such an exposure will not affect the cultural function of the story, which is to present in dramatic form an image of the origin of social reality. Indeed, the recognition by anthropologists, sociologists, and historians that mythic images are real has called into question the whole possibility of objectivity itself.

We will return to this argument in the conclusion, after the points made above have been treated in more depth, for the dream of the saga era was animated by the same principles. To return to Oehlen-schläger's poem, its text suggests themes which occupy this study. First, Oehlenschläger sees the pagan Nordic past with its own noble response to an inexorable fate; next, he considers the relationship and possible synthesis with Christianity, a perennial problem for all admirers of pre-Christian national antiquity. The Nordic gods (and Oehlenschläger) decree this synthesis, but modern man, his sense for the reality of the ineffable displaced by rationalism and materialism, fails to view the horns correctly, and with a "sated, prying eye" sees only the demythologized objects.

Before this romantic attempt to synthesize a new mythology, there were two great post-Renaissance myths of Nordic origins: one in the seventeenth century was ostensibly scholarly and historical (Olof Rud-beck's mammoth *Atlantica*), the other, in the eighteenth century, apparently primitive and epic (the Ossianic poems). Both of these attained popularity through their mythic elements, but both ultimately lost expressive force through the tension between myth and reason. Their pretense to being objective, historical documents rendered these myths fatally vulnerable to reason's impulse to demythologize. It is a curious irony that the romantic vision of the Nordic past that Oehlenschläger's poem catalyzed was itself to disappear into the darkness, joining Rudbeck and Ossian as objects for a disinterested, prying eye to examine. It is solely for reasons of length that we do not treat the reemergence of the Nordic past as myth of origins in Wagner and the Third Reich, for the animating instinct was the same as in Rudbeck, Ossian, and Oehlenschläger.

A few brief comments on methodology and aims will conclude these introductory remarks. First, although the study is historical, it is not primarily so. Readers wishing a fuller historical treatment of the Nordic Renaissance will be better served by some of the works mentioned in the Bibliography. The material is rich, for Jöran Mjöberg in his two-volume, 862–page chronicling of *The Dream of the Saga-Era* (*Drömmen om sagatiden*) apologizes for lacunae.

However rich the material, most of the works and their authors have been forgotten, existing now only in literary histories and dissertations. Generally, no claim is made here that time has been unjust, that these pastiches are undiscovered masterpieces. Recognizing that many, if not most, of the texts and authors considered will be unfamiliar, I have attempted, albeit briefly, to put them in historical contexts. Readers wishing more detailed biographical and historical data will again be obliged to turn to some of the works mentioned in the Bibliography.

The intent of this study is to explore in a systematic manner the images of the Nordic past and the series of crises and dilemmas in which the myths of the Nordic past—as an example of all myth—has found itself in its entry into the modern world. Neither the crises nor the dilemmas are resolved, for myth is a cultural symbolic structure and man seldom does more than proceed from contradiction to temporary synthesis and then to another contradiction. Yet two points should emerge from the discussion: the reality, ephemeral and however bizarre today, of these images; and the necessity of man to see his history in terms of these images.

The discovery of mythic elements in literature and society in general has reopened discussion of the problem of myth. It is hoped that an understanding of the process by which myth achieved its place in the contemporary world may be of value to scholars in the sociology of knowledge, who have often been accused of vagueness and obscurantism. The justness of these accusations stems, it seems to me, from a lack of precision in definition as well as from an intuitive respect for this aspect of art whose origins and development the critic does not always bother to explore.

Our first concern, then, will be to examine the problem of using *myth* as a term. After discussing myth as a means of organizing reality, we will see how sacred mythic patterns are displaced to regulate profane narrative. The second concern will be to show these principles at work in post-Renaissance European culture and to show the surfacing of the latent tension between myth and reason that so governs the forms of myth in contemporary social reality.

(1)

THE PROBLEM OF MYTH

The very use of the term *myth* runs the danger of arousing suspicion in the minds of the cautious, who with some reason ask whether a word which has come to mean so many things can be a useful tool for critical investigation. The popularity of the term stems in part from assertions by reputable authorities in diverse areas that myth is not fiction, and is not a primitive means of encoding empirical reality; rather, myth is a means of apprehending value in the world with its own inner logic. Indeed, it is asserted that this narrative impulse may be more fundamental to man than reason.

The rehabilitation of myth by scholars such as Ernst Cassirer and Mircea Eliade, together with work by anthropologists such as Bronislaw Malinowski and Claude Lévi-Strauss, has provided a valuable forum for scholars in fields as diverse as theology and economics to discuss the dilemmas of human experience. Yet the assertion of the reality of myth has produced reactions both skeptical and anxious. While, for instance, Reinhold Niebuhr asserts that "meaning can be attributed to history only by a mythology," historians and theologians alike have felt the necessity to "demythologize," to separate truth and fact from myth.[1]

In literary criticism, René Wellek concedes that myth is a form of truth, but he is not willing to bestow the same status on "myth criticism," fearing the consequences of reducing the uniqueness of the work of art to archetypal patterns, a sentiment echoed abroad concerning English-language "myth-criticism." Similarly, Philip Rahv, a critic with concerns different from those of Wellek, sees the protean popularity of the term as engendering a "mythomania," betraying not only literature but religion, and running counter to findings in anthropology and ethnology. Folklorists of the stature of Richard M. Dorson are distressed by the "excessive strainings" of literary scholars and would rather eschew the term.[2] Sociologists of knowledge such as Peter L. Berger and Thomas Luckmann (*The Social Construction of Reality*) and Karl Mannheim (*Ideology and Utopia*) also seem to prefer avoiding the term.[3] Clearly, it is not unwarranted to begin by recognizing myth as a scholarly problem.

Initially, we may say at least that these scholars of myth are less interested in *what* myth symbolizes than *how* myth symbolizes. Cultures and individuals within those cultures know themselves in moral and ethical terms through their orientation in a universe of value symbols, moral referents which constitute their knowledge of good and evil. These symbolic forms are organized into myths which not only formulate in narrative a culture's moral knowledge but in doing so make this knowledge accessible and capable of transmission.

When functional in myth, these symbolic forms are not perceived as being symbols—they are apprehended as an undistinguishable part of reality. Yet "the symbol gives rise to thought," as Paul Ricoeur puts it,[4] and only when the symbolic universe begins to deteriorate does an ironic relationship to the mythic universe set in and the feeling of identity, the sense of belonging to a homogeneous spatial and temporal entity, is lost. When the mythic symbol is perceived as being "merely symbolic,"[5] it either evolves into formal religion, some form of idealism, or relativism, which propounds moral alternatives as freedom from myth.

The primary function of myth is orientation. As Cartesian coordinates provide a means of locating and ordering contents in the profane world through a mathematical reference point, the mythic consciousness orders the world by providing a sacred reference point. A mythic apprehension of space-time can integrate the disparate elements of man's existence by giving a unified moral understanding of events in the profane world. The result of an orientation in the symbolic universe of myth is an understanding of reality in dramatic terms.

Another way of stating this is to recognize myth as a fundamental part of identity, man's knowledge of himself. Through myth man has access to his values and can measure his own experience in the world by sacred paradigms. These images form a reality which is a moral analogue to a culture and its individuals but at the same time stands outside them as objective truth. While it is warranted to emphasize the symbolic nature of the world of myth, it must also be borne in mind that the main function of myth is to provide not values but knowledge of them.

In this context it should be mentioned that an individual has two identities, one communal and the other personal, and herein lies one of the problems of using myth as a critical term. Man knows both these selves—or at least communicates his knowledge of them—through symbols, some of them mythic, but there is a difference in the function of the symbolic expressions of collective identity and the expressions of personal identity. The collective self is known and attains its moral orientation through the myths of its culture. In this sense myth has an adaptive function: it gives the individual a sense of community, a freedom from individuality and anxiety. Personal myths, on the other hand, objectify for an individual subjective experiences and values.

The relationship between personal and communal mythic symbols varies. When the two are identical, the ideal of any form of collectivism may be said to have been attained, in that the individual becomes free through losing the burden of his individuality. When the communal myths cease to be symbolically adequate for the individual, "alienation" (in the contemporary sense of the word) results. Now, an artist may transmit unchanged the communal myths; in this case he will be a loyal socialist realist, a son of the Mother Church, a hero in the people's struggle against bourgeois revanchism, or whatever. Communal myths give him a sufficient and dramatic understanding of the moral world. At the other extreme the artist may have a private mythology which is internally coherent but so estranged from the communal symbolic universe as to be unintelligible. This sort of personal mythology has the effect of disintegrating the individual from the community.

Minds conditioned by the Renaissance and its aftermath—having eaten the apple of scientific consciousness, as it were—find it difficult to view sympathetically a prescientific universe, even though many ostensibly scientific social doctrines and ideologies are fundamentally expressions of a mythic consciousness. In a mythic universe reality—as time and space—has neither a sense of nature governed by mechanical cause nor a sense of a transcendental world of "pure" spirit. To primitive man the world is a play of magical forces apprehended as a unified entity which does not differentiate between the material and the nonmaterial. He has no understanding of such rational principles as cause (in the mechanical sense). Death, which Cassirer holds to be the central preoccupation of the primitive mind, is a consequence of the triumph of evil—and magic—forces, not the inevitable consequence of natural decay. In such a world it is not immortality which must be established (as with modern man) but mortality, for all of life lies within this mythic mode of perception. Life beyond death is not a realm of pure spirit but a corporeal one in the same mythic space and time. This is why both time and cause to the mythic consciousness have a *narrative* quality.[6]

Paul Ricoeur has emphasized the organizing power of these narratives. To the believer, the narrative organizes and sufficiently explains the contradictory imperatives of existence in the world by subordinating them to a revealed sacred cause. While "the myth gives rise to thought," to the believer this reflection does not immediately produce doubt; rather, it provides a freedom from the contingencies of human experience.[7]

If mythic narrative reveals a sacred "why," it does so through recounting origins: of the rite, of the family, of the tribe, of the world. Eliade and others have emphasized the non-linear apprehension of time in myth; through rite and ritual the origin and its organizing power can be made a part of the present, hallowing it. The organizing of time in mythic narrative is the basis for the subordinate position of the secular event in the mythic consciousness. The secular event is true, but insufficiently so. As Raffaele Pettazzoni notes in discussing "The Truth of Myth," history only becomes true when it is sacred history.[8]

Myth's concern with genesis has directed our study of the Nordic past as a myth of origins, but our subject-matter makes the problem of myth more complex yet. Considerable research has been done on myths of origins in primitive or pre-scientific societies. Our thesis, however, is that modern man cannot exist spiritually without knowledge of origins; he apprehends this knowledge, furthermore, as mythic fact and not as empirical fact. As an instance of this, even as there developed an ostensibly demythologizing method of rational inquiry and scrutiny of once-sacred beliefs, the nostalgia for mythic origins led to a reconstitution of the Nordic past as a golden age in post-Renaissance Northern Europe. However bizarre and disparate these later reconstitutions of northern origins may appear today, humanists, rationalists, and romantics alike were able to discover and legitimize their own identity in the Nordic past and see themselves as descendants of a heroic genesis "when it shone in the North," as Oehlenschläger put it.

The early chapters of this study are concerned with the nature of pre-scientific myth and with the encounter between the mythic structures of the Germanic tribes and missionary Christianity. Besides bringing out some singular qualities of Norse myth, the encounter is a dramatic illustration of the relationship among myth, formal religion, and reason.

The remainder of the book deals with the nature and forms of modern myth. The latent conflict between myth and reason in the postscientific consciousness is illustrated by the rise and fall of two grandiose visions of the Nordic past as a golden age of origins. The element of belief characteristic of prescientific myth was sustained for a while by a methodology ostensibly based in reason. In humanism the rational method which had reinforced the conquest of Nordic primitive myth by the Church was now employed in the vision of a *Germania illustrata* to reproduce a Nordic past that was expected to vindicate both natural law and God's religion; here we observe the creation of social myth. The empiricism of the Enlightenment brought an end to these pretentious attempts but produced a crisis for man's mythmaking in a demythologized world of rational cause. Beginning with the late eighteenth century we trace the tension between myth and reason in the emergence of the Nordic past from social literary myth, culminating in Ossian and continuing into what we might call the modern literary consciousness: the programmatic attempt to synthesize myth and reason into a "new mythology" in the early nineteenth century.

To resolve the problem of myth in any significant way involves both a recognition of the confusion arising from the varied standpoints from which myth is viewed and, mostly as a consequence, distinguishing among the protean forms assumed by myth. Much of the appeal of the Nordic past to post-Renaissance men of letters was the assumption that here they had found a pure Northern European mythology, indigenous and uncontaminated by southern decadence or Christian elements. Although recent scholarship has eroded this assumption, it is possible to isolate at least some Nordic elements in the mythological texts and saga literature as illustrations of an apprehension of reality conditioned by the prescientific mythic consciousness. Moreover, in the subsequent employment of Norse mythology there are exhibited, although seldom perfectly, the nature and origins of the three principal categories of myth in addition to primitive myth. These are religious myth, social myth, and the myths of formal literature. Outside the scope of this inquiry is a peculiarly modern form of synthetic myth, where the mythmaking impulse is manipulated by images developed in advertising or propaganda.

To sort out the qualities of each of these myth forms, whose distinctions are inevitably blurred because they arise in essentially paradoxical and mostly unconscious ways in the human psyche, it is perhaps best to assess the way in which all forms of myth are similar and then to note the ways in which they differ from one another. Later chapters will study these forms as they involve the Nordic past.

First, all myth has to do with the expression of values—with feeling and form, in Suzanne Langer's phrase. If myth is viewed as a means of apprehending and organizing cultural values, the problem is no longer merely semantic, for in asserting that myth is a form for expressing this kind of truth, we are entering areas philosophical and critical. It is here, as we shall see, that myth encounters its mortal enemy, reason, for when an empirical or rational test is demanded for all truth, myth becomes unintelligible as a formulation of reality. It must either evolve into formal religion, with religion's awareness of the perpetual "other," or cohabit uneasily with reason in the secular world as social myth or ideology. Otherwise, myth is inexpressive and must of necessity be viewed by a positivist as one of man's dated entertainments or futile attempts to communicate.

Finally, myth always finds expression in symbolic form, and in describing the nature of these symbols we introduce our central concern: the relationship of historical man to his images of the genesis of his culture.

As mentioned, mythic narrative is primarily concerned with origins. In its largest scope, the concern is with the primordial establishing of order from chaos in a timeless realm prior to the complexity of man's experience in profane history. In this state of sanctity, man's will and actions are congruent with the divine models resulting from creation. But these mysteries remain ineffable until communicated. Disregarding the nonverbal communication which characterizes mysticism (our concern is with myth as a communal phenomenon), we see with Cassirer that language and myth are closely related. Indeed, one of the legacies of Cassirer's investigations has been the study of the metaphoric essence of language. I can speak of a sunrise without being accused of advocating a return to Ptolemaic astronomy; similarly, I can address "Madame Chairman" with no sense of incongruity, for the reality of language is primarily metaphoric, not empirical.

A culture's apprehension of reality is primarily expressed in metaphor, but a distinction must be made at this point among types of metaphor. Metaphor in literature is a special case of the term, for an artist employs metaphor consciously in an attempt to find some point of contact between his private symbolic identity and the communal world of his audience. He cannot be said to be "using myth" in our sense of the term, for he is aware that his representation is not real. He may be using mythology, but myth enters his work on another level.

If we agree that the artist represents reality in some way, myth enters his work through the reality he represents. The Icelandic sagas, for instance, tell a good story. But what is a "good story"? To the audience, it is a particular representation and structuring of cultural truths about the way things are or ought to be. We are entering the realm of semiology (the social context of signs) here, and we will return to it in the Conclusion, but we have argued above that the highest verbal expression of these cultural insights occurs in sacred language, in religious myth. Religious myth recognizes that its story is ontological, susceptible neither to criticism nor emendation.

Unconsciously, however, these same insights can govern the structure of secular narrative and make it into a "good story." Anyone who has tried to fathom a baroque novel (and we will be considering one) knows that what one era considers to be a masterpiece may be unintelligible to another. Myths are vulnerable, as we shall see, and so are their displacements into secular narrative. Our concern is with the reality of mythic metaphors, the work of art, and not with the private world of the author.

When myth concerns more than the momentary investing of an object with divine significance, the reality of the mythic content is given a temporal dimension, recounting in detail its sacred origin, as in the Babylonian creation story *Enuma elish*.[9] The *Enuma elish* shows that the temple of the god Marduk is the earthly manifestation of his victory over the monster Tiamat and his ordering of the universe. Similarly, the moment of incantation is more than the reenactment of the establishing of cosmos from chaos; it is felt as the act itself: in this manner creation has been made an integral part of the present and is an essential aspect of reality.[10]

This linking of a content to a time of origins is most important to the mythic consciousness. Instead of retreating into the unreal and the imaginary, the emphasis on the origin of an event or object *declares* its reality by giving it another—a temporal—dimension. But as mentioned before, just as the mythic object has a reality different from that of the empirical object, so too the mythic consciousness of time has some singular characteristics. Primarily, mythic time is plastic. That is to say that time is not expressed as a linear, progressive relationship, where an event has only one position; rather, it is possible through ritual and through myth to reintegrate a substance or action with its mythic, holy origin, or even to experience the future.[11]

Nor is time present in the mythic consciousness in the empirical sense of an infinite and unalterable progression into the future or regression into the past. When Brazilian natives bring the skulls of their ancestors to a feast, the ancestors are really *there;* Newtonian time has been annihilated. The mythic past, then, is a kind of narrative past with an absolute beginning, and there is a simultaneity between the present event and its mythic origin, invoked through ritual or charm.[12] Again, the mythic principle of identity can describe the apprehension of the past, for just as one part of a grouping is to the mythic consciousness identical with the entire grouping, an instant or event in mythic time partakes of all the other events made sacred through ritual or invocation, including, in the absolute past, the divine genesis of the event.[13]

Mircea Eliade uses the term *in illo tempore* to describe this time of sacred origins which is recoverable through ritual; in the Christian tradition, mythic time can be illustrated by the sacrament of Communion, which effects an annihilation of historical time, as it were, and a transubstantiation of substance. This allows the communicant to participate, in a real sense, in a historically symbolic event of origin. The empirical mind has difficulty coping with this mythic element in Communion unless it makes a "suspension of disbelief," because of the basis upon which it makes distinctions between true and false.

In the mythic apprehension of time the present is legitimized, to use Berger and Luckmann's term, by giving it a divine or sacred origin or culmination. Eliade cites many examples of a rite being thus validated by showing that its content originated in a nonhistorical time, *in illo tempore.*[14] It is this merging with genesis that gives the content in the present its power and efficacy. Narrative time is thus viewed not as a linear progression of events connected causally as well as temporally, but it assumes an elastic quality later adapted on a more conscious basis to literature. This temporal mobility, combined with the view of the universe as moved by magical forces which may be swayed at times by ritualistic appeal, frees cause also from the temporal series and gives it too an elastic nature. While the sacred, narrative quality of mythic space-time in one sense circumscribes the primitive mind, the primitive mind might also be said to have freedom from obeisance to an impersonal mechanical universe.

Myths provide a means of understanding the temporal, mutable present in terms of what Kerényi calls *archai,* principles from which the moral universe derives. One of the most common images of the *archai* is that of the golden age of innocence and natural virtue. The essence of the golden age as myth, Harry Levin says, is not the absence of evil but a clear temporal delineation between good and evil.[15] The fall from this state not only begins historical time, but the relationship between good and evil then becomes ambiguous. In our context a culture's image of its innocence is the central fact of its history: the rituals of some cultures (the Babylonian, for instance) see the present as integral with the original principles of moral ordering and the beginning of profane time; others might see the symbolic genesis as occurring in historical time, an incarnation of the *archai* in history (compare the discussion of Germania and Swedish Gothicism given below). In either case the result is the same: the content in the present is given a sacred quality by integrating it with an origin whose significance lies outside historical time.

While it is hardly possible for modern man to experience the world in a naive mythic manner, neither can he experience it in a wholly "demythologized" manner, that is, objectively and dispassionately, seeing the present in completely profane terms with no reference to sacred origins. To Eliade, however, the deterioration of the myths by which we understand human life in sacred perspectives produces a dread, a "terror of history."[16] For the alternative to existence conceived in terms of mythic antecedents or consequences is an isolation where the world is perceived solely in secular terms, with the roots in myth severed, lacking symbolic means to legitimize the present. Man becomes naked in time, and in this isolation his sufferings become purposeless, his fears unintelligible, his death meaningless. Though reason can see only falsehood in ancient myth, or at best a concealment of empirical content, we can see why the compulsion to mythmaking is fundamental to man. In spite of the enlightened urge to demythologize, individuals and whole cultures find in myth an escape from the "terror of history" by experiencing a sense of meaning and destiny in ahistorical terms.

At first glance it may seem odd to suggest that modern man has a mythic faculty generally associated with the primitive mind, but though there are aspects of the mythic symbol peculiar to postscientific man, the basic nature of the mythic construct is the same, and it has the same primary function: to organize value and feeling. The modern mythic consciousness shares with the primitive mind a belief in the nonsymbolic, factual reality of its contents, but at the same time it has an awareness of symbol foreign to the primitive. Combined with what Whitehead calls the "instinctive faith" in scientific method, there is a curious dialectical relationship between the mythic consciousness and empirical thought, in that the nonrational bases of modern myth are in constant danger of being exposed as untrue or as "merely symbolic."[17] The term *modern* is here taken to mean post-Renaissance, in that I am concerned with the growth of the faith that rational thought, objective and demythologized, gives us sufficient knowledge not only of the physical world but also of the moral world.[18]

This, then, is the singular and paradoxical feature of modern myth: it combines the intensity of belief characteristic of the primitive mind with the necessity to fortify the reality of its constructs in empirical terms. As long as the modern mythic symbols can be given a quasi-empirical status, they remain expressive, in that the orientation in the subjective world of value is externalized into a symbolic matrix adequately validated as "objective."

In pointing to the differences among forms of myth the nature of each can be more precisely described. While it is tempting to claim a kind of evolutionary process for myth, these qualities are relatively superficial. More interesting is the continuity and persistence of the Nordic past as a myth of origins in these different cultural forms. It will be seen, however, that Norse mythology was converted and sometimes reconstituted into different forms according to the stages of cultural history through which Germanic Europe was passing.

In the cultural metamorphosis arising from the triumph of Christianity over the elements of myth in the world of the Germanic tribes much is revealed about the distinctive mythic nature of each. The differences are both accentuated and complicated by the lateness of the conversion. By the time of the conversion, the Church had already advanced far beyond primitive Christianity and had long since accepted the wisdom of the Greeks, against which Paul had warned. This serpent in the bosom of the Church was reason, which was to prove the ultimate enemy of both myth and Church alike. First, however, reason was employed as a weapon against the Germanic tribes.[19]

In the conversion of the Germanic tribes we see the apparent vulnerability of Norse myth to the Christian culture of the missionaries as they "expose" rational contradictions in the mythic basis of the pagan Germanic world.[20] This assault is of great importance for our discussion in that the conversion was not merely on a religious plane: the whole legitimacy of the Germanic culture was undermined, its symbolic universe exposed to the assault of dialectic and supplanted by the great synthesis of the Middle Ages, the fusion of Christian myth with formal logic.

Differentiating between formal religion and primitive myth in this situation is made difficult both by the admixture of Greek philosophy with religion and by the fact that most of the available reports of Norse myth were produced by Christians and therefore filtered through the screen of the Christian *Weltanschauung*. Nevertheless, differences do emerge. The first and most important lies in the concept of symbol. Mythic thought has a basically different point of departure from that of formal religion. Primitive myth does not abstract. What to the modern mind is an abstraction, a symbol, only "is" to myth when it is given substance.[21] There is no relationship seen between the quality and its substance in the mythic consciousness; the object as myth perceives it is identical with its quality. A god or demon does not signify; he is. Where logical thought posits a relationship between its elements and abstracts general principles and laws, primitive myth posits an identity of elements.[22]

The fundamental assumption of sympathetic magic (essentially the prescientific view of the world) is informed by what Cassirer calls the "principle of concrescence," the identity of symbol and object. In the world of myth, to know the name is to have control, for "where *we* see mere sign and similarity, magical consciousness and perception see the object itself."[23] A fear of the photograph (image magic), a reluctance to name the deity (name magic), and voodoo are all predicated upon the identity of image and thing in the mythic consciousness. In general the mythic object is distinguished from its counterpart in the profane world by the quality of its efficacy. The reality of the mythic bond is a function of its efficacious bond with the subject, and mythic knowledge of a given content is precisely the full knowledge of that efficacious bond.[24]

In formal religion the undifferentiated identity of symbol and object that is characteristic of naive myth becomes a consciousness of symbol *as symbolic* of something else—another world of spirit. This distinction only gradually emerges in Christianity, however. The biblical myth of creation clearly is involved in narrative time, for creation occurs "in the beginning." The principal problem is that Genesis tells us (and the Hebrews) little about the process of creation, for the Lord executes his will by fiat, not by struggle. There is nothing overcome, no actions to imitate in human history: only faith. As Bultmann points out, this lack of detail in the account of creation in sacred writ posed problems for subsequent Old Testament narrative, for there were no coherent paradigms of divine intervention to make human history meaningful.[25] As the Hebrew conception of another world outside historical time grew over the centuries, there emerged from their tribulations a view of a timeless millenium where care would be forgotten. But the elasticity of narrative time continues at many biblical levels, with the future apprehended through prophecy and through dreams and the past integrated to the present through ritual and sacrament.

The mythic roots of primitive Christianity are obviously strong, but heaven also emerges as a realm of the spirit. In the Book of John, the Word is no longer immanent in the universe: for "the Word was with God and the Word *was* God." This spiritual revelation was later given further development in the Incarnation, which affirmed the human world as symbolic of the divine.

With the acceptance by the Church of Greek philosophy the idea of a timeless realm of spirit was refined, until by A.D. 1000 when Christianity confronted Norse myth in Iceland, a number of formal questions had been at least partially resolved. With Augustine creation had already come to be viewed as an emanation from the Godhead in a

Neoplatonic descending order of being. Here the problem of time has changed from the elasticity in primitive mythic narrative to the problem of establishing the nature of historical time in rational terms, but Augustine confronts a dualism we will meet time and again.

In Book XI of the *Confessions*[26] Augustine probes into the nature of time but finds paradox wherever he goes. What existed before Creation? God is not subject to historical time, as is man: "in the Eternal nothing passeth, but the whole is present." But what is the relationship of man's ability to make synthetic judgments about the past, present, and future to the Lord, "to whom nothing is to come?" To Augustine there must be a unified, orderly solution to these questions, and his reason despairs at resolving the dilemma resulting from the collision between a paradigmless creation myth and the Greek assumption of a fundamental regularity in creation: "it is too mighty for me," he pleads, "I cannot attain to it."

Perhaps he can find an invulnerable point of departure by considering time as the regularity of astronomical motions, but here again the disparity between time as apprehended by human reason and time as God handles it brings him to a halt: "Let no man then tell me that the motions of the heavenly bodies constitute times, because, when at the prayer of one, the sun had stood still, till he could achieve his victorious battle, the sun stood still, but time went on."

The factual reality of sacred constructs is not strange to readers of Augustine; the bishop was hardly a "savage," but Augustine's view of Genesis and Jericho has a great deal in common with Malinowski's insistence upon the reality of myth in the prescientific mind. It is "not merely a story told, but a reality lived. It is not of the nature of fiction, such as we read today in a novel, but it is a living reality, believed to have once happened in primeval times, and continuing ever since to influence the world and human destinies."[27] This narrative element in the forms of mythic thought is the basis of the view taken in myth of causality and makes possible the reality in the present of the creative energy of the gods.

While the great synthesis of medieval Christian culture was the accommodation between reason and myth, the hostility felt by Christianity toward pagan Nordic beliefs stemmed from a source other than reason's inability to assimilate myth. As Toynbee says, when the religion of a culture is refined in formal terms, it tends to become universal and is regarded as the only form of value-truth. The adequacy of a culture's symbolic universe is dependent upon maintaining its universality; aggressive conversion of the benighted thus becomes a sacred obligation of the Church and, later, a moral imperative of the State.

While rational philosophy in Christianity was one of the weapons employed in the conversion of the Germanic peoples, it was in humanism that reason began its subtle domination of men's spiritual reflexes. The humanist faith that rational inquiry into the past—in this case the Germanic past—would establish the validity of Christian doctrine proved to have far different results. During the age of humanism, however, the exploration of the Nordic past produced an early example of social myth.

Although the meticulous investigations of Ernst Cassirer show that scientific thought evolves from mythic antecedents (and both emerge from the human consciousness) the truths of myth cannot be proved by reason. Myth is real, but not empirically verifiable, as studies by anthropologists and ethnologists such as Malinowski and Kerényi show. This is why rational thought cannot approach the symbolic structures of myth save as falsehood, or as symbolizing a conceptual content. Reason, as Whitehead observed, has as its unconscious premise the rational constitution of the universe itself, and the discursive truths reason discovers are not the orderings of images but ultimate validity.

The assumption of a rationally constituted creation renders reason the enemy of myth, which makes no such assumption. Indeed, myth often posits chaos and violence as the essense of the world. Yet, the same assumption of the primacy of reason gives rise to the peculiar hybrid of modern myth. These myths are displaced: not couched in the language of primitive or religious myth, these myths employ ostensibly empirical language to regulate the social understanding of human value. Although these ostensibly objective social doctrines perform the function of myth, they can only view myths employing symbols less displaced from the sacred world as being untrue: primitive at least, pernicious perhaps, but certainly socially dangerous. Plato, for example, mounts a vigorous attack on the primitive mythic foundations of his society to clear the way for a rational Republic by showing that reason provides a superior understanding of the world. Plato employs the principles of logic to show that two truths which contradict cannot both be true. Myth is the loser in this contest, for myth does not validate its truths by the principles of logic.

Yet a form of myth develops from this rational analysis so apparently dependent upon logical or empirical validation that its essential mythic nature is hard to detect.[28] In denying the truth of Greek primitive myth, Plato at once proceeds to erect a series of social myths of which the Republic was only one. In supposing that he had demonstrated rationally the nature of justice, Plato was unaware of the power the poetic quality of his imagery had in forming his ideas, and social myths from Aristotelianism to pragmatism have had the same characteristics. The rule is that the more logical and empirical the devices employed in the explorations of social values, the more likely the validity of the result—until the use of the computer in metagamesmanship approaches the unassailable model of social structuring.

The Nordic past played a key role in the world of the German humanists and Swedish antiquarian scholars in the creation of social myth, and in their scholarly narratives may be seen a now-bizarre interplay between the rational concept of historical time and myth's legitimation of values by declaring a sacred origin. In the rise and fall of the myth of Swedish Gothicism we see displayed the central tension in modern myth: the need to maintain legitimacy in the two ultimately antithetical worlds of myth and reason.

As mentioned, we are not primarily concerned with the conscious use of mythology in literature. Rather, our concern is with the spontaneous reconstruction of the past to support the factual nature of the values of the present. In a sense this creative act of the mythic imagination is mythopoesis, but the expression of the mythic imagination is not limited to literature, nor is it an act of conscious creation. We must distinguish, then, between the ironic use of mythology and unconscious mythic constructs, for the power of the mythic symbol in both primitive and modern cultures stems from the intensity with which it is believed.

In modern myth the creative impulse is seldom literary; rather, the literary myth asserts its reality against the background of "objective" forms of narrative. Thus we deal with philosophical, historical, social, and ideological narrative in tracing the development of a literary myth of the Nordic past as a legitimation of sentimentalism in the late eighteenth century.

Contemporary myth is an offspring of the romantic awareness of the nature of symbol, even as the critical suspicion of myth stems in part from the collapse of the romantic belief in the transcendental reality of the symbol. Though in romanticism art was liberated from the imitation of empirical nature, contemporary research into the nature of social behavior and cultural symbol has produced a darker legacy. It may well be that modern man "hungers after myth," but as Cassirer feared in *The Myth of the State* (1946), knowledge of the nature of man's mythmaking impulse and cultural symbols has been fused with technology and techniques of mass persuasion to create synthetic myths which are no longer spontaneous but are fabricated for purposes of controlling or manipulating public opinion.

The study of a myth of origins, as expressed in images of the Nordic past, shows not only that the study of myth cannot be confined to one discipline, but is closely allied to structuralism and semiology, a point which will be developed in more detail in the Conclusion.

The myths of contemporary literature are marked by a developed consciousness, a consciousness produced by the rise of literary criticism as well as the heightened consciousness of the nature of a physical world ordered by principles of regularity expressed in mathematical symbols. On the other hand we have become aware of the world of self and of the different worlds which consciousness experiences and creates through experience. The reality of these worlds is expressed in nonrational symbolic modes: literature, religion, ideology, and, basically, myth. The discoveries of Einstein, Gödel, and Heisenberg have demanded a reevaluation of the objectivity of the scientific symbol, while rational discourse is still developing a methodology of coping with the reality of suprarational experience. In the myriad of individual experiences and expressions of those experiences the consequences of leaving this essentially mythic world unordered would be to leave much of human experience unintelligible.

Recalling the distinction made above between communal identity and private identity, I would suggest that much of the task of literary criticism is to provide just such a translation from a private matrix of symbols into a shared communal world. Though much is lost in translation, explications of texts provide one means for effecting this rapprochement.

Guiding principles are necessary, however, for "myth criticism,"

whether based upon the discovery of Jungian archetypes or on elucida-
tions of the private world of the poet, can be rewarding and fruitful
only if it does not fall into the neoromantic trap and elevate myth into a
transcendental hotline to the Absolute—the "mythomania" derided by
Rahv. Our approach to literary texts will be governed by this distinction, in that we are concerned with the text primarily as a formulation
and expression of communal myths. As such, our treatment of literary
texts makes no claim to completeness, for we will give only secondary consideration to the personal mythology of the author.

Our central concern, then, is with myth as a means of apprehending
value in dramatic terms. Here we must take into account what Northrop Frye and Joseph Campbell call the archetypal myth, a myth so
fundamental and enduring in the human spirit that it has found recurring expression in all great literature. The term *mythopoesis* has meaning here, for it is dealing with the heroic quest which takes place in a
universe in which there exists an ironic relationship to the communal
myths but where the process of alienation is not yet complete.[29] One
function of myth, ancient or modern, is to make heroism possible, for
the protagonist of the heroic mode cannot exist outside a framework of
myth, in that it is myth that expresses the *archai,* the sacred paradigms
he strives to fulfill or transcend. Sometimes he succeeds, transforming
his society by remythologizing it with the divine knowledge attained
on his quest, descent, or ascension. The sense of tragedy in the heroic
mode, however, comes when the hero, be he ancient or modern, is no
longer confident of his orientation in myth and confronts the uncon-
querable monster, the "terror of history."

In various forms the idea of a golden age of the North provided just
such a background for social or literary heroism. Though the action of
modern myths does not take place in a divine world where the *archai*
are explicitly established, the mythic pattern of the golden age was
couched in Gothic images and governed the structure of both scholarly
and literary narratives. Though today there is little serious emotional
identification with what Jöran Mjöberg calls "The Dream of the
Saga-Era,"[30] this was not the case for the timespan of this study. From
the Renaissance through the era of romanticism the idea of a golden
age of the North played a role as myth, often minor, sometimes major,
in the intellectual life of Northern Europe, and was reconstituted spon-

taneously by historians, philosophers, and men of belles lettres. It was seen as fact, the genesis and legitimation of their own values. Our first task, however, is to examine the relationship between myth, heroism, and narrative by analyzing the source of Gothic nostalgia: the Norse mythic consciousness and its displacement into saga narrative.

(2)

NORSE MYTH
AS SYMBOL AND PARADIGM

The apprehension of reality expressed through myth has a dual function. On the one hand myth objectifies and hence makes accessible the values of a culture, while on the other hand it serves as self-evident truths, unquestioned paradigms for subsequent generations. The social forms of the present are legitimized, while moral certainty is provided for choice in the future. Eliade cites the story of a mariner in New Guinea who before setting out dressed, danced, and spread his arms to imitate the winged hero Aori. Whether or not he actually became Aori, he did not set out alone; his human act had become charged with a sacred power and the potential uncertainty of an action in "open" historical time had been avoided by the invocation of a sacred action that is in one sense already complete, but is still accessible to mortals.[1]

There is a fundamental difference between the constitution of the mythic universe and the rational one, and also between the kind of knowledge presented by the mythic consciousness and that presented by rational-empirical thought. The mythic universe has a narrative dimension lacking in the Cartesian one: it has a beginning, often an end, but always a meaning.

Although the mythic consciousness experiences a collapsing of temporal and spatial distance between genesis and the time of ritual action, narrative sequence is of necessity involved in the representation of this consciousness. It does not immediately follow, however, that techniques for explicating profane narrative can indiscriminately be applied to mythic narrative lest its reality, its representation of the sacred, escape in the process. In a sense, such criticism has been levelled at Lévi-Strauss in the name of hermeneutics.[2]

Our critical problem does not just center upon the distinction between the sacred and the profane, a distinction maintained so persuasively by Eliade, but the relationship *between* the sacred and the profane. When a narrative takes place in a world recognizably sacred, peopled with gods, monsters and transmitted through incantation, we are perhaps more willing to accept myth's view of space-time than we would, say, in discussing a novel or a treatise in social science. When mythic patterns are implicit in narrative rather than explicit we may use the term *displacement* to describe the power of myth to regulate the structure and content of a profane text, organizing chaos into a "good story."

Use of the term *displaced myth* raises the question of "undisplaced myth." Unarticulated intuitions of the sacred or of animism may be said to be undisplaced myth, in that these "gods of the moment" (to use Usener's phrase) have not been subjected to thought or organization. Examples of this preverbal cognition of mythic space-time in primitive societies are easily accessible, but we might also mention the familiar reflex of body english, an attempt to control an object spatially which certainly does not have its conceptual basis in Newtonian mechanics.

Insofar as mythic intuition becomes verbal, it must of necessity involve narrative, and a degree of displacement from the ineffably sacred world to the human sets in. In subsequent chapters we will deal with narratives where the action takes place in a completely human world (social myth) and even in a world explicitly announced as created by man (formal art).

Yet the social acceptance of even literary myth was predicated upon its verisimilitude; this verisimilitude was in turn predicated upon a dramatic apprehension of human history. Sacred mythic narrative (relatively undisplaced) asserts ultimate objectivity and distinguishes between the sacred and the profane. As myths took narrative form in eras where the sacred was no longer recognized as being the source of ultimate objectivity, they were expressed in narratives which the culture could accept as being objective.

The organization involved in whatever degree of displacement of the sacred of necessity introduces an element of the human, of the profane. The greater the degree of displacement of myth, the more explicitly human becomes the language of that narrative, and the pretense of these narratives to discursive methodology makes them fatally vulnerable to exposure and demythologizing. Although nostalgia for Viking heroism animated historians, philosophers, and men of belles lettres to see their own present in terms of a northern golden age, the values of

Christianity, humanism, rationalism, and idealism were basically alien to the mythic world of their sources. Consequently, many of these modern displaced myths are now bizarre and comic, yet the mythic universe of their sources informed a profound vision of human existence that could allow conquest to evil but triumph to men.

The problem of displacement enters into any discussion of Norse myth, not only because of the narrative form, but these largely Icelandic sources date from a period after the conversion of the Scandinavian countries and were written down by at least nominal Christians.[3] Some of the sources present reasonably reliable accounts of pagan customs, however, as archaeological findings attest. Furthermore, although the degree of Christian "contamination" in the Eddas and sagas has been a matter of heated debate for generations, it should be kept in mind here that the distinction to be made is between the mythic consciousness and formal religion, with the "Christian/pagan" debate of only secondary importance. Although aspects of Christian culture were absorbed into the pagan Norse culture (indeed, elements of syncretism proved to be problems for religious authorities in Scandinavia and on the Continent even down to the present century), it is possible to isolate some stylistic traits of a mythic consciousness not informed by the medieval Christian apprehension and representation of reality.

Formal religion has an awareness that its objects are symbolic, that the phenomenal world is but an inadequate expression of truth. Thus in the saga of Saint Olaf (*Oláfs saga helga,* chap. 113), when Olaf destroys an idol of Thor, the sun is described as a symbol of the Christian God. King Olaf comments, "You think it strange that you cannot see our god, but we expect that he will soon come to us. You terrify us with your god who is blind and deaf and cannot save either himself nor others and cannot budge unless he is carried." As the sun rises, Olaf says, "And now look ye to the east, there comes our God now with great light."[4] The author (and Olaf) realize not only the symbolic nature of the action but also the difference between symbol and object, for the author and the king are conscious that the idol of Thor is not divine (he "cannot save either himself nor others, and cannot budge unless he is carried"), but that divinity is pure spirit. The mythic consciousness, however, has no such awareness, and when Olaf destroys Thor's idol, to the pagans this in a very real sense is an assault upon Thor himself. This consciousness that divine truth cannot be fully expressed in substance constitutes a basic distinction between the naive mythic consciousness and the myths of formal religion.

Mythic narrative does not view elements in terms of their relationships but projects its truths into an absolute past, into creation, and lacking the concept of pure spirit expresses this quality in substance. An illustration of this tendency can be seen in the "Völuspá" ("The Sibyl's Prophecy") which is the central poetic document for the Norse creation myth and the basis for Snorri Sturluson's elaboration in the *Prose Edda*.[5] The sixty-five stanzas of the "Völuspá" give the impression of an incantation, in that they are narrated by a "Völva" (prophetess), who is asked by Odin to reveal the beginning of the world and its end. She does this, telling of the time of beginnings, before creation. The Völva tells of the golden age of the gods. After recounting some of the main events in the history of the gods, the Völva speaks of Ragnarök, the final battle between the gods and their enemies, in which both are destroyed, and fire and flood demolish creation. Some much-debated stanzas vaguely describing a new creation rising from the ruins of the old conclude the poem.

The unity in the "Völuspá" stems from the theme that the eventual destruction of the world (and of the gods) is implicit in creation, that ultimate defeat is inevitable, and that all of Odin's wisdom (and, by implication, man's) only serves to postpone the final confrontation. But how is this vision expressed? First of all it should be mentioned that the matter of creation itself had an essentially malevolent quality, being the body of Ymir, a frost giant slain by the gods. But technical devices also facilitate the manipulation of time so that the reader-listener is involved both in the creation and in its consequent catastrophe.

In the first stanza the poet places the poem in the historical (profane) present through a rhetorical device. The Völva says, "Hearing I ask from the holy races, / From Heimdal's sons [i.e., man] both high and low." The invocation is a formula used normally by poets in heroic verse to demand the attention of his audience. Kees Bolle discusses the presence of a teller in sacred narrative, however, in terms of "subjective reservedness." That is, the subjectivity of an announced or implied narrator underlines the authority, objectivity, and mystery of the myth: "the myth is there, almost in spite of the people who are, nevertheless, also there."[6] But it is also clear in the first stanza that the narration is directly spoken to Odin in an indefinite time and deals with a sacred subject; thus the poem is established in the historical present of the audience, then immediately removed from it, and from the second stanza the poem changes tense from present to preterite.

Then comes the narration of creation, again in the past tense. At stanza 27, however, the Völva completes this tale of the past and in the present tense asks Odin if he would know yet more. At this point the Völva begins to tell Odin of the future, and the preparation for Ragnarök. For a while this narration too is in the past tense, as the Völva recounts her vision, but at stanza 41 she again asks Odin if he would know more and continues in general in the present tense. Ragnarök is experienced directly, as though the future is happening as the poem is spoken: "All Jotenheim [the home of the giants] groans, the gods are at council; / Loud roar the dwarfs by the doors of stone, / The masters of the rocks; would you know more?" Thus the reader-listener participates in the whole of creation climaxed by the immediate experience of Ragnarök itself. But the significance of Ragnarök only becomes clear when the inevitability of the ultimate destruction is understood as a direct consequence of creation.

In myth only that which is created is; in the Norse creation myth the world is not formed ex nihilo, but from the body of a slain giant, and order is established from a preexisting substance. The act itself is less one of creation than of transformation. Chaos is described in terms of a lack of means for measuring historical time: after their creation out of Ymir's body, the sun, moon, and stars "knew not what their stations were" (stanza 5). The gods establish temporal order, and they also give *megin* to the heavenly bodies and to the first man and woman (stanza 17), an immanent, dynamic principle, a power of control.[7] In the Norse genesis the gods establish historical time, but they also create what is the latent power in any object to control and form myth's efficacious bond.[8]

The inexorable nature of existence seen in the "Völuspá" is projected into the very stuff of genesis, for the giants are the enemies of man and the gods. Thus matter itself originally has a fundamentally hostile quality. This characteristic of Norse cosmogony is also reflected in Odin's moral ambivalence, for he and all the gods were created from the same matter as Ymir; Odin himself is described as being partly of giant ancestry.[9]

Part of the realism of sacred mythic narrative is that values of the present are reified, given substance and ontological status. The legitmation of this ontology is accomplished through the narrative nature of mythic time, in that reality is described in terms of its genesis. In Norse myth even the gods are not immune from the basically inimical nature of creation, since they are a product of genesis and are not instigators of it. Through breaking their oaths to the giants (*jötnar*), they end the golden age and begin the strife which eventually leads to Ragnarök. Destruction, symbolized in the myth of Ragnarök, is seen in Norse myth as a necessary consequence of the singular quality of creation.[10] The struggle between the gods and the giants, though expressing a fundamental dichotomy, is complementary in a sense, for gods and giants are both *vættir* (creatures), as are tutelary spirits (see below).[11] This grim view of the unified discord characterizing mythic time is not rendered conceptually, however, but given substance and made a part of creation.

We have argued above concerning the reality of myth and characteristics of undisplaced mythic narrative. Poems such as the "Völuspá" are explicitly sacred in tone, and however much displacement has necessarily intruded as a result of individual artistry, the setting and realism give the effect of being sacred rather than profane.

When the narrative situation no longer takes place in a sacred world the problem of analysis becomes more complex, in that the mythic patterns become implicit rather than explicit. It is in this displacement of the sacred world to the human world that myth's legitimizing function attains its primary importance, however, providing an absolute with which to regulate human choice. Though we might see moral choice as being made on the purely theoretical level of philosophy or ethics, more often choice is actually made with a displaced mythic referent. At such a time, there may or may not be an overt invocation of sacred paradigms. On the human plane the stern view of existence objectified by the gods is borne out by some of the family sagas, where the attempts of good men to intervene in a causal chain of events and retaliations are never successful for long. Human actions can delay but not prevent a final disaster, which is an inexorable consequence of the usually innocuous incident which often begins a saga. Yet the saga world is more than a realm of inevitable defeat, for in the possibility for human assertion lies the concept of heroism that provides a kind of triumph for the human spirit, in that the mythic world subtly conditions the representation of reality in the human world.[12]

The problem of saga realism has been vexing scholars for decades. The verisimilitude in the family sagas employs strikingly modern devices, and the illusion of objectivity is so persuasive that the sagas were long thought to be "history" in our sense of the term. Since the 1940s the reliability of the sagas as sources of historical data has been increasingly challenged. The realistic illusion remains, however, and contemporary scholars have urged that the sagas be considered "as literature."

Perhaps the discussion of realism in the sagas can be approached with a methodology primarily literary, but without abandoning historical considerations. M. I. Steblin-Kamenskij, for instance, has suggested that the saga style is indeed realistic and historical, but that the Icelanders' concepts of reality and even fact were not the same as ours. Steblin-Kamenskij describes the realism of the sagas as stemming from a view of reality which ignores our distinction between historical and artistic truth, and he calls it a "third entity."[13] This discussion might be of use here, for this "third entity" might well be a fusion of space-time conditioned by empirical reason and space-time conditioned by the norms of myth. The artistic effect stems from the former, while the thematic effect stems from the latter.

The family sagas provide a unique complement to the discussion of Norse myth in that all the events take place in historical time, but the representation of reality is conditioned by displaced mythic paradigms. As the *ættesögur* take place in the human world of medieval Iceland, the role of myth is quite subtle and complex, but uniquely revealing. The sagas do not ignore the historical world, as does the "Völuspá," nor is there a retreat from the historical world into the mythic past, as, say, in the *Nibelungenlied;* though the sagas offer a possibility for greatness and heroism in a world recognizably human, rational, and historical, the apprehension of reality incorporates the dramatic quality of the mythic world as part of a unified perception. The rational-empirical world is not consciously rejected—quite the contrary; it is only that there is an unconscious dimension in saga realism that incorporates the world and paradigms of myth.

A distinctive feature of realism stemming from displaced myth and the nature and possibilities of heroism within it is illustrated by this passage from *Njáls Saga:*

One day Njál and Thord were sitting out of doors. There was a goat which used to roam about the home-meadow, and no one was allowed to drive it away. Thord said, "That's very strange." "What do you see that seems to you so strange?" asked Njál. "The goat seems to be lying in the hollow there, drenched in blood," replied Thord. Njál said that there was no goat there, nor anything else. "Then what is it?" asked Thord. "It means that you must be a doomed man," said Njál. "That was your fetch (*fylgja*) you must have seen. Be on your guard." "That will not help me much if that is to be my fate," said Thord.[14]

Shortly after seeing his dead *fylgja,* Thord is killed.

This is usually described as an introduction of the "supernatural" into the narrative, but in this passage it is clear that the goat "used to roam about the home-meadow," so we may infer actual existence in the past. Further, it still exists in the real world for Thord, though it does not to the "wise" Njál. Njál, though, knows something that Thord does not: that "you must be a doomed man." Just what is the nature of this knowledge and what does it imply?

First, Njál perceives the goat to be a portent and consequently the historical reality of the situation—Thord's involvement in a web of murderous retribution—is intensified. Though Njál cannot see the goat, he accepts the fact that *Thord* sees it: in this acceptance, which admits both the empirical and the nonempirical, there is apparently no sense of inconsistency or contradiction.

Njál also sees the goat as a *fylgja. Fylgjur* take differing forms, but they are guardian or tutelary beings, either animals or women (*fylgjukonur*). Of significance here is the nature of the *fylgja* as a material extension of a character, spatially independent but connected to the person in an efficacious manner. An analogous though not identical principle is that of the voodoo doll, in which the two objects (person and doll) are similarly related.

The acceptance of the *fylgja* as part of the real world suggests immediately a different view of reality, a world in which rational and nonrational elements interact in an apparently capricious but effective way, a world in which cause (in this case, the death of the goat and the death of the man) is viewed as a bond between two seemingly unrelated objects. There is little distinction here between things spatial and nonspatial, nor does there exist a strict adherence to the logical concept of time.

This interaction through the *fylgja* of an "other" yet nonempirical world with "this" world to intensify in a concrete manner the reality of the situation can find illustration through another example from chapter 23 of *Njála*. Here it is in the dream state (still not differentiated from the "empirical" world) that the character perceives reality, while rationally the situation is deceptive. Gunnar of Hlidarend is staying disguised at Hrut's farm. Höskuld, who is searching for Gunnar, awakens from a dream and asks if anybody noticed anything unusual about the big man who was at Hrut's. One man noticed his gold ornaments, whereupon Höskuld sees that the figure in his dream is the *fylgja* of none other than Gunnar of Hlidarend. "*Now* I see it all: We must ride at once to Hrut's."

In the dream of Gunnar's *fylgja* the setting is in this world, and the dream is the apprehension of an actual event; the dream, however, depicts a situation *more* real than the empirical one. Höskuld's dream is a perception through the *fylgja* of a qualitative world of reality in which the empirical validation plays a secondary role.

The relationship between Thord and his *fylgja* and Gunnar and his is not "magical" in the sense of voodoo (actively exercising powers over a person) but effective in much the same way as a hero's armor or weapon is considered to have an autonomous efficacy. Nor is the *fylgja* a religious object in the formal sense,[15] for as it is described in the sagas and from folklore evidence, it does not exist on a fundamentally different plane of reality from that of its human counterpart. Although it is to the modern reader (and in typical medieval narrative) a symbolic representation of the quality of character, there is little awareness in the sagas that the forms covered by the term *fylgja* are symbolic; the *fylgjur* are sometimes concrete enough to be tripped over (even when empirically invisible), substantial enough to be transferable, but still a part, an extended projection of the person to whom they belong. Saga realism is thus able to do something that the empirical view of reality cannot, or that formal literature with its conscious manipulation of metaphor and symbol cannot. It can bring, at times of crisis, a directly apprehended and undifferentiated cognition to a situation and incorporate the quality of its significance into the total view of reality.

Though the degree to which mythological references and saga

sources depict detailed beliefs is debatable, resistance to abstraction finds support in linguistic and archaeological evidence. The inability of a mythically constituted universe to conceive a spirit beyond symbol can be seen in the introduction of a Christian concept of soul into pagan Iceland. The Icelandic language in pagan times (before 1000) had no equivalent for unsubstantial quality of this sort, and the word *sál* appears to have been imported from England.[16] Archaeological evidence also indicates that the dead were not thought to be in a fundamentally different world but on the other side of a by no means unbridgeable divide in which the character exists in a state similar to that in life.[17]

Communion with the dead was not only thought possible, it was not especially out of the ordinary. Just as at the sight of the *fylgja* there is none of the *mysterium tremendum* at the sight of a holy object, the dead were very much a part of the society of the living. *Draugar* (corpses that will not stay buried) provide an illustration. The troublesome Hrapp in *Laxdoela Saga*—a *draug* considered to be as obnoxious dead as he was when alive—can only be dispatched from the world of the living by burning, but this was more a social rite than a formally religious one.[18] There is some evidence of cremation in Scandinavian folk customs, but according to Christiansen the rite of cremation did not play an integral part in folk belief.[19] In general the concept of the afterlife was either of a physical existence of the body in the grave or of a journey to another place.[20]

This inability to imagine abstract spirit and the incorporation of the supernatural into the "real" world form the distinguishing features of the prescientific mind as compared to the modern mind. Often the presence of what would be considered supernatural is more real than the mundane world,[21] but the characters in the sagas, at least, accept *fylgjur, draugar,* and the continued existence of the dead in a matter-of-fact way as part of that unified perception of reality. In *Njála* the reaction of Skarphedin and Hogni to seeing the dead Gunnar sitting on his grave mound singing a verse is not one of terror at an event they cannot assimilate into their understanding, but a rather practical observation that "they could see Gunnar was happy." They recognize this as an intensification, that Gunnar in concrete terms is telling the living it is better to die than to yield. The moral point, however, is not made externally by a narrator but by introducing the mythic element as part of the characters' experience of the real world.

In a dream the real world often takes on this added dimension, for in the literary representation of the dream the realm of the dead merges with that of the living, again intensifying the empirical world. The distinction between saga realism and the medieval consciousness of a separate "other" world of spirit receives vivid illustration by contrasting the Old English story of Cædmon with the similar story of Hallbjörn. In the Cædmon story, an agent from the Christian "other" world gives him the gift of poetry in a dream, and after the dream Cædmon retains the inspiration and sings many songs to the glory of God. In the story of Thorleif Jarlaskald, the shepherd Hallbjörn sits on the grave mound of the poet Thorleif, hoping for inspiration. Hallbjörn had had no success as a poet, but one night he dreamed that Thorleif emerged from the grave and taught him a verse that would make him a great poet. When Hallbjörn first awoke, he thought he saw Thorleif returning to this grave. The dream functions here as a gateway for the reentering of the dead into what we would call empirical reality; like Gunnar on his grave mound, Thorleif can communicate directly with the character.[22]

Occasionally, however, the use of the dream in saga literature appears to have a consciously symbolic aspect, and this is usually coupled with recognizable elements of medieval Christian morality. Consider the remarkable dreaming of Gísli, the hero of *Gísla Saga*. He dreams of two *draumkonur* (dream women), one good, one evil; in his dream he walks up to a house, sees seven fires, and is told by his good *draumkona* that those were the years he had to live; she advises him to be good to men less fortunate than he. Unlike Höskuld's dream, and unlike the typical appearance of the *fylgjukona*, Gísli's dream has a symbolic relationship to reality: he is aware that his good and bad *draumkonur* exist *only* in his dreams, and that their existence is one of signification. There is a barrier between their world and his.

It might be noted that this sort of dream is also seen as unusual by the characters in the saga, in that they feel there is something occult about Gísli and his dreams, that "he was a man with spirit in him." Though *Gísla Saga* is free from the hagiographic elements of sagas of Christian heroes where the truth of an action or object in this world lies in a higher, a different world of spiritual verities, a comparison of the depiction of Gísli's *draumkonur* to that of Thord's dead *fylgja* shows that the *fylgjur* exist in an objective sense, not as allegory or conscious symbol, which are foreign to the mythic apprehension of the object. Although the death of the *fylgja* is prophetic, its existence is not exhausted in its signification.

It is apparent, both from the discussion of the potential heightening of the reality of the object and the prophetic role of dreams, that saga realism implies an apprehension of space-time different from either the "open" empirical view or the Christian concept we saw in Augustine, where spiritual time is eternal, while rational time is a sequence of events in space. The death of Thord's *fylgja* introduces a plastic element of time into the saga, for though Thord sees the goat in space, Njál sees it in time: " 'It means that you must be a doomed man,' said Njál. 'That was your *fylgja* you have seen. Be on your guard.' 'That will not help me much if that is to be my fate,' said Thord." This apprehension of the future has great implications for the depiction and possibilities of heroism.

As we have seen, in the mythic consciousness of time an event is not isolated or unalterably sequential as it is in Newtonian time: in practical terms, it can have more than one "when."[23] This tendency to project the qualitative aspect of the present into mythic time may be illustrated by recalling the Norse creation myth as described in the Völuspá.

The mythic intuition of time intrudes into the saga style to intensify reality, much as does the mythic consciousness of the object, and plays an integral part in the realism of the sagas. Consider the extensive practice of introducing a character through his genealogy, a counting of generations so distracting to some translators that they omit them as disgressions. But if we continue to approach the saga style with the norms of myth, the use of genealogy becomes a part of the representation of a unified perception of reality. As Steblin-Kamenskij has noted, the preoccupation with names does not indicate a concern for the individual, but with the organic unity of time. As myth lacks the concept of pure spirit, and as qualities must be objectified, they can often be transferred from one person to another. In *Hallfreðar Saga*, Hallfred's *fylgjukona* declares that the bond between them is broken, and it is passed on to Hallfred's younger son who bears the same name. The older Hallfred suspects he has not long to live.

The custom of naming after dead ancestors (often grandparents) is widespread in the sagas; this may have had myth's transference of quality as its basis.[24] This has been debated, but it seems likely, considering the nearness or presence of the dead in the mythic consciousness and the tendency in mythic time for the past to become a real and actual part of the present. In *Njáls Saga* genealogies have the stylistic function of developing early the tension between violence and social interaction based upon self-control. As Richard Allen has shown, the great clash in *Njála* between human law and human nature begins in chapter 1, with the comparison of the genealogies of Mord Fiddle and the half-brothers Hrut and Höskuld.[25] The brothers' lineage goes all the way back to the days of great warriors, while Mord is described only as the son of Sighvat the Red. While it is the man of heroic lineage, Hrut, who is attuned to something ominous in Hallgerd's "thief's eyes" (chapter 1), it is significant, considering that Icelandic law was more a free creation, less bound to mythic roots than Continental Germanic law,[26] that Mord's excellence is not based upon origins, but "he was so great a lawman, that none considered a case properly executed unless he was consulted."

In the genealogies there is a mythic causal operation which implies that no character exists without innate characteristics, no character is independent of the past. In literary terms, he has a reality by accretion before he enters the action, a potential underscoring his acts. If there is one theme running through the great sagas, it is that no event exists in isolation,[27] that in spite of the will of the best men the slightest event can have an effect which culminates in catastrophe; past and future are an integral part of the present.[28] At times of crisis, as I have suggested, a mode of realism intrudes into empirical reality to underscore this point by "annihilating time"; the death of Thord's *fylgja* is a case in point.

Several have observed that *Njála* is a saga about law,[29] and what it has to say about law is interesting in the light of the previous discussion. Icelandic law was apparently less a codification of tradition than a free creation of relationships. The first heathen law is from 930; in *Njála*, the conversion is described, and there is apparently an attempt to invest the law with Christian myth—Christianity is officially adopted at the Althing, the saintly Höskuld is made a formative power in society through being made a goði, the powerful chieftain Hall of Side waives the legal atonement for his son and with communal approval offers peace to his enemies. At the end, Kári foregoes killing

Flosi, the last of the Burners, and Flosi does not revenge the death of his accomplices upon Kári. This upturn at the end of *Njála,* with its note of reconciliation, is convincing. If we consider the relationship of the hero to the law, though, these are individual acts of magnanimity in refusing violence; so far as human institutions go, *Njála* does not present much hope for collective attempts to control destruction. The law does not provide an alternative to hostility; rather, it catalyzes it. However much the theme of "turn the other cheek" runs through the narrative, these individual actions are as futile to check the chain of vengeance as is Njál's adoption of Höskuld and Hall of Side's magnanimity. Similarly, the two great collective attempts to settle the conflict at the Althing only fan the hostilities, first as Flosi refuses settlement for Höskuld, which was urged by the community "for God's sake" (chapter 123), then as the prosecution of the Burners results in the Althing itself becoming the site for a pitched battle (chapter 145). Indeed, even Njál is more concerned with legal form than justice (chapter 97) and sets up the fifth court for Höskuld's sake.

So it does not appear that there has been any transfiguration of the law; the positive note of *Njála* is that of free acts of nobility by individuals, but this does not break the causal pattern of violence, and only after all violence is spent can Kári and Flosi be reconciled as individuals. Flosi is not legally bound to avenge the deaths of the Burners after all, and there is no collective pressure left on Kári to continue his vengeance.

The Norse myth of creation and the family sagas provide an introduction both to the nature of Norse fate and to its corollary, heroism, for it is in the interaction of the realities of the human world with the truths of the mythic universe that men define themselves.[30] Through mythic time, Thord knows his death is accomplished with the death of his *fylgja.* He can approach his existence in historical time with several options. He can be passive and wait for his time to run out; he can also attempt to avoid his fate by escaping the cycle of vengeance. He does neither; he behaves as though he had freedom of action. He wills to honor his obligations and dies. Yet there is a meaning, a self-definition in his death which neither of the first two choices would have allowed. He runs neither from his fate nor from evil, and though he is killed, his defense is heroic.

In *Gísla Saga,* Vestein, accepting the ominous truth that the empirical world has taken on a mythic aspect, events being signs which point to his death ("all rivers are flowing one way"), continues his journey with this knowledge from mythic time and does not let it affect his actions in historical time. He acts as though the future were open, a product of his free will. The same stance is true of Gunnar of Hlidarend, who chooses to remain in Iceland in spite of the fact that his only chance for survival is to leave the country. In electing to remain true to his values, he resists his murderers, many of whom have been forced by obligation into this act they know is evil, and Gunnar attains heroic stature in his death.

Though intrusions show that all these actions are "fated," as we see, the characters assert their freedom from this determinism and define themselves by resisting. This is possible, because, unlike Augustine, they saw the paradox of historical time and mythic time as a unified perception of reality. The paradigms of this apprehension exist in the mythic universe: in the "Völuspá," the gods' function in creation is one of ordering and name-giving, but the world of the historical present is a transformed product of the mythic past, and in the Norse creation story the essence of matter itself is evil. The myths of creation and of Ragnarök suggest that there is a kind of entropy, a tendency toward disorder in the universe, a gradual disintegration which the gods themselves play a major part in implementing.[31] Here is the connection between the mythological narrative and the realistic narrative of the sagas. The singular fact of Norse myth, as W. P. Ker noted, is that though the Norse gods are on the right side, this is not the side that wins. Unlike *Enuma elish,* the forms of order will finally be destroyed, and the monsters, the forces of "chaos and unreason," will ultimately overcome both gods and those men chosen to oppose them. This outcome is inevitable, a necessary consequence of genesis. Displaced to the human world, the myth of Ragnarök shows that it does not take a great assertion to bring on calamity; rather, small incidents or words feed the potential for disorder (in human terms, violence). In *Gísla Saga,* idle womens' chatter brings on the death of the hero, while early in *Njála* the author senses the pernicious potential of daily triviality: "there was much chatter, for they were unwise" (chap. 8). Later in the saga, as mentioned above, descriptions of nonempirical reality (the *draumkonur*) dominate the narrative, until at the end the hero psychologically lives more in the mythic world than in the empirical world.

Yet destruction is not defeat. Returning to the human world, we can see Vestein accepting destruction as an ontological principle, yet he is not reduced to passivity; neither is Gunnar, neither is Njál, until he is too old to resist. Njál does not *see* the bloody *fylgja* of Thord, but he knows the reality of the situation: that ultimate truth incorporates a paradox. Though mythic time has announced that Thord is dead, Njál still suggests that he defend himself, knowing at the same time that it will be of no practical use, since he is a "doomed man." Thord then asserts his freedom so well that not only does the author of the saga comment on the quality of his defense, but Thrain Sigfusson, one of the murderers, recognizes that in yielding to the historical necessity that has obligated him to commit a dishonorable act, he has implemented the deterioration of human resistance to chaos: "we have done," he says, "an evil deed." Njál and Gunnar will continue to affirm individual human freedom in the face of evil by maintaining their friendship, in spite of the forces working to drive them apart. The other characters fall victim to legal necessity and vengeance which augments the spreading degeneration of human value. "I wish I knew," says Gunnar, "whether I am less a man than others because I am more reluctant to kill than they are," yet Gunnar is the greatest of warriors.

In the displacement of the symbolic universe of myth to the human world of historical time we are at the heart of the drama of the Norse apprehension of reality: personal excellence need not triumph historically to have a satisfying mythic base. The myth of Ragnarök suggests why nobility lies not in the confident expectation of triumph but in the resisting of the latent tide of chaos, and why superiority to evil is not predicated upon its defeat.

The paradox of a cultural respect for law and the literary depiction of violence, outlawry, and the demonic supernatural as normal is basically the coming together in one style of a realism based upon secular criteria for freedom with a realism based upon a displaced myth. Law, the secular assertion of rational human order in historical time, is the alternative to surrendering to the violence and anarchy which is not a departure from a fundamentally ordered creation, but is an ontological fact. Collectively, man partakes of a profane irony; individually, the hero partakes of a mythic tragedy.

The singular quality of Norse heroism arises, therefore, as a consequence of the Norse view of reality, a symbolic universe given form both in mythology and in the sagas. The unified apprehension of empirical and nonempirical objects produced an undifferentiated world, a world in which both space and time could be—and were—annihilated by the mythic consciousness, a world in which the supernatural as portent was directly perceived as heightened reality. By these means, too, cause could be understood as an active relationship between objects and events which to the modern mind would seem unrelated. This view gave the world a wondrous quality, for in it man was not a prisoner of a natural process governed by rationally determined law, but was able to appropriate the past, the future, and the "other" world (especially that of the dead, again involving time) into the consciousness. This did not leave him wholly free, however, for his vision of his own future—and the gods' vision of the world's future—allowed him to perceive his fate. In a sense, then, the individual was a prisoner of the past and the future, of mythic time, yet paradoxically he was also free to choose the quality of his conduct, to succumb to historicity or to define himself heroically by imitating mythic paradigms. By rising above determinism, the extraordinary man could achieve a kind of victory, though resistance to moral anarchy often took the form of negating civil law. Indeed, legal process in many sagas furthers the deterioration of human value, and good men execute evil deeds.

This is the wisdom of Njál, "who was wise and could see into the future." He is not wise in terms of being able to influence or control the future; as a hero, his world is too displaced for such power. Rather, he is wise because he sees that no event exists in isolation, that the chain of causality winds inexorably from genesis to apocalypse. He also knows that good men will impose their freedom upon chaos and fate, transcending the ultimate disintegration by choosing to resist it.

The paradigm of paradoxical victory in defeat makes the heroism of Norse saga-narrative more subtle than other examples of medieval heroic literature. Myth makes heroism possible; perhaps it is the very displacement of the myth of Ragnarök that makes the sagas "good stories" in a way that saints' legends, the Bishops' sagas and continental narrative informed by a developed religious consciousness are not. Such a style, while incorporating abstraction and reflection, cannot embody antinomies as can displacements of myth. Ricoeur touches upon a literary limitation of the religious consciousness in noting, "If, then, the religious consciousness hesitates to *formulate* the tragic theology, that is because elsewhere it professes 'the innocence of God,' to speak in Platonic language, or his 'holiness,' in Biblical language. Explicit formulation of the tragic theology would mean self-destruction for the religious consciousness."[32]

Yet religion also has strong roots in myth, and makes myth's claim to ultimate knowledge. To reinforce this claim, however, missionary Christianity of the middle ages could expose paganism, much as did Saint Olaf with the temple of Thor. For a style representing theologically regulated reality to govern narrative, for triumph to replace tragedy, the explicit antinomies of pagan undisplaced myth had to be either neutralized and transformed, or destroyed. This was the mission of the conversion.

(3)

BROKEN MYTH:
REASON, SYMBOL, AND
CONVERSION

One of the functions of myth is to legitimize human actions by letting them be understood as embodiments of sacred paradigms. These paradigms, it will be recalled, exist as extensions of human value, yet are apprehended as something suprahuman. Man finds security in integrating the historical world with the sacred, for the mythic universe is one of moral certainty, in which affirmation of the reality of divine or heroic archetypes is not only possible but intrinsic. In the universe where mythic images constitute a coherent whole, a sufficient explanation and orientation, myth, religion, and rational inquiry are complementary parts of what Tillich calls "unbroken myth."[1]

Space-time in this unbroken universe is in a sense a four-dimensional continuum, in that the sacred past is an integral part of the reality of the present. The truths of this four-dimensional mythic continuum are vulnerable, however, to a dialectical principle as inexorable as entropy to the empirical universe. Discussing the dialectic of man's perpetual dissatisfaction, Berdyaev says that "every culture at a certain stage of its development discloses a principle which saps its own spiritual foundations,"[2] The contact between the pagan Germanic tribes and the Christian missionary culture disclosed three aspects of just such a principle: first, the further erosion of myth already begun; second, the revelation produced by confrontation with the formal quality of Christianity; and third, the employment of Greek philosophy as an ally of the Church. These tensions, both within myths and between myth and reason, form a theme central to this study.

The first danger to myth is the empirical "marginal" experience which disturbs the mythic world of the individual or culture. In the rational world, an object which would fall up would be such an experience; a phenomenon, though unintelligible, since it is outside reason's norms of space, time, and cause. The sacred efficacy of the principle of concrescence has some elasticity, of course. If one mariner, having become the hero Aori, fails to return, it is possible that he did not imitate the paradigm exactly. As more mariners do not come back, however, an element of contemplation sets in; sooner or later enough "violations" of the mythic causal principle accumulate to achieve overload, and the order is disrupted.

Another development also emerges from the interaction of myth and marginal experience: a gradual subordination of the power of the gods to "destiny." Such a separation does not negate the efficacy of sacred paradigms but subjects them to a higher, inscrutable power—fate. We saw this in the discussion of Norse myth above, where the gods order but are victims along with men of an inimical cosmic process. In this apprehension of fate, myth maintains a delicate equilibrium between the images of order and orientation and the potentially patternless nature of marginal human experience. Although Norse myth never achieved the level of intellectualization which resulted in the Greek concept of *moira*, it offers nonetheless a profound insight into the significance of human assertion of value.

But reason (or theoretical thought)—not the idea of fate—is myth's real enemy. The narrator of the "Völuspá" does not go into the *why* of creation, but as narratives of genesis are subject to inquiry seeking to ascertain the degree of their truth, the absolute knowledge given by myth receives its mortal blow. "Where philosophy first raises this question—where, instead of seeking the foundation of reality, it asks after the meaning and foundation of truth—the bond between being and time seems to be severed at one stroke."[3] Plato sees "true being" as having neither beginning nor end; neither does truth.

Philosophical reflection can have several relationships to myth, ranging from an uneasy accommodation with images felt to be no longer quite adequate to express truth, but "symbolically true" (that is, expressing a lower degree of truth than reason), to out-and-out atheism. Once being and truth are seen as timeless, " 'logos' has torn itself away from myth—pure thought has declared its independence from the mythical powers of fate."[4]

The consequences of theoretical thought for myth are radical, for the abstraction of rational principle and law ultimately sever man's bond to the sacred. Yet the sundering of myth's concrescence of genesis with the present is not done absolutely, for a completely rational cognition of experience produces a terrible estrangement from the past and a deterioration of the legitimizing power of myth's symbolic universe. A peculiar paradox of modern Western culture is the reluctance of rational man to leave the universe of myth, preferring to transform myth's constructs so as to give them an ostensibly empirical base. The Hellenic, the Hebrew, and the Christian cultures all developed to a point at which the principle of concrescence was no longer sufficient to explain the diverse nature of human experience, but a universe completely severed from its roots in myth appeared so intolerable that each managed to reach some accommodation between the morally neutral world of space-time as apprehended by reason and the expression of the world in mythic images.[5] The concept of symbol, though retaining much of the efficacy of the mythic construct, deprived it of its objectivity. It was in this fashion that the peculiar nature of the Christian symbol developed an accommodation between myth and reason that colored the Church's confrontation with the Germanic tribes.

Through its symbolic view of the phenomenal world Christianity had developed from its base in Old Testament Judaism, but it also had moved to incorporate some of the rationalism of the Greeks. The basic axiom in the Hellenic world view was the rational constitution of creation;[6] order, the world and *kosmos* were essentially synonymous, and the cyclical nature of astronomical motions was an indication of regularity and perfection in creation.[7]

As we have seen, Augustine sensed the danger attendant upon viewing the motion of the heavenly bodies as constituting time, precisely because of the consequent unhallowing of history. Although in the *Confessions* Augustine's Hellenism is at odds with the mythic traditions of Judaism, in *The City of God* he was to synthesize a new mythical view of human history. This synthesis of myth and reason, which was to be such a potent weapon in the conversion of the Germanic tribes,[8] was made possible through the distinction between the religious symbol and the mythic symbol.

By "religious symbol" we do not mean regarding creation-narrative as a *mythos,* as Plato regards his *Timaeus:* a set of images, recognized as only "probable."[9] The religious symbol retains the power latent in the mythic construct, but the construct is recognized as being not sacred in itself—it is a lens through which the sacred is apprehended.

Thor's image can be destroyed, and his cult vanishes; the ark of the covenant must be jealously guarded, lest harm befall the Deity; the name of Jahweh must be disguised, lest enemies gain control of the Sacred. A destruction of the Cross, however, has no effect upon Christ: the image is recognized as sacred, but not identical with it, as in the mythic consciousness.[10] Central to the success of the conversion of the Germanic tribes by medieval Christian culture was just this dual nature of the religious symbol: with its roots in myth, the contest could be one of power (St. Michael versus Thor); with the element of reflection necessary for such a symbolic awareness, the pagan faith could be assaulted through reason.

This understanding developed slowly, and as in any accommodation of myth and theoretical thought it was not without tension. We mentioned above that the Hebrew creation myth differs from the other creation myths in several respects, one being that nothing is overcome in the act of creation, though the initial power is, again, oral. The result of this creation by fiat is a lack of paradigms: as Bultmann suggests, the Old Testament does not reveal the operating principles of creation, in that the law is announced, not established.[11] The God of the Hebrews constantly intervenes in human history, but not as a periodic actualization of sacred archetypes. Neither man nor the symbolic universe of the Hebrews is rationally constituted, and herein lies the necessity for unreflecting belief.[12]

In one sense, theoretical thought has no place in a universe where the divine *creates* matter and time, and is not a shaper of chaos into cosmos, subject to a quality existing "when above the heaven had not been named." Kant saw what Augustine had feared: that rational contemplation of time ends in paradox. One can see, however, an attempt to accommodate the implications of the Hebrew creation myth and historical time even in the Old Testament. This accommodation begins with the dawning realization that the divine is not *contained* in the object (as in primitive myth) but that the divine expresses itself through the phenomenal world. Isaiah for instance recognizes that an adequate representation cannot be made of the Creator (41:18), and rejects idolatry, where the sacred object is identical with the divine, as a "lower" form of consciousness: "Shall I fall down to the stock of a tree?" (45:19). Saint Olaf, it will be recalled, challenges his opposition of Thor worshipers with the same concept of symbolic divinity when he compares an idol that "cannot budge" to the divinity that cannot be seen.

In the Old Testament the lack of paradigmatic knowledge accessible through a ritual integration with genesis, coupled with the realization that the Creator did not reside, but was immanent in creation, has several consequences. First of all, faith in the Old Testament is not based upon propositional knowledge but on renunciation of self-will and consequent confident submission to a divine will whose causal principles are often ineluctable.[13]

Pursuing this further, we may say that what distinguishes both Isaiah's concept of the object and his view of history is an awareness of the symbolic nature of the mythic content. This is, of course, far from articulated, but Isaiah's reluctance to worship a tree indicates the inadequacy of primitive myth for him to express the divine. At this stage the religious object and the religious event retain the efficacy of myth, but their reality is not complete in themselves; they point to an ultimate reality which is recognized as transcendent. Tillich thinks here is the fundamental distinction of the religious symbol.[14]

This nascent awareness of the prophets of the symbolic nature of the human world is both foreign to the primitive mythic consciousness and a development of it. Early Christian culture developed the dual roots of the symbol in myth and transcendence into a vision of man and time. Keeping the linear and eschatological elements of the Hebraic view of history, Christian thinkers rejected the Hellenic view of time as cyclical and elaborated Christendom's fundamental fact—the Incarnation—into a philosophy of historical fulfillment.[15] This synthesis had its roots both in myth and in rational thought, and as we shall see, was able to mount a twofold assault on the pagan world.

The Incarnation of Christ provided the paradigmatic legitimization for the Christian symbolic universe, but this sacred event takes place in historical time. Here again we see not the abolition of historical time, but the sanctification of it. If in the prophets the magical nature of the empirical world is rejected as a lower form of worship, as idolatry, in Christianity the fallen world is first renounced, then reclaimed and rejuvenated through faith. Here lies the singular potency of the Christian symbol, for the incarnation of Christ as a humble figure provides a mythic paradigm asserting the simultaneous reality and transcendance of the rationally trivial act. When Matthew reports that "whosoever

shall give to drink unto one of these little ones a cup of cold water only
in the name of a disciple, verily I say unto you, he shall in no wise lose
his reward" (10:42), he is announcing a stance toward the historical
world which gives sacred power to the humble content by declaring its
symbolic reality.

This affirmation of both the reality and the symbolic nature of the
object was extended into the apprehension of time. Though the historical event was again asserted to be unique and nonrecurring,[16] the
mythic basis of the symbolic view provided a complex concrescence
with the sacred that served to legitimize the historical world in mythic
terms. Time not only has a beginning and an end but through the
Incarnation a midpoint. As in the concept of the divine object, this
event does not exist outside time but occurred in historical time, and
hence is not recoverable as a primitive myth. In the Epistle to the
Hebrews, Paul emphasizes both the unique character of the historical
event and its anticipation of the end to history; unlike gods in rites of
cyclical generation, Christ did not "offer himself often, as the high
priest entereth into the holy place every year with blood of others; For
then must he often have suffered since the foundation of the world: but
now once in the end of the world hath he appeared to put away sin by
the sacrifice of himself" (9:26–27).

The Council of Nicea in 325 emphasized this conquest of historical
time through the human-made-divine, the Resurrection. Christ's death
is both a finite, human succumbing to the determinism of historicity
and a free conquest of it, a regaining and anticipation of the "kingdom
with no end," which is extended to the believer through the Savior.
The peculiar tension latent in the Christian symbol can be seen in the
debate as to whether the Son was "of the same substance" as the
Father (*homousios*). Was the Son temporal or eternal?[17]

Similarly, the view of sacred intervention is a symbolic concept of
time alien to the Hebrews, for as was mentioned, Jahweh did not
manifest himself in a paradigmatic manner. In the Christian outlook,
however, God became historical, fulfilling genesis and anticipating
salvation. The Old Testament is not a genesis but a prelude to the
fundamental fact, the death of Christ.[18]

This concrescence of mythic time and profane event became an
elaborate method for understanding history in the Middle Ages, and
Augustine played a great part in the synthesis of myth and theoretical

thought. All pre-Christian historical time, then, was considered symbolic, prefiguring the time of Christ, which was both historical and sacred. In the figural interpretation of history, as described by Auerbach, we see a combination of mythic concrescence and the abstract intellectual relationships of theoretical thought: figural interpretation, Auerbach says,

> establishes a connection between two events or persons, the first of which signifies not only itself but also the second, while the second encompasses or fulfills the first. The two poles of the figure are separate in time, but both, being real events or figures, are within time, within the stream of historical life. Only the understanding of the two persons or events is a spiritual act, but this spiritual act deals with concrete events whether past, present, or future, and not with concepts or abstractions; these are quite secondary, since promise and fulfillment are real historical events, which have either happened in the incarnation of the Word, or will happen in the second coming.[19]

Thus the full reality of an Old Testament event requires a temporal dimension linking and sanctifying it by connecting it to Christ. In *The City of God,* Augustine sees Noah's ark as *praefiguratio ecclesiae* (15, 27), while Moses has an extension into Christ himself.

We have outlined the process by which myth emerges from prescientific cognition and is to some degree incorporated into the symbolic awareness of the religious consciousness. We have also hinted at a basic tension which eventually renders a mythic universe inadequate to absorb and integrate human experience. Though Augustine was finally able to solve the problem he posed in the *Confessions* concerning the two means of apprehending time,[20] the accommodation between myth and reason conceals a dialectical principle which ultimately undermines the symbolic universe of myth. Berdyaev describes the process as the repudiation by a culture of its own symbols,[21] an awareness that the rites and symbols are not constitutive of truth but are "merely" representations of truth. In the world of broken myth, reason, myth, and religion are no longer operating under a unified apprehension of reality but are validating truth by different criteria. Reason, contemplating mythic symbols, can accept them as truth only by seeing them as embodying a content ultimately rational; in this broken universe the objective reality of the mythic content erodes, passing from the sacred to the demonic, crossing the border to the untrue as superstition and finally so displaced from the sacred as to be comedy and travesty.

As an integral aspect of the reality of the mythic universe is its temporal dimension, the undermining of the truth of myth by this dialectic process leads to a crisis where a culture "begins to doubt and criticize the premises upon which it rests." Berdyaev continues that a culture eventually makes communion with sacred times inaccessible: "It prepares its own destruction by separating itself from its sources."[22] This had begun to happen in the pagan Germanic world; the conversion facilitated the process.

We pointed out earlier that one of the functions of myth is to legitimize the heroic act—without an orientation in myth there is no significance to heroism. We now continue the exploration of the dialectic between myth and rational thought in a specific context. The complex symbolic universe of medieval Christian culture outlined above employed both reason and its own mythic origins in the encounter with the less displaced mythic world of the Germanic tribes. In effect, the assault was upon the pagan concept of the object and of time; the result was a shattering of the legitimacy of the pagan world and a partial transformation of the hero.

The first important phase of the Church's strategy of conversion was the use of Christianity as a "counter myth," employing the elements of naive myth in the Church partly in an attempt to transform the Germanic social structure based upon the *comitatus* into one based upon the social myth of the Church. In effect, this tactic became an effort to compete in practical terms with the efficacy of the pagan gods—and myth knows the divine through the efficacy of the mythic object—by opposing them with the temporal power of the Christian God. The conversion of Clovis in 496, for example, was achieved by agreeing to have the issue decided in battle. If the king's prayers to the Christian God were answered with victory, this to the king would be sufficient proof that the pagan gods were inferior and that the Christian God was the true (that is, the stronger) power. The battle was won, and Clovis' conversion formed the political foothold of Christianity.[23]

Although this sort of "conversion" involved actions more political than religious, the effects of such tactics in the long run had great impact upon the mythic consciousness. Initially, the effects of the political phase of the conversion was to replace what Baetke calls the Germanic "cult and legal religion" with a similar one stemming from the theology of Gregory I, whose ultimate source was Augustine.[24] Gregory's dogmatic emphasis lay not upon the death of Christ but upon his life; salvation from the power of the Devil and sin. As this affected the Germanic tribes, the pagan gods were not relegated to nonbeing but had their "true" nature exposed—as demons, a clear and present danger.[25]

The superficial demands of the Church were externally quite simple—baptism and individual submission to Church ritual and dogma[26]—but it was a mark of acuity on the part of the missionaries that they quickly recognized these as essential means to break the continuity with the pagan mythic past, to destroy the temporal dimension of the mythic consciousness.

The effects of this assault upon the world of pagan myth can be seen both in the documents of the Church and in the internal ones, documents which describe the reactions of the mythic world to the new faith. The act of baptism, the first of the Church's demands, was often facilitated by the broadsword, but to the pagans the act was regarded not as symbolic but as a rite of real magical efficacy, often giving the baptizer power over the convert, and several converts are reported to have been killed in this manner. The social effect of baptism was generally viewed as cutting the person off not only from the old gods and totems but also from dead pagan kinsmen as well, severing the magical bond between them;[27] thus baptism, in disrupting the continuity with the past, had a devastating effect upon the mythic consciousness of the pagans.

Olaf Tryggvason's bride-to-be, for example, refuses baptism by saying that she does not choose to give up that faith (trú) held by her forefathers (frœndr mínir), though Olaf can believe in whatever god suits him. In the mythic image world, the reactions to the change in faith by the pagan tutelary spirits, to use an example from the previous chapter, also show an awareness of the danger the new faith will bring to the world of pagan myth. Several instances are related where the tutelary spirit complains to the individual that baptism has broken the bond between them and that he can no longer be of use.[28] In

Tháttr Thorvalds ins Víðförla, the bishop's persecution of Kodran's *spámaðr* leads it to object that the treatment is cruel and barbaric; after three nights of this the *spámaðr* has wasted away to such an extent that he is forced to leave.

Baptism was also often described as a shame to the family (*frænda-skömm*), and there are recorded instances of the dead kinsmen (who were still a part of the community) appearing in dreams and taking vengeance for the breaking of the temporal continuity. After Gest in the *Bárðar saga Snæfelsáss* has become a Christian, he is blinded in a dream by his dead father, Bard, who says that he has shamed the faith of his forefathers by his paltriness.[29]

The second demand made by the Church of its converts, submission to the dogma of the Church, had a similar effect, for Christian customs ran directly counter to the pagan social order, which had its basis in the sacred world of myth.[30] Indeed, the very eagerness of some of the early converts was deemed by pagans to be in bad taste and not a little silly: "Ketil was an eager Christian and the heathens called him Ketil Foolish."[31]

The consternation on the part of the tutelary spirits over baptism is reflected in the opposition of the farmers to subordinating themselves to the institutions of the Church. It was not only the obvious forbidding of sacrifice and worship of the *landvættir;* these were but symptomatic of the aversion to the disruption of tradition resulting from the breaking of continuity with the past. Asbjörn of Methalhús speaks to King Håkon the Good for the men of his area in saying that when they chose him to be their king they thought they were regaining their ancestral rights, but now they are not sure, for he demands that they relinquish the custom of their ancestors, who were better men than they.[32] In general the effects of both aspects of Christianity were seen by the heathens as a scandal to kinsmen, living and dead.

The Church attempted to cope with this aspect of the mythic consciousness of time not only by forbidding ancestor worship but also by instituting the counter myth of the saints. The powerful chieftain Hall of Side is converted by being convinced that St. Michael can better look after his interests than the pagan protective spirits. But the goal of breaking the Nordic continuity with its heathen past was not accomplished merely by transference. Rather, the pagan rituals were gradually secularized—divested of their mythic role. An illustration of this can be seen in the attitude of the Church toward the ritual of libation and the customs surrounding the grave mound, which under various names were viewed as two exclusively pagan practices, in that they implied the nearness and presence of the dead.

The initial approach to the first practice, that of veneration of grave mounds, was to isolate them linguistically as "heathen." Quite early the grave mounds are called "sacrifice mounds" (*blóthaugar*) or "heathen mounds" (*heidnir haugar*), heathens being described by one commentator as being those who sat out on mounds and aroused trolls.[33] This might explain the number of citations in the early laws concerning the grave mound and the practice of "sitting-out."[34]

In Norway at least the Church disposed of the practice ostensibly by compromising on the problem. Fines made it impossible to bury the dead outside hallowed ground (hence the traditional grave mound as a burial place was outlawed), but for a while it was allowed to place runestones on a mound; later the stones too were transferred to the Christian grave.[35] The solution, then was to allow the symbol of the custom to remain but to remove the physical presence of the dead which was the animation of the symbol.

The libation ritual at a wake (called by several names, but usually *gravøl*) was as much a problem to the Church authorities as the grave mound, and was handled in a similar fashion. In Norway, the Church attempted to dispatch the *gravøl* by splitting it in two, so to speak; as a ritual libation to the dead, the *gravøl* was customarily held on the seventh day after death, and marked the turning-over and continuity of family property. The laws under the Christian administration kept the legal function of the *gravøl* ("When a man is deceased, the heir is to seat himself in the highseat and gather together all the beneficiaries to meet on the seventh day, so that each can receive his inheritance so that witnesses can testify") but attempted to divorce it from homage to the dead, and eradicate the mythic base to the legal ritual.[36]

One way of doing this was to decree that if the heir wished to celebrate an inheritance with a *gravøl,* this could be done on the seventh day, but if it was to honor the dead it must be called a "libation for the *soul*" (*salo øl*), and a priest must be invited who must be paid for the religious services. The attempt to Christianize the old custom, held on the seventh day, evidently had little success, judging from later statutes against it.[37]

More effective was the method for handling the grave mound customs. The seventh day was kept as the day of inheritance, but religious practices were forbidden on that day. In all the laws the day for the *religious* rites for the dead was changed to the fifth day after death ("The corpse of a Christian is to be brought to the church within five days' time"), so that by removing the dead person physically from the *gravøl,* placing him in consecrated ground, the ritual establishing continuity with the dead had no means to sustain itself.[38]

The proscription of ritual forming a link with the mythic past and with the community, a bond vital to the survival of the naive mythic consciousness, was a primary goal of the Christian mission in its tactic of establishing a counter myth—the substitution of Christian rite and Christian symbols. This interruption broke the sense of immediacy with the dead and with the present world of efficacious images and was on the whole successful, as was the adaption of pagan rites into Christian festivals (as was done with the rite of Easter, for example).

The attack on the pagan practices of maintaining contact with the dead was not just an effort to break the tie with the mythic past but was also an attempt to introduce the concept of the immaterial soul, with an existence after death in a mode fundamentally different from that in the profane world. Here the Christian culture operated not as counter myth but as formal religion, for to explain the concept of a world of pure spirit involved not just a manipulation of the primitive mythic consciousness but its destruction. To effect this the Christian culture could avail itself of a weapon whose ultimate nature and power were not yet fully appreciated—logic. By confronting the pagan mythic consciousness with logic's criteria of validating truth the missionaries could show the inadequacies of mythic thought. A letter of Daniel, Bishop of Winchester, to Boniface sometime between 723 and 725 indicates the strategy of this approach, for not only is Daniel conscious of the vulnerability of the mythic consciousness to the rational method of checking and proof, but he also sees that myth's weakest point is its concept of a narrative, absolute past. Bishop Daniel's letter is a remarkable description of the dialectic relationship between mythic thought and logical thought, a dialectic which continued through the eighteenth century.

"You may most readily overcome the resistance of those uncivilized people," he says, not by "arguing with them about the origin of their gods," but by letting them "affirm that some of them were begotten by others," and taking as a point of departure the argument that "since they did not exist before, they must have had a beginning," he continues:

> Then, when they have been compelled to learn that their gods had a beginning since some were begotten by others, they must be asked in the same way whether they believe that the world had a beginning or was always in existence without beginning. If it had a beginning, who created it? Certainly they can find no place where begotten gods could dwell before the universe was made. . . . But if they should argue that the world always existed without beginning, you should strive to refute this and convince them by many documents and arguments. Ask your opponents who governed the world before the gods were born, who was their ruler? How could they bring under their dominion or subject to their law a universe that had always existed before them? And whence, or from whom or when, was the first god or goddess set up or begotten? . . .
>
> At intervals you should compare their superstitions with our Christian doctrines, touching upon them from the flank, as it were, so that the pagans, thrown into confusion rather than angered, may be ashamed of their absurd ideas and may understand that their infamous ceremonies and fables are well known to us.[39]

Bishop Daniel is suggesting that the theoretical assault not be made frontally, that is, by attacking the value-truths of myth, but by exposing the means by which myth asserts truth as inadequate. The Christian missionary, arguing from the logical basis of Greco-Roman thought (which, since Augustine, was assumed to be consistent with revelation), offers the apple of self-consciousness to the pagan myth by showing its inadequacy in the alien realm of empirical truth.

Some of the vernacular literature from the Old High German period perhaps indicates an effect of this tactic, for since Daniel bases his logical argument upon the fallacy of begotten, temporal deities, it is possible that there is a tie-in to the subsequent emphasis in much of the religious literature upon God, the creator out of nothing. For example, the "Wessobrunner Gebet," a poetic fragment from the late eighth or early ninth century, says: "I heard tell among men of marvels the greatest, that the earth once was not, nor the heaven above, nor tree . . . nor hill was, nor any stone; nor shone the sun, nor did the moon shine, nor the great sea. When there was nought, of end or boundary, then was the one almighty God, the most merciful of men."[40]

A prose prayer following the poem asks God to help the author "resist devils" and hold to the "right belief." This reflects a transitional state of religious faith between paganism and Christianity, for by "right belief" is meant in part a negative belief: *not* believing in the heathen gods. When the writer prays for help in withstanding the Devil, he refers to the still-powerful heathen deities, which is the sense in which he uses *arc* (evil).[41] Although some of the formulas are similar to those of the "Völuspá," the emphasis upon a conscious creation of matter as opposed to the "unexplained" formation of, say, the giant Ymir might suggest the attempt to introduce a concept of spirit beyond substance.

On a more mundane level, it was in the idea of the hero in which Christian literature was able to introduce the concepts of signification implicit in formal religion.[42] The sagas indicated that the ideal of the self-willed hero was the rule rather than the exception. The Church transmuted the mythic base of the *comitatus* into one with Christian images—the "thane of God." This can be seen in Continental literature particularly, where the actions of the individual hero are portrayed as but historical analogues of divine will. The Germanic ethic of the *comitatus*—the traditional relationship of man to man, thane to lord—was transformed and replaced by a similar relationship of hero to God. This transformation of the pagan ethic finds illustration in the Old High German poem "Ludwigslied" (ca. 881–882).[43] The poem deals with a battle between the Frankish king Ludwig and pagan Norsemen and uses conventional motifs from heroic poetry. The hero, the younger son of a king, is trained by a renowned master; attacked by a foreign enemy, he arrives on the scene at the last moment, exhorts his troop of heroes, and wins a great victory.

The thematic emphasis, however, is not upon the ruler as hero but upon him as an agent of God and the Church, defending "God's people" (1. 23). The battle is not just between Franks and Norsemen but between Christians and pagans and is described as having a higher significance—it is really a test of the king and a chastisement of his people (II. 9–10). Ludwig is not a hero defending his kingdom and liegemen but a Christian knight, ordained to serve God (I. 2), who was Ludwig's weapon-master (I. 4). The warriors are Ludwig's retainers only incidentally; basically they are knights of God also (I. 36), fighting not for fame but to work God's will against the heathens in the continuing battle against idolatry (I. 30). The *comitatus,* with its roots in myth, has been replaced by a formally religious relationship, where the power and authority of the hero come neither from his own will nor from the sacred past, accessible through rites, traditions, and other social structures, but from God, and events in historical time are understood as being "really" part of God's plan. The *kraft* is not the hero's innate power but flows from God (I. 55); similarly, the reward for fealty comes not from the hero's hand but from God, through being freed from historical time and entering eternity.

The sagas show little of this concept of the Christian hero, for they are not generally emancipated from the mythic perception of reality. Yet the era of conversion was a time of uncertainty, conflict, and doubt, a shattering of the old gods and a lack of familiarity with the new. In the saga literature, there is some evidence of this period of transition, and one character type—the "noble heathen"[44]—might be regarded as the product, or perhaps the victim, of the change from naive to Christian myth, or at least of a sense of formalism (a feeling that the pagan myth is inadequate to confront the Christian mission).

The noble heathen as a type is illustrated by such characters as Njál in *Njáls Saga* and Gísli in *Gísla Saga* who, although lacking a formal conception of a transcendent deity, are at least partially emancipated from attachment to mythic deities. To what extent these characters, who have attained a certain rational monotheism (or at least skepticism), are creations of the saga writers in the thirteenth century or mirror the "marginal experiences" of the tenth is not easily determined, but they are often men of exceptional wisdom or heroism.[45] As described by Lars Lönnroth, their "natural religion"—a belief in "him who made the sun"—is sometimes portrayed as the result of undirected reflective contemplation, with contact with Christianity later providing the necessary element of revelation. Yet even though these characters are often distinguished through their wisdom (Njál, for example), critics have found this natural monotheism out of place in the sagas and anomalous and suggest that it was a means later Christian writers employed to establish the moral excellence of pagan heroes. Modern critics are not alone in this feeling, for even other characters in the sagas, whose sense of reality is conditioned by different norms, also find these "noble heathens" a little peculiar.

Another character type which shows a detachment from the world of myth is the "godless man."[46] This character claims that no gods are adequate and believes only in himself. Such a growing separation from the primitive belief is perhaps natural, considering the relative lateness of the conversion (tenth century) in Norway and Iceland; also, in the ninth and tenth centuries Norway experienced violent social upheavals which displaced many of the former landowners. Although some emigrated to Iceland, literally taking their gods with them, others went abroad, some as far as Byzantium, and perhaps exposure to the multitude of beliefs was the source for the skeptical view of both primitive myth and formal religion. At any rate, it appears that Norse myth for some individuals had time to reach what Cassirer calls a "crisis"—that is, the traveler became aware that the primitive mythic forms could not absorb and express in myth his broadened range of experience, and the forms thus lost their quality of objective reality without ever evolving—for this character type at least—to the metaphorical state of formal religion.

Berger and Luckmann hold that "identity is ultimately legitimized by placing it within the context of a symbolic universe,"[47] so that a realization by these "godless men" of the contingent quality of the old order isolates them by making them wander in a meaningless historical world. Thus Christian culture, instead of forcing this awareness upon the pagans in the manner Bishop Daniel advocates, in some cases filled a cultural vacuum already developed with an orientation in a superior mythic universe. To some of the "godless men," however, for whom the complexities and contradictions of the historical world had become evident, the mythic elements of Christianity seemed no more sensible than the old belief.

If the conversion be considered as a test between two forms of mythic thought, the Christian culture won a clear victory over Norse pagan myth by interrupting rite and symbol which formed the essential bond for the mythic consciousness, then by substituting Christian rite and symbol, assimilating elements of pagan myth into Church festivals. Nevertheless, the pagan mythic consciousness displayed a resilience and obduracy which indicates that although the forms of myth are vulnerable to attack by more sophisticated modes of thought the mythic impulse is disposed of less easily. This can be seen first in the problems of syncretism, which in the mission to the Germanic tribes plagues the authorities from the start. Around 737 or 739 Pope Gregory III had to admonish bishops in Alemannia and Bavaria to "hold themselves completely away from offering to the dead,"[48] and even though the gods were largely diabolized, Church officials found that the mythic aspects of Christianity were at times absorbed into the pagan mythic consciousness. One problem, judging by the *Indiculus superstitionem,* was that individuals began to regard their ancestors as saints and continued to sacrifice to them.[49]

Nor does the strategy of cutting off the symbolic roots of the libation and the grave mound appear to have been completely successful, for as late as the eighteenth century in Norway clerics registered complaints concerning the continuation of these customs.[50] Folklorists have noted that in later folktales the dead return and behave in much the same manner as they do in the sagas,[51] and they record many survivals of both the libation ritual at the wake and the veneration of the grave mound. These customs are not always recognized by the participants as worship of the dead, but the correspondence is so striking as to indicate the perpetuation of prescientific mythic forms even into the twentieth century. As an indication of the survival of the idea that the dead are still a part of the community and are present in the grave mound, A. W. Brøgger tells of an excavation in 1909 of a grave mound from the migration period. The owner of the farm in all seriousness maintained that "garvorn" lived in the mound and that it had been the custom in the past to give him a butchered animal (*slakt*) whenever anyone on the estate died. When asked how long it had been since "garvorn" had been fed, the farmer replied, "Oh, we butchered a heifer for him when my father died."[52]

This and other instances appear to support the suggestion that the mythic consciousness retains in some degree its formative principles even in confrontation with a "superior" kind of knowledge. The history of the conversion of the Germanic tribes indicates that although logical thought can expose the *forms* of myth, often rendering them untrue in the eyes of those who previously believed in them, the mythic consciousness giving symbolic structure to the intuitions of value is likely to seek other—but similar—forms within the norms of myth and thus absorb the attacks made by logical thought.

Although elements of Norse myth displayed a striking ability to persist in primitive form as a sort of "outlaw" cult and other elements crept into Christianity itself, the Christian religion was ultimately dominant both through its effective advancement of a counter myth and through its use of formal logic. Yet Paul's warning that the use of reason as a criterion for establishing religious truth poses dangers for faith ("the letter kills") will be seen in the historical writings of the humanists. The growing role for reason in the demonstration of truth was finally to be employed not just against the "superstitions" of the pagans but against Church doctrine itself. For the time being, however, reason and revelation maintained an increasingly uneasy equilibrium, complementing each other in the creation of social myth, discussed in the next chapter. In the development of the vision of Germania by German humanists and of Gothicism by Swedish historians of the Great Power Era of the sixteenth and seventeenth centuries not only was the myth of the golden age expressed in Nordic images, but the element of belief took its modern form. Though the myths of Germania and Gothicism became inexpressive to the point of being comic, in the validation of a mythically constituted nostalgia by an ostensibly empirical methodology we will see the basis of modern mythic forms.

(4)

NATIONAL IDENTITY
AND SOCIAL MYTH: GERMANIA
AND SWEDISH GOTHICISM

In a sense all myth is social, in that one of its functions is to give identity by providing an orientation in a sacred, created universe. The truths of myth are cultural truths, for a culture knows its values through the images given them. Like mirrors, these images and sets of images are seen existing independently of the observer, yet they give him a means of understanding existence in dramatic terms. To the primitive, there can be myths for the most minute details of daily life, each rooted in ultimate reality and in turn anchoring the believer in a universe of meaning and significance. Although the scope of myth can range from static intensifying of an object in space to sanctifying of the present by placing it against the backdrop of the creation of the universe, the function is the same: to provide knowledge, knowledge which is apprehended as objective and absolute. This knowledge constitutes man's private and communal identities.

One form of identity that the mythic consciousness makes possible is heroism, for the hero has paradigmatic reasons for his assertions. In the postscientific world, however, the problem of heroic legitimation is more complex. Truths developed by the mythic consciousness cannot withstand logical and empirical scrutiny, but the desire for moral certainty in man leads, even in an era where rational inquiry is deemed sufficient to ascertain truth, to the production of value theories so ostensibly dependent upon reason and empirical method that their origin in myth is for a time wholly disguised.

The primary distinction between modern myth, whether social or literary, and other forms of myth we have discussed is in the kind of narrative employed. The narrative world of modern myth makes no overt pretense to being sacred: though the moral function is the same in all forms of myth, modern myths are apparently completely displaced from both the sacred world of prescientific creation narratives and the interaction of the sacred with the profane in heroic literature. Though the factual status is asserted, the objectivity is expressed in ostensibly demythologized language, rather than language explicitly religious.

This collapsing of the distinction between the sacred and the profane makes modern myth, particularly social myth, difficult to approach. The conception of a Nordic golden age by German humanists and Scandinavian scholars of the sixteenth and seventeenth centuries had the function of legitimizing contemporary assertions of heroism, but the dialectic between myth and reason was incorporated into the very symbolic matrix of these social myths. In a sense the fusion was similar to that of medieval Christianity, but the myths of Germania and Gothicism are nearly completely displaced into the secular world of human history. In a striking amalgamation of reason and the mythic imagination the Nordic past was recreated as a divine archetype, as a sacred genesis of the social values of the present. This golden age of the North shared with primitive myth the necessity to be thought objectively real, but the criteria for determining objective reality had changed by the time of the humanists, for reason was evolving into a self-conscious method, ostensibly "objective," developing its symbolic structures in a manner supposedly independent of myth and religion.[1] The Church, which had incorporated much scientific discovery into its apprehension of reality,[2] was having to cope with a radical transformation of man's understanding of the physical world which insisted upon a new method for validating truth.

For centuries the Church had successfully subordinated scientific inquiry to mythic truth, reason to faith, but by the time of Copernicus enough marginal experiences had occurred to put the medieval synthesis in the position of a "broken myth." Copernicus' main achievement was not the presenting of new data or facts—even his conclusions were highly suspect[3]—rather, he provided a new way of imagining the world, a new means of understanding both extant data and new data. The Church correctly saw what Copernicus and Galileo did not—that this new universe would be ultimately incongruent with the traditional Christian understanding of reality. It would be oversimplifying to suggest that the Church feared that the world would lose its symbolic quality. Instead, its authorities saw that the unconscious assumptions about what the world was symbolic *of* would change. By Galileo's time the fear had surfaced. Copernicus had not insisted upon the reality of his hypothesis (published in *De Revolutionibus Orbium Coelestium*, 1543), and thanks to a prudent preface added after his death the work did not arouse the immediate hostility of the authorities.[4] Galileo, however, not only asserted the absolute reality of the theory but assumed that scientific validation produced absolute truth, an idea which would undermine the whole medieval cosmos.[5]

In this context Kepler might be more accurately regarded as the true "demythologizer," for by positing the elliptical orbit of Mars he broke an originally mythical axiom thousands of years old: that the most perfect motion is circular. As Georges Poulet has shown, the circle has been one of the fundamental images of perfection,[6] and though Kepler simplified creation by his analysis of Tycho Brahe's data, the effect was demythologizing in that there was no "sacred center" in Eliade's sense, there was no absolute reference point (even Newton will assert the existence of absolute space), and there was no moral symmetry.

This emerging set of images of the physical world came to constitute a symbolic universe whose relationships and means for establishing truth were basically at odds with that of the Church. The Book of Nature, Galileo maintains, "is written in mathematical symbols."[7] As we have seen, however, demythologizing is not done instantly. For the time being, reason and revelation maintained an increasingly uneasy partnership, with the tacit assumption that the truths produced by scientific inquiry were coexistent with the mythically based images of Christian culture, truths held in common with the divine mind.[8]

This peculiar cohabitation of mythic images and rational constructs distinguishes early social myths, such as those of Germania and Swedish Gothicism, from prescientific myths. Modern myths must maintain their status as reality in two realms: first, as narrative constructs expressing more or less spontaneously the world of value, and second as historical, empirical fact. We will find that such myths are made by historians, philosophers, and other empirically oriented investigators and not by what we would call a formal literary consciousness. To oversimplify, if prescientific myth attains conceptual status as philosophy, modern myth develops its mythic concepts from a basis in philosophy. One area in which the two forms of truth complement each other is social myth.

Social myth may be defined as the intermingling of mythic images and rational inquiry in the apprehension of human value. As such, the constructs of social myth retain myth's quality of being objectively real to the believer, but the reality must be sustained by an appeal to scientific validation. Unlike prescientific myth, which portrays in narrative fashion an animistic universe, social myth is the product of the reflecting logical mind to which myth is falsehood. Thus the value-truths of social myths are assumed to be facts, attained through a putative scientific methodology and subject to empirical verification. Yet some of the same characteristics of prescientific myth also regulate the "objectivity" of social myth, principally the projection of contemporary value-truths into a symbolic genesis. While functioning as myth, these projections are legitimized as historical truth by methodologies thought sufficient to validate them as objective.

The two social myths of the Nordic origins—the vision of Germania of the German humanists and the later construct of Swedish Gothicism—took form in an era dominated by chiliastic myths. On the most primitive level the chiliastic movements of the sixteenth century, the Anabaptists, for example, completely rejected historical time, seeing the immediate revolution, the Apocalypse, as inducing the end of time, the Millenium.[9] The escape from the complexities of historicity into myth is the basis for what Mannheim calls the "absolute present-ness" of chiliastic movements, in that the Millenium is seen as immediate, revolution the only possible creative principle.[10]

Though it may be that all forms of utopias are chiliastic,[11] utopian constructs of a golden age imply order not destruction. The immediacy of the myth remains, but meaning is established as a reassertion of the order latent in the *illud tempus* rather than in a negation of historicity in anticipation of the New Jerusalem. In general the social myths of the Nordic past reconstituted the historical data of the Germanic world through the symbolic matrix of the golden age, reestablishing these archetypes as "sacred" and fixing them in historical time.[12]

The social myths of Germania and Swedish Gothicism may be seen as instances of what Mannheim calls the "spiritualization of politics."[13] Though expressed as heroic narrative, the present being understood as a reenactment of the definitive struggle of Teutonic (or Gothic) valor, these myths were presented in the form of history, with a quasi-factual basis derived from rational inquiry. In these historical visions of a primitive Germanic society there was no conscious attempt to alter a recognized body of historical material. Rather, the German humanists employed techniques (described below) thought sufficient to validate historical truth. In discovering contemporary value-truths in a time of genesis, humanist scholars did not find what they wanted to find; they found what they *had* to find.

Two main elements supported the creation of a myth of Gothic genesis: first, an understanding of history which saw the northern nations as the place of origin of political freedom; second, a methodology for establishing historical truth. Both of these stem from German humanist scholarship, though with medieval precedent,[14] and we will first consider the *topos* of *translatio imperii,* then the related myth of northern freedom.

The reestablishment of a mythic communion with the national genesis required first of all a schema of history entirely different from that of the Italian humanists, who saw their own era as the renaissance of a classical golden age and viewed the fall of Rome under the onslaught of the Goths as the fall into the dark "ages in the middle."[15] This new schema was provided by the medieval *topos* of *translatio imperii* (transfer of empire).[16] The Book of Daniel (2:40) prophesies four empires of the world, a statement explicated in the fifth century by Jerome to mean that the conquest of Rome in 412 by the Goths was a legitimate transfer of the authority of the Empire to the North.

Seeing the *topos* in moral terms, scholars could easily assimilate it into divine history: Jerome interprets the Goths as God's instrument for chastising Roman decadence; Augustine sees the fall of Rome as a historical demonstration of the sinful nature of the City of Man in comparison to the City of God.[17] With these two views of the past northern nations not only reestablished a continuity between the present and the time of cultural origins, but they injected a moral element in which the classical past came off decidedly second best—indeed, an illustration of the vices associated with tyranny and corruption. German humanists such as Ulrich von Hutten took as a symbolic genesis of the *translatio imperii* the defeat of Varus' Roman legions in A.D. 9 by Arminius, and the subsequent history of Arminius (or Hermann) in German intellectual life is an integral part of the myth of Germania.[18] For Swedish Gothicism, however, national pride found its symbolic event in the conquest of Rome in 410 by the Goths (assumed, as we shall see, to be Swedes).

The result of this understanding of the *translatio imperii* was a symbolic universe whose temporal dimension saw northern freedom conquering southern tyranny, a myth later disseminated by Montesquieu. The central document used to provide the facticity of Gothic moral superiority was Tacitus' *Germania,* discovered in the late fifteenth century. Tacitus, seeking to expose the vices of first-century Rome, ascribed to the Germans the virtues he thought lacking in his contemporaries. Though Tacitus failed in his moral mission, fifteen centuries later he was to serve as mythmaker. Two of his statements accepted uncritically as historically accurate became "sacred" texts which fired the imaginations of northern scholars to conceive of the Protestant present as a reincarnation of a golden age of the Goths.

First, they found in Tacitus documentation that the Germanic chiefs were democratic, leading by "example rather than their authority," with the whole community debating major issues (chapters 7, 11). This statement was of great importance, for it revealed that the northern countries were the originators of political freedom.[19] Second, scholars found in Tacitus a way to cope with the problem of their ancestors' paganism. Tacitus contrasts Roman idol-worship with the religion of the Germanic tribes, who "do not deem it consistent with the divine majesty to imprison their gods within walls or represent them with anything like human features," and he continues by noting that "their holy places are the woods and groves, and they call by the name of god that hidden presence which is seen only by the eye of reverence" (chapter 9). Tacitus complements this description of the Teutons' latent spirituality by mentioning their "ancient songs," celebrating the "earth-born god, Tuisto" (chapter 2).

As might be expected among those whose literary taste was conditioned by classical style, the idea of a literary merit in the "ancient songs" that Tacitus mentions was seldom broached among the humanists, nor was there at this time any attempt to recreate these songs in contemporary literature. In part this was due to the power of the dominant myth of the Renaissance which still saw the Goths as the destroyers of classical culture. North of the Alps, for instance, Erasmus blamed the Goths not only for the destruction of Greco-Roman culture but also for the introduction of illiteracy into medieval society.[20] By Shaftesbury's time, the "Goths" had become symbols of a timeless esthetic peril, "for even Barbarity and Gothicism were already enter'd into Arts, ere the Savages had made any Impression on the Empire."[21]

With Tacitus as a document, however, the historians and scholars of the northern nations such as Conrad Celtis (1459–1508) were able to construct and support with some logic a narrative beginning to their culture which showed that humanist values, derived from classical culture, existed not only in the sixteenth and seventeenth centuries but were present *in illo tempore,* with their own ancestors. This catalogue of virtues was essentially the same as those Tacitus ascribes to the Germans: chastity, piety, valor, love of nature, democracy.[22] Humanist scholars fashioned from all this a nonclassical *Urzeit* legitimizing their own values, amplifying the hints in Tacitus into a fully articulated vision of primitive humanist Teutons through accepted scholarly methodology. The ultimate goal was a northern *Germania illustrata,* modeled upon Biondo's famed exaltation of the Italian past;[23] although this was not realized in Germany during the time of the Reformation and the Thirty Years' War the vision became ever more real to the national historians, from Conrad Celtis through Philip Cluverius (1580–1622).[24]

With its scholastic origin providing historical respectability the theory of *translatio imperii* formed an effective basis for projecting humanist values into the mythic past: the "arch-humanist" Conrad Celtis exhorted his contemporaries to take up once more "that ancient spirit of yours, with which you so often terrified and confounded the Romans."[25] In going just a small step beyond the idea of the heroic North and a decadent South, Jacob Wimpfeling in 1505 was able to account for the noble qualities in his ancestors by noting that if "nobility is born of virtue, the early Germans were certainly in no way the inferiors of the Romans, for they always prided themselves on fidelity, honesty, justice, generosity and veracity."[26] By 1518 Celtis' idea of a *Germania illustrata* had developed to the extent that the historian Irenicus could legitimately challenge even the Italian concept of history by asking "Quis dicatur Barbarus?" and document at length the humanity, fidelity, chastity, and proto-Christianity of the ancient Germans.[27]

Yet this vision of the noble northern past continued the duality present in its genesis: the nobility ascribed to the early Germans was a moral, natural one and not a cultural one. The prestige of classical culture was too great, its accomplishments too evident, the lack of German cultural development too obvious, and the historical fact of Rome's destruction too well known for even the enthusiastic humanistic mythmakers to make a complete analogue of the past. The idea of German moral excellence (and low cultural status) and Roman cultural excellence (with moral decadence) was almost as attractive, and it had the advantage of squaring better with the obvious realities of the present. Not that there was entirely lacking a mythic effort to create an early Germanic intellectual life, but this had to be done virtually out of whole cloth.

A social myth, though, is not just fantasy: to maintain its "objective" status, an up-to-date methodology is required. Even though supported by an uncritical acceptance of Tacitus, the elevation of the *topos* of *translatio imperii* to mythic status was not enough in itself to legitimize northern national identity. The methodology for establishing the reality of the myth in this case was a combination of several techniques which, first, validated the myth of Germania in "scientific" terms and, second, connected the mythic genesis of the present northern heroism to a time sacred in a Christian sense to biblical history.

The first of these techniques was chronology, a demythologized view of time as mathematical sequence. Usually, chronology was employed to tie modern historical time first to a Gothic genesis and second to biblical history through an unbroken succession of rulers. As a technique to legitimize myth it served to give an empirical link from modern, profane time to a sacred time. Furthermore, the contrast of the heroic northern past with the decadent South was reinforced by the assimilation of the North into biblical history.

Central to the connection of the profane present to the sacred genesis was the forgery of Annius of Viterbo in 1498.[28] His document, ascribed to the Chaldean scholar Berosus, connected the Germanic god Tuisto (mentioned in Tacitus) to the time of Noah by changing "Tuisto deus" to "Tuyscon gigas," one of Noah's postdiluvian sons. According to this widely (though not universally) accepted document, Noah divided the world, assigning Tuyscon the area from the Danube to the Rhine, and Tuyscon's son Mannus (also in Tacitus) translated into profane, historical time the moral authority of his grandfather. The Pseudo-Berosus not only served to link the secular history to sacred history by connecting Tacitus to the Bible, it also defused the religious problem of Germanic paganism: Tuisto was not really a false god but was euhemerized into a national hero.

Chronology was one technique by which the present was linked empirically to the idea of Germania (the genesis of social value) and to the Bible (the genesis of religious value). The device of etymology served the same function. Although the invention of the Germanic languages had been ascribed to Tuisto, most northern scholarship of the sixteenth century sought to project the origin of the vernacular languages back into biblical times; the goal was to overcome the prejudice against the nonclassical culture by establishing its sacred origin.[29] Basing conjectures upon the assumption that the most natural and the purest language had monosyllabic roots, German scholars showed that the classical languages were not only inferior in beauty to the "Celtische Uhr- und Ertz Sprache" but in some cases made the ancient languages derivative of this proto-Celtic, which was in turn shown to be related etymologically to Hebrew.[30]

English historians, searching for the roots of their national language, were immensely impressed by Continental hypotheses concerning the "Cimbrian" or "Scythian" language. The effect of the developing myth of Germanic origins can be seen in Camden and especially Verstegen as they abandon the theories concerning the classical genesis of Britain and concentrate on "Saxon" origins.[31] Here the same mythologizing tendency was at work, and etymology played a central role in connecting the English-Saxon language to its Continental progenitor. Tacitus had extolled the representative institutions of the Germans, and English historians began to connect England's parliamentary democracy to this golden age of martial heroism.[32]

Etymology also helped solve the most crucial problem of the social myth of the Nordic past—the thorny matter of the pagan religion. Making idolatry acceptable was not easy for Christian historians, especially during the Reformation when "idolatry" had a pejorative connotation vis-à-vis the Church. Although for a while the Pseudo-Berosus provided scholars with documentary evidence that the early Germans' idolatry was merely the gratitude shown to illustrious heroes, the main clue to the religion of the Germanic forebears was provided by Tacitus' statement that the Germans did not imprison their gods within walls. In contrast to foreign (southern, i.e., Catholic) idolaters, then, the humanists could by a relatively minor feat of the imagination posit a primordial intuition of monotheism among their Germanic ancestors. Etymology provided one way. Cluverius, in his *Germaniæ Antiquæ libri tres* (1616), the most erudite work of the time, showed that the word *Tuisto* was originally *Deus,* by tracing its connections through various imagined sound shifts.[33] What is important here is the ostensible demonstration that the primitive Germans really had an innate sense of biblical monotheism and were not idolaters at all. These "scientific" techniques connecting secular history to divine history are aspects of the tendency of the mythic consciousness to establish the essence of a particular content by revealing its origin.

These were the major techniques by which the German humanists sought to provide facticity for their attempted historical vision of the political myth of Germania. From the time of Ulrich von Hutten, the event symbolic of the northern ideals of freedom in conflict with southern tyranny had been the defeat by Arminius of the Roman legions in the battle of Teutoburg Forest.[34] It is not surprising, therefore, that the first major literary treatment of the myth of Germania should be the monolithic novel *Arminius* (1689–1690) by Daniel Kaspar von Lohenstein, and that it should be influenced by the humanist vision.[35] In three thousand quarto pages Lohenstein constructed out of the materials of current scholarship a massive synthesis which approached the ultimate humanist goal of the *Germania illustrata.* Since myth is essentially indifferent to empirical time, the ideals embodied in the symbolic event are extended throughout history. The moral polarity between freedom and tyranny is decided in favor of Germany over Rome in a manner hardly different from the social myth Lohenstein draws upon. Spartacus, for example, is shown to have been a German, leading a freedom-loving band of Teutons in the constant fight against Roman oppression.

Exercising the literary temporal elasticity in myth, Lohenstein has his characters oscillate symbolically between the distant past and the present or recent past.[36] Sparing his readers any exercise of the imagination, Lohenstein makes clear that Divitiacus in the novel is an analogue of Luther (also Henry VIII of England), and that one event in the time schema of the novel is also the Parisian Bloodbath, while another is the English Revolution of 1688.[37] This curious literary device, with its obvious attempt at a sort of historicity, is not unnatural if the nature of time in the mythic consciousness be kept in mind and if

the novel be approached in terms of social myth insufficiently transferred to the sphere of formal literature.

The setting of the novel also appears to occupy a middle ground
between the seventeenth century and the time of ancient origins, for
just as the time of Hermann/Arminius serves as a temporal analogue to
the seventeenth century, so too are the characters aware of their descent from the dim days of Tuyscon (Cluverius appears to have been
Lohenstein's principal source). Although Lohenstein's use of time in
Arminius strikes some commentators as "mindless,"[38] it is apparent
that Lohenstein is giving symbolic representation in a crude way to the
sense of time handled only abstractly by the historians: the values of
the seventeenth century can "exist" in an earlier, heroic era, and gain a
"sacred" character because of the temporal distance. But the heroic
age—the setting of the novel—is in turn constantly aware that it too is
a product of the ultimate beginning of things, of the time of Tuisto, and
also that it is a producer of future values. What is amazing, however, is
that this had been attempted as *history*, as truth; in this *Gelehrtenro-
man* Lohenstein appears to have been as knowledgeable about Germanic antiquities as anybody in Europe at the time.

Arminius is interesting not only for the sense of time which seems so
strange today but also as a stage in the development of the archetype of
the Nordic hero. In *Arminius,* although the reader is to believe that the
difference between the noble primitive Germans and the decadent,
opulent Romans is an absolute one, Lohenstein's style is too much a
product of pseudoclassical rhetoric and bombast to make this distinction convincing.[39] As the myth of the Nordic past developed, the
attempt to depict a distinctively "northern" character was vitiated by
classical literary conventions. This is evident in *Arminius* in the dual
view of the Nordic hero. The warlike qualities of Germanic heroism
which formed the basis of the political myth conflicted fundamentally
with other cultural values which formed literary conventions.[40]

To the humanists, because character was thought to be an illustration
of moral absolutes, the archetype of the Nordic hero split, in a sense,
and the Germanic hero illustrating political virtue acquired an exotic,
barbaric counterpart. In *Arminius* this duality follows the humanistic
myth of the Germanic religion: Lohenstein tells us that the "Ur-
religion" of the Germans was indeed nonidolatrous, for prayers were
addressed to a "single, eternal, and invisible Divinity" (I, 980), and

the supposed worship of Tuisto and Hercules was merely the gratitude of the people and a desire to follow the heroes' example. There were even indications that a triune godhead was worshiped.[41] The falling away, says the author, occurred because the Bards—preservers of the old belief—lost power to the Druids, who had become integral accessories to the idea of the Germanic past through the works of Aventius.

The Druids, corrupters of the Germanic monotheism, introduced barbarism and foreign idolatry, but this was not Roman idolatry—rather, the Druids introduced Scandinavian gods, such as "Thür" and Thor (I, 977), and an eyewitness describes the bloody barbarism of Scandinavian rites at the temple of Uppsala (II, 878ff.).[42] Lohenstein incorporated this humanist idea of the fall of German monotheism at the corrupting hands of Scandinavian barbarism into the fluidity of narrative time: the contrast between the Bards and the Druids is portrayed as an analogue to the contemporary conflict between the Evangelical faith and Catholicism, with the author's sympathy of course on the side of the Evangelist-Bards.[43]

The work of seventeenth-century Scandinavian scholars facilitated this view of the Scandinavian role in the primitive retreat from native Germanic monotheism. Lohenstein was evidently acquainted with Saxo Grammaticus and Resenius' edition of the Edda; with these and other sources rapidly becoming available, an internal documentation was accessible. Before the seventeenth century (with the exception of Claussøn's edition of Saxo), references to Northern Europe's pagan past had been gleaned from Latin authors; now, however, samples were available of the "ancient songs."[44]

Scandinavian scholarship contributed two important motifs to the social myth. The first result of the (largely Danish) philological research was to give a definite form to the barbaric half of the dual Nordic archetype. In 1689 the Danish scholar Thomas Bartholin produced his *De causis contemptae a danis adhuc gentilibus mortis libri tres*, which was an anthology of hitherto unpublished texts, as well as an examination of the alleged fearlessness of the Danish (Germanic) people in the face of death. These examples were widely read.[45] Codifying this warlike half of the Nordic hero was a poem attributed to Ragnar Lodbrok, who became the embodiment of this fascinating savagery of the Norseman.

Ragnar's death song, the "Krákumál," was included in Ole Worm's

Runir (1628), one of the indispensable sources for Norse documents, and was the source for two of the most common "realistic touches" in the depiction of the hero. One of the appealing bits of imagery is that the hero "dies laughing" ("ridens moriar," p. 206). The other cornerstone in the concept of the Norseman stemmed from a mistranslation of a skaldic circumlocution: Ragnar says that in Valhall he will drink ale "ór bjugviðum hausa," meaning "from curved skull-branches," i.e., drinking horns. This was mistranslated into "Sperabant heroes se in aula Othini bibituros ex craniis eorum ceciderunt," by which Ragnar is made to say that in Odin's hall he will drink from the skulls of those he has slain. Perhaps because this mistranslation fitted so neatly into the developing idea of the Nordic past, Ragnar's drinking habit was an indispensable part of the myth of the warlike character until well into the nineteenth century and was probably the most widely known single aspect of the Scandinavian past.[46]

Another important result of the early Scandinavian scholarship was the documentation of the idea of a unified northern people under the rubric "Goths." The myth was based upon a general moral polarity between North and South, discussed above, but Tacitus had described a dismaying number of Germanic tribes. The demand that the temporal projection be justified factually received a great boost with the editing of Snorri Sturluson's *Heimskringla* and his *Prose Edda* in the seventeenth century. Snorri, writing in the thirteenth century, euhemerized the Norse gods, probably to justify his preserving of the pagan legends, and wrote that the historical Odin migrated from Asia; hence, he says, the Nordic progenitors were called "Æsir." This unified genesis and migration from the East was seen as a complement to Jordanes, who had said that the Goths came from the "womb of nations" (*Getica*, 25).

In general, the discovery of internal, primary sources by Scandinavian scholars enabled antiquarians (particularly in England) to unite the moral vision of the German humanists with what was thought to be a detailed explanation of "Gothic" origins: the result was that Old Norse was called the "lingua Gothica," the poems edited by Resenius and Worm were "libri antiqui lingua Gothica scripti," and the origin of all the northern nations were linked to Odin's migration.[47]

The most important result of the spate of editions in the seventeenth century was the beginning of a subsequent breakdown of the contrast between the political estimation and the esthetic condemnation of the Nordic past. Although the majority of educated gentlemen by the late eighteenth century considered "Gothic" the equivalent of "tasteless," the "runic poems" (particularly that of Ragnar Lodbrok) served to document new theories of the role of spontaneous primitive imagination, genius, and the "marvelous."

Initially, however, the appearance of these "wild runic odes" in the seventeenth century served to crystallize the dual view of the Nordic past. Sir William Temple was apparently aware of the new Scandinavian scholarship and was one of the first to popularize it. In his essay "Of Heroic Virtue" (1690), Sir William described the migrations of Odin and the Scythians/Geats/Goths and praised the valor of the Germanic tribes, contending that the founders of the governments of modern Europe could not have been "unreasonable or unthinking men. It is more likely, that there was among them some force of order, some reach of conduct, above the common strain."[48] He even suggests that there is a truly poetical, even Pindaric quality in the runic poetry and cites two stanzas from Ragnar's poem.[49] But in the same collection of essays he laments that with the fall of Rome "almost all learning was buried in its ruins: the Northern nations, that conquered or rather overwhelmed it by their numbers, were too barbarous to preserve the remains of learning or civility more carefully than they did those of statuary or architecture, which fell before their brutish rage."[50] Sir William did not appear to feel that his view of the Germanic past, informed on the one hand by social myth and on the other by cultural values, was in any way inconsistent.

The runic scholarship provided a philological base for the second myth of the Nordic past, Swedish Gothicism, in the sixteenth and seventeenth centuries. If Danish and English research gave an ostensibly clear picture of the origin of the "Gothic" nations, as well as a few strokes of realistic character depiction, Swedish historians used accepted methodology to construct an epic link between the present and the heroic past that surpassed the dreams of the Germanic humanists for a *Germania illustrata*. Gothicism formed the second aspect of the Nordic past's social myth, and was one of the most bizarre visions of European historiography.

The contemporary analogue was more precise than that of the German humanists': Sweden's intervention in the Thirty Years' War in

1630 under Gustavus Adolphus. But the research to give a mythic dimension to Sweden's claims to European greatness had been going on for almost two centuries and continued until Sweden's era as a great power (called the *stormaktstid*) ended in the early eighteenth century.[51]

The basis of the social myth of Swedish Gothicism was the Goths' conquering of Rome in the fifth century A.D., and this to the Swedes played a role as a symbolic event analogous to that of the defeat of Varus by Arminius. The Swedish historians had more precise data to support their historical fantasies than did the German scholars, however. First of all there was Jordanes' statement that the "Getae" (Geats, but mistaken for Goths and later assumed to be Swedes) stemmed from the "womb of nations,"[52] and second, there was tangible evidence—the runic inscriptions. These were generally thought by nationalist scholars to be thousands of years old, some conjecturing that owing to "manifest" similarities between the runes and Hebrew, "Runic" might have descended directly from the language of the Bible, its purity unaffected by the Tower of Babel.

There is evidence for the social myth of Swedish Gothicism as early as 1434, when Bishop Nicolaus Ragvaldi at the Council of Basel cited the Gothic (Swedish) origin of the European peoples as his reason for demanding primacy in seating over the southern nations, and his narration of the glorious deeds of the Goths became a sort of Volksbuch back home.[53] By the sixteenth century the idea of an ancient Swedish greatness had become an established myth, and this was largely due to Johannes Magnus' ten books on the *History of the Gothic and Swedish Kings (Historia de omnibus Gothorum Sueonumque regibus,* 1554), the first major documentation of the *stormaktstidens* Gothic past, "a Gothic Iliad." Johannes Magnus pictured the Goths as a simple people whose natural virtue surpassed the artificial learning of the Greeks and Romans.[54] But the conflict of values in the vision of the Nordic past was also present in Swedish Gothicism. In Johannes Magnus, the resentment of the stigma of barbarism takes the form of a defensive note, the proof of the Goths' literary attainment centering in the imagined antiquity of the runic inscriptions: "But you must not think that the Northerners had no writers who chronicled their manliness: for the Goths had letters and writings long before the Latin were invented ... we may easily assume that before the Flood or shortly thereafter valiant heroes were celebrated."[55]

But even the characters in Johannes Magnus are conscious that they are cultural barbarians, and a Gothic "King Berik" describes the duality in the Nordic character in direct address to the reader: "For we by nature had a too-great lust and proclivity to violence," he admits, "but we were no less concerned with virtue and honor: furthermore, there never lacked among us learned and wise men who freed and delivered us from all base barbaric customs and ignorance."[56]

Again, the *translatio imperii* served as a schema for putting Swedish antiquity into world history, but it was not until the reign of Gustavus II Adolphus (1611–1632) that the historical vision received its modern analogue, its objective correlative. As the antagonism between Catholic and Protestant took the political form that resulted in the Thirty Years' War, a growing number of portents appeared that a heaven-sent knight would come to save the day for the Protestants. Some of the signs were deduced from the Bible, and most were interpreted as pointing toward an overthrow of southern tyranny by a "Lion from the North." When Gustavus landed in Germany in 1630 his success demonstrated that the prophecy had been fulfilled, and a *translatio imperii* (in religious terms) was once more in process.[57]

This sense of time permeated the intellectual life of Sweden for years and was widespread abroad.[58] Again, it was the contrast in values between North and South—between freedom and tyranny—which animated the myth, yet in the *stormaktstid* the contemporary relevance was more precise than in Germany. Thus, in Georges de Scudéry's epic *Alaric ou Rome vaincuë* (1654), Alaric is the instrument of God against

> Rome, whose pride tyrannized the world;
> Rome, who dared bring war to our homes;
> O shameful remembrance of suffered outrages!
> Rome, who conquered us, and put us in chains.

Alaric's victory is an allegory of the conquest of passion by reason, and Scudéry at the end makes it clear that his battle is a perpetual one, that Alaric will be reincarnated in Gustavus Adolphus: "That glorious Phoenix who will rise from your ashes / Will surpass by far the great feats of Alexander."[59]

Lévi-Strauss has suggested that the myth dims oppositions. Both Johannes Magnus and his brother Olaus sought to portray the heroic past in chivalric terms (as did their German counterparts), but the attempt to synthesize chivalric romanticism and primitivism never succeeded. The warlike qualities of the Goth fitted poorly with the Christian ideal of the *bellum iustum,* which governed much of the rationalization for contemporary foreign policy.[60] Indicative of this is the appearance in the literature of Swedish Gothicism of the split image of the Gothic hero. The dramas of Johannes Messenius feature a pairing of characters, one peaceful, one warlike. In *Disa* (1611) the gentle queen Disa is set opposite the amazon Pentisilae, the embodiment of war, who decides to emigrate to Sweden. In *Suanhuita* the peaceful king Signill is paired with the bellicose hero Starkater. The aggressive side of this dual character, however, has a further refinement, again indicative of the inability to internalize the conflict in the myth of the Nordic past: when Starkater appears as a chivalric warrior he has a counterpart in the barbaric Moorsgrijs.[61]

The most spectacular expressions of the creative imagination were not those of poets but of historians. Their investigations established not only the assumed objectivity of later social myth but a set of "Nordic" literary images for writers wishing verisimilitude. We have alluded to Ole Worm's legacy of Ragnar Lodbrog; Olaus Magnus relates that to this day in Sweden swallows frozen in winter thaw out in the spring and fly away. Though used as a metaphor in poetry, this image was not considered "fiction" but as warranting serious investigation by the British Royal Society.[62]

It would be misleading to imply that only Sweden was involved in the creation of a Gothic past; Denmark, as mentioned earlier, also contributed such scholarly works but lacked Sweden's contemporary political referent or a symbolic event upon which to base the temporal projection. Danish historians, to be sure, used the same techniques for projecting the present into the past as did the German, English, and Swedish historians, and even produced their own pseudo-Berosus, the Gulland document. This linked Denmark's progenitor "King Dan" (mentioned in Saxo Grammaticus, but demoted by Johannes Magnus to a vassal of the Swedish king) to Noah, for Japhet's son Gomer was the leader of the Cimbrians, the Goths stemming from a Danish descendant, "King Guthi" of Jutland. But these attempts to connect secular history to sacred were too weak and too late, and for a while the Swedes had successfully nationalized the *illud tempus* of the Scandinavian past.[63]

The Danes struck a more serious counterblow in the late seventeenth century through the philological work of Ole Worm, Thomas Bartholin, Arne Magnússon and others, and their efforts in bringing out a great many important sources in the vernacular prompted a Swedish effort at saga-editing. But the sagas having to do with Sweden are in general the *fornaldarsögur,* those sagas with little or no historical content and a large admixture of fairy-tale fantasy. Still, they were accepted as historical documents and uncritically ingested into the social myth of Swedish Gothicism. Verelius, one of the leading scholars in this effort, admitted that there was much in these sagas which appeared to be fanciful, but "one should therefore not regard this saga as untrue when it tells of such things."[64]

All these elements form a mosaic and were fused into a unified understanding of history in Olaus Rudbeck's *Atlantica (Atland eller Manheim,* 1679–1704). These four volumes solved the cultural problem of the relationship of the national, northern past to classical antiquity in a stunning display of erudition: at once, the myth's greatest imaginative expression and the beginning of its demise.

There had been a growing suspicion among Swedish scholars that the classical legends about the Hyperboreans (literally, "those who live beyond the North wind") were really hidden references to Sweden.[65] The figure of Abaris, the Hyperborean who flew to Greece on a magic arrow, attracted some attention in this regard, and illustrates how Swedish Gothicism as social myth established its facts. It was known that runes were engraved on sticks, and the poet and scholar Stiernhielm saw Abaris (his Swedish name was supposedly Ewart or Iwar) as a "Runa-madr," a priest who knew Odin's magic arts. Abaris, said Stiernhielm, taught this Nordic wisdom to Pythagoras, and Stiernhielm was able to find Swedish idioms in Pythagoras' mystic symbols.[66]

This was the line of endeavor Rudbeck's contemporaries were pursuing when he turned his genius (as it must be called) from medicine to philosophy. Utilizing all the scholarly tools of research at his command, Rudbeck in a grand tour de force assimilated the entire classical culture into Swedish history, establishing the North as the symbolic genesis of Western culture. He connected the stories of the Hyperboreans with Plato's tale of Atlantis, and identified them both with Sweden. "Hyperborean," he says, is "a good Swedish word, coming from 'King Bore'" and meaning "nobility"; "Boreades" was the Greek mispronunciation of "Bores ætt," the descendants of Bore. Atlantis, furthermore, had had its capital at Uppsala.[67] With this, Rudbeck destroyed at a stroke the assumption of the cultural supremacy of classical antiquity vis-à-vis the barbaric North: what matter if the Goths were later receivers of classical learning? All the wisdom of the ancients, all their legends and tales were shown to have been *Swedish* in origin.

Like Stiernhielm, Rudbeck considered Abaris (in Swedish, Habor) the bringer of northern culture and religion to Pythagoras, who later (along with Orpheus, Hesiod, Homer, and others) visited Sweden. Since the Swedish philosophy was so profound that the primitive southerners were unable to grasp its complexities, what they later presented to the West was, alas, the flickering shadow of a shade.

It must be kept in mind that this expression of social myth was not "fiction"—in the four massive tomes (only a prelude to the planned work, and the fourth volume was partly destroyed by fire in 1702) the author diligently and exhaustively calculates, etymologizes, and proves each of his conjectures with all the contemporary scholarly methods available. When he says, "We have now through the grace of God shown Sweden's various names, and what they were in ancient times," he is, given his criteria for obtaining truth through etymology, correct. Thus Hercules was really a Swede, Här-kalle; Troy was founded by Swedes, as was Memphis in Egypt (built by Njörd, called Mannus by Tacitus). In the chapter "On our Runic Letters and how the Greeks got them from us," he shows how not only astronomy but letters and writing were of Swedish origin. Even the cult of Apollo was to Rudbeck but a faded version of the Nordic Balder religion.

I see the *Atlantica* as the climax of the subconscious humanist attempt to legitimize a heroic universe by proving that its values were *archai,* established at genesis. With Rudbeck, the glory of Sweden's *stormaktstid* was shown to be the central fact of world history from the sacred time of Noah to the present. As social myth, the *Atlantica* gave the myth of northern freedom its most elaborate expression and was the supreme effort to cope with the duality implicit in the myth of the Nordic past.

Though modern myth relies upon reason for its acceptance as truth, reason is the sworn enemy of myth, and it was reason which deflated Swedish Gothicism as a means of understanding historical time. The very immensity of Rudbeck's fantastic demonstrations attracted considerable attention (if not approbation) outside Sweden and he was proposed as a member of the British Royal Society. Although he had been internally consistent with his "proofs," the era when his methodology would be sufficient to establish truth was over, and the dialectical nature of myth in a world where science and reason were becoming constantly more independent and skeptical of a priori methods and systems began to assert itself, destroying the grandiose structure of humanist social myth. The evolution in the criteria for validating truth's objectivity created marginal experiences which could not be assimilated, and an element of contingency entered the myth of Gothicism. In an age where reason was becoming the sole measurement of veracity, however, there was no possibility for Gothicism to exist as a broken myth—no synthesis could be made, though the longing for the vision to be reestablished as truth continued.

By the early eighteenth century not only had the means for establishing fact evolved but historians had come to demand that the study of the past yield things other than hypothetical chronology and origins. Leibniz criticized the a priori nature of Rudbeck's investigations, commenting that it would be possible for any country to do for itself what Rudbeck had done for Sweden. Rudbeck, says Leibniz, approached his material with his conclusion already formed and not only chose his sources to prove his theory but accepted them uncritically. With this approach no historian can distinguish the true from the false.[68] A reviewer of a book on Swedish runestones commented in 1771 that the humanist approach to history must not be called a search for fact: "Should one imagine," the reviewer asks, "that one can find upon the runestones the time of Odin, Magog, the Ark, the Sea of Galilee, and Sodom and Gomorrah, when clearer eyes can now read something quite different?"[69]

The final degree of displacement from belief, a certain indication that a mythic construct is no longer symbolically adequate, is the appearance of irony, particularly parody. Ludvig Holberg writes that, having read Rudbeck, he is incensed that ancient writers have robbed Scandinavia of its historical glory, and in the mock-serious tone of the *Spectator* says that through etymology and other "reliable" techniques he has discovered that the Trojan War actually took place in Norway.[70] Holberg says, however, that he will restrict himself to the "certain" area of postdiluvian studies in order to be sure of his facts in his examination of Nordic antiquities; this was meant as a commentary upon Swedish and Danish antiquaries whose antediluvian studies were more bizarre than those having to do with Noah. (Bishop Petrus Bång in 1675 attempted to prove that Adam lived in Sweden and discussed the possibility of Adam being a bishop; this was not rejected by Rudbeck.) Holberg, taking the illusion of fact from under the Rudbeckians, relegated them to the same category as poets, dealers in fiction.[71]

The undermining by empiricism of the myth of Gothicism was not confined to its conclusions. Leibniz, Holberg, Lessing, and Swift all criticized the faith in speculative etymology and the misuse of sources. But the most biting assault on Gothicism was made in Sweden by Olof Dalin.[72] During the same years as Rudbeck's disciple Biörner was publishing his collection of texts *Deeds of Nordic Heroes* (*Nordiska kämpadater,* 1737), Dalin began his attack. In 1739 he produced his "Tests of Wisdom, or Herr Arngrim Berserk's Remarkable Thoughts Concerning a Discovery in the Earth," wherein learned parallels are adduced to claim that a copper pot was the helmet of the hero "Bo the Fat." In the same years that Johan Göransson wrote a genealogy of Swedish kings from 2200 B.C. until 1749, Dalin remarked in the Introduction to his own *History of the Kingdom of Sweden* (*Svea rikes historia,* 1747) that although Rudbeckianism requires a sort of genius, it does not yield fact, and wherever Atlantis was—if it ever existed— will never be decided.

Thus the methodology of the Enlightenment, in the name of reason and fact, attempted to put an end to the extravagances of national historical fantasy; after Dalin and the death of Charles XII it was no longer possible to imagine heroism with the *stormaktstid* images of Swedish Gothicism. But the destruction of the forms of myth did not destroy the impulse to mythmaking nor the central value-truth, particularly in the case of the myth of northern freedom. The moral polarity remained and took new forms, expressing current secondary values. Curiously, Dalin was to be an integral part of this next generation of mythmaking in that, in contrast to the fallacious conjectures of the Rudbeckians, Dalin considered *his* history of Sweden as one "which has its strength not in ancient sagas, but in Nature itself" and did not fail to cite Newton. This was not only a reaction to the earlier historical methodology but to a general way of thinking as well.[73] The heroic fantasies were deflated by an extension of the same epistemological assumptions that created them—fact, but the new methodology was to prompt new fantasies.

The duality remained—Voltaire wrote that the northern peoples lived in disgusting idolatry, worshiping Odin, "and fancied that after death the happiness of man consisted in carousing in the hall of Wodan, and drinking beer out of the skulls of their enemies. We have still extant translations of some of their old ballads, in which this notion is expressed."[74] Dalin, the scourge of the Rudbeckians, writes that on the contrary the religion of Sweden's first inhabitants was based upon the pure knowledge of God by Noah and his descendants but was effaced by time and human additions; "its main tenets, the Chief Good and the Chief Evil, a blessed and innocent time before the coming of evil, a Fall and a Redemption through a Middle-God, were accepted not only in ancient Sweden, but in all pagan peoples' theologies."[75]

We have dwelt at length upon the two dominant social myths of post-Renaissance Northern Europe because they display in such easily identifiable form the basic qualities of social myth. Before one smiles condescendingly at the grotesqueries of German humanistic scholars, however, it should be recognized that they were seldom consciously practicing deception or fraud. They had begun with the faith that rational inquiry into the Nordic past would reveal both the truths of God's words in the Bible and the noble qualities of their ancestors. If their mythmaking impulse created a fabrication of scholarship which today appears comic, it must be remembered that given these scholars' criteria for validating data, their treatises were considered discoveries, not inventions.

Nor should we feel that social myth disappeared with the exposure of the discredited means by which the Germanic and Swedish social myths were propagated. In the dominant social myths of our day we have seen the power of fascism, with its theory of a superior race, and of dialectical materialism. It is not always so easy, however, to detect the mythic qualities of liberalism, when genetics have questioned equality and psychology assaults the basic postulate of autonomous individualism. The methods of the social sciences, however, given ultimate sanction by the computer, will later be seen by different eyes as social myth with perhaps the same ironic view we have of the social myths of Germania and Gothicism.

Some of the very critics instrumental in the "exposure" of the social myth of the Rudbeckians were involved in the creation of another idea of the Nordic past, one which eventually functioned as myth in formal literature in the late eighteenth century. We will now turn to the role of the Nordic past in the Enlightenment, as well as the development of the myth of northern freedom into a literary myth, objectifying and projecting into a Nordic golden age new ideas about the nature of primitive man, the creative process, and "natural" poetry.

(5)

FROM SOCIAL MYTH TO
LITERARY MYTH:
THE NOBLE NORDIC

Because empirical thought of necessity regards myth as "fiction" (hence untrue), Enlightenment rationalism, as Erich Heller says, "deprived the language of religion as well as art of part of an essential degree of reality."[1] In spite of manifold discussions of "genius" and the "je ne sais quoi," an Enlightenment empiricist could hardly consider "monstrous fictions" as an independent, nonrational means of knowing, as being truth rather than concealing truth. Whatever the pride taken in emancipation from these primitive chimeras, it was through a complex myth that the Nordic past (usually regarded as an illustration of raw barbarism) came to play a small but legitimate part in the Enlightenment, both in a social myth of origins and to a degree as a literary myth of the golden age.

To clarify the term *literary myth* we must distinguish the ironic use of mythology in literature from the spontaneous reality of literary myth, a reality it shares with primitive and social myth. Mythological figures could swarm like gnats in rococo idylls, but no degree of reality was attached to them. The poet was no longer an oracular transmitter of divine truth but a free creator, limited in neoclassicism only by the precept to "imitate nature": nature, of course, being demythologized. The poet, not under the spell of myth as reality, might dot his manuscript with decorative allusions or demythologize it completely into allegory, as poetic language was merely "cunning artifice" and not in any way related to undisplaced myth.

As with the social myths of Germania and Gothicism, however, mythic symbolic structures continued to be smuggled into literature and to have their effect, despite contempt at the conscious level for any claim that might be made for them as truth. Northrop Frye holds that archetypal symbols of myth emerge compulsively from the subrational depths of the poet's mind (which itself is a bearer of tradition) in a creative process of whose nature he is not always aware.[2] But we have seen in the social myths of Germania and Gothicism that archetypal elements of mythic narrative appear in works which are neither mythological narrative (in its more restricted sense) nor formal literature. So our concern is not immediately with the free use of Nordic subject matter in formal literature—the Swedish poet Bellman's use of "Freyja" in his rococo songs implies no element of belief—but another, deeper level of the literary consciousness, where symbol is not perceived as being such. For this discussion, we will restrict "literary myth" to the moral facts of the poet as expressed in communal symbols. Mythic expressions may draw their power from archetypal patterns, but different eras operating under differing symbolic universes will express these recurring patterns in varying forms. A singular instance of this was the symbolization of primitivism in Nordic images—the noble savage of the northern seas.

In viewing the noble Nordic as a mythic expression of sentimental primitivism we may recognize the transition from social myth to literary myth as well as the peculiar tension between the mythic role of the Nordic past and eighteenth-century literary convention. Given the Enlightenment estimation of myth as fiction or euhemeristic distortions of historical events and personages, there would appear to be little likelihood that the discredited social myths of Germania and Gothicism could inform Enlightenment writings save in a negative displacement from the sacred world—as parody. Yet given also the power of the mythmaking impulse, particularly the need for a myth of origins, it is not too surprising to see some attempt made to refurbish the "Gothic" past in language acceptable to the Enlightenment and made part of rationalism's regulating images.

The Nordic past, as might be expected, therefore found expression on both an empirical-rational and a mythic level. Consciously, Nordic subject matter was either derided in formal literature or, when seriously studied, searched for concealed historical or conceptual content and treated as allegory, conforming to neoclassical esthetics. On the mythic (unconscious) plane the Norseman became the central figure in a major social myth of Enlightenment origins—the myth of northern freedom—and developed from this into a minor literary myth of the golden age. This myth, however, ran counter to the controlling myth of the Enlightenment—progress.[3]

The first protagonist in the tension between progress and primitivism was the Enlightenment view of history as a linear advancement of mankind toward a perfect (and demythologized) society, a process which was "natural," provided that reason was employed both to instruct mankind and to reshape the environment. The second protagonist may be called the sentimental primitivism stemming from Rousseau, who in brief saw progress not as an advance but as a backward evolution to a desirable but primitive condition. It is in thus looking backward that the Nordic past reemerged as part of a golden age; we will treat this in more detail subsequently, but the barbaric Viking was also assimilated to some degree into the mechanistic world view of the myth of progress. To understand the process by which this was accomplished, one must outline the development of the idea of human progress which defined so much of the Enlightenment stance toward the world of value.

It may not be too startling to consider Newton and Locke as the basic mythmakers in the development of this myth if "mythmaker" is defined as a pivotal figure who surmounts the basic conflicts of his time by distilling new metaphors through which an era understands and subsequently expresses its values. Newton showed how the apparently bewildering complexity of the physical world could be satisfactorily understood as instances of a few mechanical principles; Locke extended this mechanistic understanding of the physical world into the operations of the human mind.

Newton's *Principia* (1687) was a culmination of the epistemological revolution which had produced such brilliant successes for rational inquiry into the physical world and served as a propaedeutic for subsequent investigation—not only into the physical world, but also into the human world.[4] The success of the Newtonian world view and its development into ideology created, in a way that humanism had not, a crisis for the mythic consciousness which has continued to the present. Galileo believed that the truths of science and the truths of Christian myth were reconcilable—if only the latter were "rightly understood."[5] After Newton, Enlightenment investigators extended Galileo's method of apprehending nature through reason rather than through a priori revelation from the realm of number and quantity into the areas of psychology, sociology, and finally religion.[6] Two truths cannot contradict each other, as logicians from Aristotle through Galileo to the present have asserted; since truths of the mythic aspect of religion are expressed in a fundamentally alien symbolic mode, that of reason, as truth they were essentially unintelligible to Enlightenment empiricism.

As investigators from Galileo to Newton developed a symbolic universe based upon mathematically intelligible regularity and mechanical law, empiricists of the Enlightenment generally assumed—and demanded—that all inquiry be conducted with an open, scientific mind, generalizing laws from data derived from experience alone. To be abandoned were what Newton called "occult qualities"; in human terms, revelation, tradition, and authority which could not be "rightly understood" by mechanical principles.

In such a universe, where rational method has the ultimate authority in determining all truth including that of human values, the fantasies and figments of the nonrational or prerational mind could only fall on the wrong side of a timeless distinction between true and false, reason and superstition. Illustrative of this attitude are the comments by Thomas Sprat in his *History of the Royal Society* (1667). Sprat, buoyed by the successes of the empirical method of reducing the physical world to data knowable through rational (not divine) natural law, views the eras before Galileo and his own as periods when magic and superstition held sway. "But from the time in which the *Real Philosophy* has appear'd," says Sprat, these horrors hardly remain. "Every man is unshaken at those Tales at which his Ancestors trembled: the course of things goes quietly along, in its own true channel of Natural Causes and Effects." Although experiments have not yet discovered the ultimate truths of the physical world, "they have already vanquish'd those wild inhabitants of the false world," and since the "wit of the Fables and Religions of the Antient world is well-nigh consum'd . . . it is now high time to dismiss them." Since Sprat measured truth by the norms of science, he gives as the reason for dismissing the fables that "they were only Fictions at first; whereas Truth is never so well express'd or amplify'd, as by those Ornaments which are True and Real in themselves."[7]

In terms of the idea of the imagination, the criteria for truth expressed by Sprat, combined with the psychological theories of Locke, were of immense significance. If one accepted with Hobbes the consequence of the Lockean view of the mind as a mechanical recorder of sense impressions, imagination was essentially the same as memory: "after the object is removed, . . . we still retain an image of the thing seen. . . . And this is it, the Latins call *imagination,* from the image made in seeing." Thus the primary merit of a text lay in its verisimilitude, its depiction of historical reality.[8]

As truth was determined by a mode of thought and a theory of the mind fundamentally at odds with that of myth, empirical assumptions rendered poets, critics, historians, and philosophers alike incapable of recognizing myth as an independent form of cognition. In other words, although it was agreed that the "marvelous" was persistent if not essential in literature, writers conditioned by empirical thought were unable to explain just *why* this was so. Dryden, noting that the "greatest part of mankind" expressed itself through myth and that this fact "is foundation enough for poetry," could only describe the nature of nonempirical elements in poetry by saying, "You are pleased with the image without being cozend by the fiction."[9]

It was of course legitimate to study myth to discover in it historical cause or empirical content, as Newton does in his *Chronology of Ancient Kingdoms Amended* (1728), in which he is able to impose chronological sequence upon any mythological reference by decoding it into a datable event and reveal any god as a primitive savant. Another way of coping with the barbarous was to show that it really disguised nobler, enlightened values and could be treated as allegory. This method was acceptable even to Voltaire, as can be seen in his virtually unreadable *Henriade.* Still, material from what Fontenelle called "fabulous history" could only be explored for the truth it concealed, not as truth itself.

Under the constellation of these assumptions, it might seem strange that "Gothic" barbarism could develop into social myth (much less literary myth), but Montesquieu and, more particularly, Paul-Henri Mallet succeeded in reimagining the North in language acceptable to the philosophe and satisfying to the mythic need for origins. Preliminary to any reestablishment of the Nordic past in terms of a golden age, however, was the development of a new view of what history was a history *of.* Ludvig Holberg, so devastating in his parody of the social myth of Gothicism, comments that those who merely scribble chronologies ought not be called historians; he demands that the study of data be approached from the standpoint of rational law, so that one may learn to know countries, men, and oneself. Reiterating Fontenelle, Holberg asserts that just to *know* the extravagancies of the past is useless: what one must glean from fabulous history is what *led* the past to the extravagance.[10]

It was Montesquieu, however, who, in exploring the *spirit* of the laws (not just the laws themselves), developed a historical method which relied neither upon eccesiastical tradition nor upon "fabulous" data but could explain both by empirical means. One of the achievements of *The Spirit of the Laws* (*L'Esprit des lois,* 1748) was a reformulation of the humanist myth of northern freedom and southern decadence in just such Lockean terms. Montesquieu comments that Rudbeck appears to have ignored this essential virtue of the northern nations—that they were the source of European liberty, "the factory where the tools were made to break the chains forged in the Mediterranean."[11] With this means of understanding the Nordic past, Montesquieu gave the philosophes an acceptable way to regard it as symbolic genesis of contemporary assertions of social and literary freedom from the stifling tyranny of the South.

Montesquieu was not interested in the primitive-as-abstract, as were the earlier theorists of natural law.[12] Rather, he explained the moral antithesis mechanically, analyzing the freedom myth as a product of the northern environment: the climate of the North produced among other things a different sort of person, the cold dampening the passions, naturally creating a people with few vices and an abundance of virtues, while in the South "the more lively passions multiply the vices."[13]

Although the interest in the effect of the environment upon the mind ("mind" in the Lockean sense of a passive receiver of sense impressions) was of fundamental importance in the subsequent revaluation of the esthetic worth of primitive poetry, it was not directly through Montesquieu that the world of "Celtic" antiquities was absorbed into the polite literary circles of the Enlightenment. Paul-Henri Mallet, one of Montesquieu's disciples, wrote his *Introduction to the History of Denmark* (*Introduction á l'histoire de Dannemarc,* 1755–1756) and *Edda; or, Documents of the Mythology and the Poetry of the Ancient Scandinavians* (*Edda, ou monuments de la mythologie et de la poésie des anciens Scandinaves,* 1781) explicitly for the man of good taste who would not find it unreasonable to have a new area of study opened to him, particularly as it was the past not of the southern nations but of the northern "Celtic" nations, founders of contemporary freedom.[14] He was followed in this by Bishop Percy, who translated Mallet and also took three out of the influential *Five Pieces of Runic Poetry* from him, observing that the "runic" poetry (as documents) is not a mere antiquarian curiosity but affords "matter of philosophical reflection, by showing the workings of the human mind in its almost original state of nature."[15]

Neither Percy nor Mallet viewed the Nordic savage as dwelling happily in a golden age, however. Although the Nordic peoples were raw and strong, Mallet's concept of history is progressivist: he notes that those who would describe as a golden age what was really a time of misery are falsifying history (I, 140). Mallet made the Nordic past amenable to "serious reflection" by emphasizing Montesquieu's point that the chief "cause" of the northern culture was mechanical: climate. Hence the allegedly famous northern veneration of women (extracted from Tacitus) is explained by the cold, which again "naturally" made the Norsemen less passionate and more protective, and here is the origin of northern chivalry. Mallet calls this trait "to this day the distinguishing characteristic of European manners" (I, 315). Instead of treating the Nordic past as cut off from the present by its barbarity (as did Hume and others), Mallet views the "Celtic" tribes as the founders of contemporary institutions. He explicitly rejects the humanist chroniclers, particularly the Gulland forgery, and maintains that establishing the connection to the northern past is of interest not just to the pedantic antiquarian but to the gentleman, the philosophe.

Mallet does not suggest that there is any poetic merit in the Eddaic fables, but he is concerned to justify their study by the modern scholar. By extracting the kernel of ancient philosophy from the specious fictions of poets (I, 103), Mallet discovers that the religions of the North were an enlightened deism. From Snorri's mention of "Allfather" as a kenning for Odin, Mallet describes a "natural" worship of the "père universel" as indigenous to the Celtic tribes, explaining the falling away into idolatry as being the fault of Odin and his Asian interlopers.[16] Mallet, like Lohenstein in his *Arminius,* explains that the simple Scythian religion was first altered by southerners, but accounts for the fact differently, referring to their climate-conditioned lively imaginations, and "hence that chaos of extravagance, in some respects ingenious, known by the name of mythology" (I, 75–80).

Mallet's works, written in a clear, lucid style, free of antiquarian and humanist Latinisms, achieved their purpose of bringing the north-

ern history and mythology to the attention of the world of polite learning in the acceptable context of Montesquieu's method. Mallet was
Madame de Staël's principal reference and probably the source of
information about the North for the editors of the *Encyclopédie*.[17] Also
(and this was of great importance later), Mallet used images of the
Nordic past to popularize the notion of primitive monotheism, thus
making the potentially objectionable "Celts" acceptable for salvation
by contemporary Christians.

Although the problem of idolatry in the classical past had long since
been solved through allegory, there were ticklish aspects of it in dealing with the Goths, particularly when it came to using barbaric subject
matter in literature. To the writers and artists of the Italian Renaissance, there had been a sense of continuity with classical antiquity, and
mythology could express a feeling of identification with the national
past. This is not to say that the gods were believed in, but classical
mythology could function in a symbolic manner for the Italian
humanists as an expression of identity.[18] In the North, however, there
was no mythology in a national sense, for the subordination of the use
of the "marvelous" to the scientifically probable was allied with the
inherited label of barbarity to inhibit the development of a distinctively
Nordic genre both elevated in style and national in subject.

A common distinction in the employment of the marvelous, however, was in the depiction of a "true and actual event," where the
unbelievable was rejected as violating verisimilitude, and "legends,
tales, and romantic adventures"—i.e., fiction—where the marvelous
could be justified on *historic* grounds, since the unenlightened peoples
of those times believed it: this, though, was not "serious literature."[19]

This distinction helped in incorporating the Nordic past into two
genres of neoclassical literature. To Carl Gustaf Leopold, the arbiter of
Swedish neoclassical taste, the migration of Odin and the Æsir from
Asia was a fact (the euhemeristic explanation was not questioned) and
the freedom myth thus could be treated seriously, which means historically. Leopold dramatized this event in *Oden* (1790), the high point of
Swedish neoclassical tragedy. In order to treat the subject seriously,
however, Leopold subordinated his material to the canons of neoclassical literary taste, which were in turn informed by the doctrine of
progress. It was obvious to him that the barbarism of the Nordic past
was objectionable, and that Odin's manners had to be polished up a bit,

for the "raw, sensuous nature-descriptions of wholly barbaric eras" were unsuited to the "entire nobler nature" of contemporary tragedy as he understood it.[20] But his assimilation of the freedom myth into the abstract neoclassical style draws no real distinction between the freedom-loving northern "Scythians" and the villainous tyrants of Rome. In this respect, Leopold's *Oden* illustrates in miniature a basic paradox in the Nordic past as literary myth: the tension between the value-truths animating the myth and literary conventions which could neither express a "gothic" style of writing nor see value in northern barbarism. In Leopold's case, his strict but unimaginative approach and his pompous, abstract language negates the stylistic expression of any difference between North and South and vitiates the putative theme of the play. Artistically, Oden is a much less believable character than his Roman antagonist Pompey, who acquires a kind of credibility through Leopold's style and his association with classical literary convention.

In neoclassical literature where the Nordic universe was treated as "fanciful" and no pretense to historicity is made, the most interesting attempt to employ the Nordic past was Christen Pram's Danish epic *Stærkodder* (1785). This warrior hero had been used by an earlier generation of Swedish historians, but they were unable to resolve the dual view of the Nordic hero. Pram was more successful at this (although there is still the pairing of the bellicose warrior Stærkodder and the sentimental lover Halvar with the addition of a morally omniscient heroine), but Pram's attempt is a conscious imitation of Wieland's *Oberon,* and his muse is basically the same: "Thou, o Phoebus, whom Scandia's men / Called the god Mimer, you simple Reason." Indeed, Pram explicitly rejects a Nordic muse, saying that

> Your rumbling voice will be of no avail;
> Who would wish to hear your booming thunder?
> One flees you in dread, or pays you no heed.[21]

Since Pram's epic is not "serious," he allows the marvelous, but even though he is not obliged to include euhemeristic explanations of the gods, the water from Mimir's well, the ship Skibladnir, and Skirnir's sword (the three things the hero must bring back) are only shallow allegories illustrating the contemporary political situation in Denmark.

Neoclassical esthetics, predicated upon the exemplary methods of mathematics and mechanics, in the certainty of eventually ascertaining the universal principles by which good art corresponds to nature, was implicitly hostile to the use of the Nordic past in formal literature. To accept the possibility of an intrinsic merit to the "runic" poetry independent of the canons of neoclassical taste would imply a rejection of neoclassicism's very claim to universal principles of taste. Whether the attempts were serious or fanciful, there was no concerted effort among the neoclassicists to discover and imitate a particularly "Nordic" style of writing, nor could there be. Although the social myth of northern freedom, as reformulated by Montesquieu and Mallet, had some impact on neoclassical literature, no techniques of imagery or characterization developed which could allow the freedom myth to become a myth in formal literature. If the bellicose Viking half of the archetypal Nordic hero was too unrefined for men of good taste, however, his landbound alter ago underwent an important metamorphosis and emerged as a lasting literary myth—the *odalbonde*.

It might be expected that the Nordic freeman farmer would serve as the lens through which the myth of northern freedom would develop from social myth to literary myth. Certainly the man of the soil was more congenial to the eighteenth-century mentality than the barbaric Viking conqueror. Also, the *odalbonde* could share an identity of space with the writer in the present that the restless seafarer could not. Both these images of the Norseman—the Viking and the *odalbonde*— are integral to the Nordic past as myth, but it is the *odalbonde* that has continued to the present as a potent literary and social myth. In the world of sentimental primitivism the golden age was defined in terms of Arcadia rather than warfare, and it is here we must consider Rousseau as a mythmaker.

Rousseau, though attuned to empirical thought, gave a new formulation of the relationship between primitive emotion and modern intellect:[22] if through scorn the Church had been neutralized as an expression for enlightened social values, and if the pagan gods had been neutralized for literature through euhemerism and allegory, Rousseau did give definitive formulations of a relationship between nature and the "sensitive heart." Nature, which when defined mechanically was producing such dramatic results for rational inquiry, was now redefined as a satisfactory path for man's inescapable emotions.

Rousseau approached the idea of the nonreflective naive experience from an anthropological, not a literary, standpoint. The inexorable consequence of the self-awareness of rational thought was, for Rousseau, the separation of the mind from the heart, thought from action, the concept from the thing perceived, individual identity from communal identity. This self-awareness was one of the unfortunate products of civilization. At some point, however—the golden age—the separation from spontaneity had not taken place.[23] While man fulfills himself (in the "véritable vie") only in community with others, this awareness of self cuts him off from a direct apprehension of nature, as do products of intellection, such as harmony and grammar. There lies poised between a state of solitude and civilization a state in which man's expressive faculties were unified, when the contemporary fragmentation had not begun. This state, mythically and historically poised in an ahistoric *illud tempus,* was a golden age—an age man should aspire to recapture.

The temporal location of the golden age was between savagery and civilization—not in the "state of nature," but "between the rude essays of uncorrected fancy, on the one hand, and refinements of reason and science on the other."[24] Richard Hurd, who made this assessment, was one of the principal apologists for "runic" poetry, and conceived of the poetic golden age in vaguely Nordic terms. As the idea of a particularly Nordic muse grew, its temporal projection—its mythic element—couched this hypothetical instant of symbolic genesis in Nordic images.

This mythic instant was elaborated by writers who, following Montesquieu, were less concerned with the primitive and his "monstrous fictions" than they were with the environment that shaped them. Diderot, for instance, in the *Supplement to the Voyages of Bougainville,* sees the primitive through the myth of "soft" primitivism: the unflattering accounts of the contemporary savage went unassimilated, while the primitive was understood with images and conventions stemming from classical descriptions of the Age of Gold. Diderot extended Lockean psychology into what would now be called environmentalist sociology by describing how beneficent, uncorrupted nature results of necessity in a benign, uncorrupted primitive.[25]

The idea of a primitive, emotional, unified relationship to nature was widespread in the late eighteenth century and was often used polemically to imply a sense of degeneracy from this perception.[26]

Primitivists understood the distinction between primitive emotion and the "objective" nature of modern rationality with language stemming from descriptions of a golden age. When couched in quasi-literary terms and "Gothic" images, this mythic instant provided the temporal setting for the myth of the noble Nordic—the Bard (see chapter 6) and the *odalbonde*.

Although Rousseau viewed the Germanic tribes as barbarians, the potential of his understanding of time for the mythic consciousness can be found in the preface to Justus Möser's *Arminius* (1749), in which Möser interprets the descriptions in Tacitus (as filtered through humanist social myth) as having a temporal bond to the present: they "can be used to this very hour to describe our farmers in Lower Saxony."[27] It was in Scandinavia, however, that the views attributed to Rousseau were from the first couched in "Gothic" images, and Rousseauistic primitivism found mythic expression in the figure of the *odalbonde*.[28]

Central to the development of the *odalbonde* myth was Olof Dalin, who will be remembered as being instrumental in the remorseless dismantling of the Rudbeckians. But Rousseauism, in Sweden particularly, had many connections direct and indirect with the scholarship of the *Stormaktstid*. Dalin's attack on Rudbeck had been less a rejection of his mythic vision than of his methodology and criteria for truth. In his *History of the Kingdom of Sweden* (*Svea rikes historia*, 1747–1762), meant as the final blow in the dialectic exposing Rudbeckianism and appearing three years before Rousseau's *Discourses,* a newfound myth is latent. Dalin described the ancient Swedes as "Herde-Skyther" (shepherd Scythians) and said that they had retained the purity and innocence of their ancestors, the postdiluvians. Unconcerned with material goods, their simplicity and justice had been models for all. In morality, these "Herde-Skyther," with their intuitive knowledge, surpassed the Egyptians with all their technology. Since the soil belonged to all, there was no sense of property; indeed, according to Dalin (and Rousseauism), the golden age came to an end when a sense of possession developed.[29]

Though Dalin was recreating a social myth different from that produced by humanist historians, he still had the problem of assimilating marginal facts into a mythic universe: the remolding of the pagan religion into acceptable forms. Dalin began with the assumption of innate primitive monotheism, but there was an important difference in his treatment of Norse mythology. While Mallet and others had seen Norse mythology in terms of disconnected "fables," Dalin perceived an underlying unity, a consistent world view. This unity was an artificial schema taken from Ramsey's *Discourse on Mythology* (*Discours sur la mythologie*, 1727), where the author demonstrates to his satisfaction that all mythologies are based on the knowledge of a supreme god, a trinity of power, love, and wisdom, a golden age of innocence, a fall from grace, and salvation through a mediating god.[30]

Since Snorri Sturluson had mentioned "Allfather" as a kenning for Odin, writers even before Dalin made the pagan past acceptable (turning it into an image of their own time) by separating "Allfather" from Odin and suggesting that the Norsemen really had an innate concept of monotheism, with "Allfather" as the supreme god. Dalin filled the positions of the trinity with Odin, Thor, and Frigga (there was some precedent for this in Adam of Bremen's account of pagan practices in Uppsala), but the schema had the curious effect of making Thor the god of love. This was necessary, since Thor was assigned the role of savior, but Dalin was obliged to apply some agile allegorizing.[31]

As did Rousseau, Dalin placed the golden age in a mythic instant between savagery and the alleged tyranny of institutions, and thanks to Dalin, ideas associated with Rousseau were given Nordic form in Scandinavian literature, even though images were taken from Haller's description of the Swiss in *The Alps*.[32] But the redevelopment of a myth of a Nordic golden age did not obviate the duality in the character of the Nordic hero; rather, it sharpened it. However pastoral the images of the "Herde-Scyther," writers who extolled the "noble simplicity" of their *odalbonde* ancestors still felt attracted to the violence of the barbaric "Goth," and remarked that "it was with blood alone that they thought themselves able to buy happiness in Valhall."[33] In Denmark, P. F. Suhm warns his readers in the introduction to his Gessnerian *Idylls and Conversations* (*Idyller og samtaler*, 1772) that in the Nordic pastorals he has allowed himself to "write a little more wildly" than in the other pastorals, although exactly what he means by this is difficult to determine.[34]

Just as the contemporary reports of the noble savage and the assumptions about human nature in the golden age complemented each other and provided reciprocal documentation,[35] the Nordic counterpart, the *odalbonde*, received similar legitimation. Gerhard Schøning, whose

History of the Kingdom of Norway (Norges riiges historie, 1771–1783)
was one of the principal catalysts of Norwegian nationalism,[36] found
his version of the freedom myth (he uses etymology to assert that
Montesquieu's "Normans" were really Norwegians) confirmed by the
contemporary Norwegian farmer. The *odalbonde*, he says, presents a
"proof, that the fire and warmth, the courage and bravery which made
the Norwegians in the old days a source of terror for all of Europe,
glows today in the breast of the Norwegian farmer."[37]

Not all versions of the *odalbonde* myth introduce this temporal
aspect of his Viking ancestry, but central to it is the objective correlative of the soil. Where the earlier myth had depended upon etymologi-
cal deductions for proof, and easily disprovable conjectures about the
runestones (plus tricks such as substantiating the idea of *translatio
imperii* by pointing out that Gustavus was an anagram of Augustus),
the myth of the freeman farmer did not rest solely upon a current
political situation.

The *odalbonde* began as a social myth of origins, a projection of an
ideal of freedom the northern countries wished they had, and a moral
continuity from the heroic past to the not-so-heroic present. By the late
eighteenth century, however, the *odalbonde* had become an established mythic element in formal literature, as comparison of two
examples from Swedish literature, Johan Gabriel Oxenstierna's *The
Harvests (Skördarna, 1796)* and Erik Gustaf Geijer's poem "Odalbonden" (1811) illustrates.

In *The Harvests,* Oxenstierna not only describes peasant life with a
superabundance of benign nature scenes, but through the *odalbonde*
connects the present to the Nordic golden age. Taking many of his
examples from Dalin, he depicts the peasants' beginning in the Gothic
past. But here the duality in the myth of the Norse hero comes into
play.[38] Oxenstierna attempts to harmonize the two aspects of the Nordic myth by seeing the noble, sentimental half as a transformation of an
earlier barbaric race. The brutal sacrifices of the warrior, says
Oxenstierna, were replaced by peaceful rites under Queen Disa. This
changed the national character, although the freedom myth ("all were
of equal station, all were equally free") remained. Now, though, the
Norseman was to offer his harvests and not his blood, and the warrior
(*kämpa*) was to become the *odalbonde*. With this metamorphosis the
rocky landscape became fruitful, and the peasant has tilled the soil
until today.[39]

This attempt to give a mythic dimension to the idea of a contemporary golden age by seeing it as an extension in (mythic) time of the Nordic past is not very successful. One reason is the unconvincing attempt to synthesize the duality in the Nordic hero, but the other is Oxenstierna's effort to recreate the naive experience by introducing nature gods into the poem. Here Oxenstierna is a product of his time, for his concept of "nature" is a scientific, empirical one, and his mythological decorations appear sterile and unnecessary.

Erik Gustaf Geijer had a deeper understanding of the nature of myth and a different concept of the nature of symbol. In his "Odalbonden" we can see how social myth can be absorbed into formal literature and still convey the simultaneity of mythic time. The more sophisticated use of the *odalbonde* myth as symbol by Geijer stands in sharp contrast to Oxenstierna's crude attempt to fuse the historical present and the mythic past. In "Odalbonden" the farmer narrates eighteen of the twenty stanzas of the poem, and for fourteen of them there is no definite indication of when the narration is taking place. The narrator shows an awareness of his own psychological makeup ("Honor's name tempts me not. She lives, though, in my breast") which is inconsistent with the deliberately inelegant and abrupt language, but for seven-tenths of the poem Geijer is consciously describing a type that exists outside historical time: "The solid earth, she's my hope, She'll always be true."[40]

In stanza fifteen, however, the narrator says, "I wander up to Svea's council / With shield upon my arm," which establishes the distance in time ("Svea" is heroic language for "Sweden"). But this is the only definite indication that the narration is taking place in the heroic past. The remainder of the poem shows that the free Nordic hero "sanctifies" the historical present by existing both in the past *and* in the present:

> Our lawman doesn't use many words
> For the King in common things.
> But strong is the people's yea or nay
> During weapons' ringing clash.

The last two stanzas are narrated by the poet, who concludes by saying

> He sits and whittles his walking-cane
> May Sweden n'er see his race's end!

The Odalbonde's name may sink in the grave,
But his deeds will last through time.

The development of the *odalbonde* from a vague "Scythian" in Dalin's Rousseauistic formulations to a myth in formal literature is indicative of the persistence of the mythmaking impulse in an empirical era, but the quasi-factual status of this myth of the Nordic golden age also animated at least a partial breakdown of the negative status heretofore assigned to the barbaric "runic rhyme" and the emergence of a style of writing thought to be peculiarly "Nordic." The formulation of a symbolic universe in which literary values could be expressed in terms of the northern muse is the concern of our next chapter.

(6)

THE BARD
AS ORIGINAL GENIUS:
THE NORDIC MUSE

The previous chapter outlined the development of an enlightened Nordic golden age couched in terms of the myth of northern freedom. Though this social myth did not successfully express neoclassical literary tenets, after the writings of Rousseau and Dalin some form of a golden age was thought to have had an empirical existence. In the *odalbonde* we saw the emergence of one literary myth from this social myth; the use of the Nordic past as literary myth will now be examined in a wider perspective, in that the concept of the Nordic golden age formed the basis of a brief and relatively ill-starred attempt in the late eighteenth century to recreate a way of writing thought to be both "Nordic" and national.

Although the mythmaking impulse was to create an empirically satisfactory theoretical basis for a Nordic muse, the validity of myth in the literary consciousness involves imagery as well as a body of theory. Expressive of the gradual revaluation of the esthetic validity of the prescientific mind were techniques of imagery and narrative, as well as the development as literary myth of the incarnation of Rousseau's "mythic instant": the Bard.

In 1769 the Danish critic Jacob Baden voiced concern over the emergence of this myth (which to him was alien, a potential debasement of European literary standards) by ruefully observing that "it looks as though Norse mythology is about to become the 'in' thing."[1] The explicit rejection of a "Nordic muse" on the part of the neoclassicists Pram, Leopold, and others further indicates that in this period there was a literary style considered to be particularly "northern" and savage. As we have seen, the combination of antiquarian scholarship (itself mythically based) and social myth provided so-called documentary evidence which "proved" that in the Nordic past there flourished a sort of national poetry. Though the majority considered this poetry barbaric, a growing number found it to be vigorous, manly, and "naive," a spontaneous sort of lyric expressing an immediate, passionate view of nature. Baden's fears were largely unjustified, or at least premature; this new view of the Nordic past could not yet compete with the empirical spirit. Yet it is perhaps an indication of the persistence of the mythic consciousness that even the scholarly, classically trained Thomas Gray could bring himself to imitate the barbaric "runic rhyme" in his widely read poems "The Descent of Odin" and "The Fatal Sisters." Despite the political-esthetic duality in the idea of the Germanic past, the "runic rhymes" and savage fables which had shocked and disgusted an earlier generation were read by some later in the century as forms of vitality, if not of truth.

We have seen the rationalist relegation of mythology to falsehood and of the "Goths" to historical and esthetic barbarity, which prevented neoclassicists from finding literary merit in Nordic poetry. How, then, did the turnabout in literary taste occur which resulted in the positive evaluation of primitive poetry in general, "runic" poetry in particular, and the consequent notion that it might be possible and even desirable to recreate the spirit of a Nordic muse in the present? This Nordic golden age was reconstituted both as a legitimation of late eighteenth-century primitivism, where virtue animated the world and was clearly distinguished from vice, and as an escape from the modern subject-object dualism into a naive past yet unfallen into the moral complexities of the historical world. The reformulation of the myth expressed a new awareness of the nature of the primitive mind and of the esthetic value of its creations, an awareness which would culminate in the self-conscious romantic attempt to create Friedrich Schlegel's "new mythology."

The "new mythology," however, involved a valuation of the symbol foreign to the Enlightenment, where nonempirical poetic constructs were "merely symbolic." Though the post-Kantian generation of Wordsworth believed that the poet could discover and experience nature by looking inward ("We receive but what we give / And in our life alone does Nature live"), the reflective literary consciousness of the early eighteenth century assumed nature was an objective order, inspiring, but generally separate from the emotion of the poetic perception. The "laws" of nature were thought to have been discovered (hence, objectively true), while the literary symbol, having lost its objective, oracular power, was merely invented. The symbol, then, could not be the basis for literary creation in the early eighteenth century, and the constructs of the primitive could only be seen as fictions.[2]

In the latter half of the eighteenth century, however, it was pointed out that the implied analogy of art to mathematics was not necessarily valid.[3] In a larger sense the whole epistemology of the Enlightenment had begun to be undermined by Hume's skepticism, and new ideas about the nature of the mind, the creative process, and "true" poetry were voiced by Herder and others. This did not mean, of course, that the mechanistic view was rejected at a stroke; but in terms of literature, the "Age of Sensibility" attempted to assimilate some of the new ideas by extending the older critical boundaries into the realm of myth and the irrational. We shall see how the expansion of assumptions concerning the definition of truth, when coupled with the mythic apprehension of time following Rousseau—the "mythic instant" described in the previous chapter—formed essential aspects of a literary symbolic universe in which a way of writing thought to be wild and Nordic could attain myth's objectivity and express a confidence that it was possible to recapture a "sacred" time of noble vigor thought lost with the fall into unbridled rationalism.

The first aspect of the new symbolic universe was the application of Lockean psychology to the primitive mind. Curiously, the scientific basis for the revaluation not only of primitive poetry but of the nature of mythology stemmed from the same scientific method that had earlier relegated both to exempla of man's prescientific barbarism, superstition, and folly. Using Locke's theory of the mind, theorists of the mid-eighteenth century launched extensive investigations into the nature of the primitive mentality and its product, mythology, and also into the nature of the creative process.[4] Although initially it is misleading to couple these two areas of inquiry, it was suspected later in the century that the two might have something in common.

Locke, of course, had maintained that man is born with no innate ideas, ideas coming about when the mind reflects on sense data, knowledge when the mind becomes the "object of its own contemplation." The relationship of primitive, unreflecting man to the world was essentially a passive one of sense perception. The unreflecting mind of the savage was assumed to be a photographic recorder of empirical reality, the allegories and fables being a "natural" result of the inability to abstract. Before Hume the customary approach had been to apply the theory to decode the fables into either higher concepts or historical data. Later in the century a more sophisticated view of nature allegory was developed, but toward midcentury investigators expanded the psychological implications of the Lockean assumptions into a picture of the savage that portrayed him more as a human being participating in the growth of human culture.

The basis of this new psychological explanation of mythology was an assessment in empirical terms of the reaction of the primitive to the world around him. Where previously the savage had been used to illustrate the idea that deistic Christianity was "as old as Creation"[5] Hume reversed this premise by studying religion as an aspect of *human* nature. To Hume mythology was not concealed truth but a fundamental manifestation of unreason. The primitive mind, devoid of rationality, projects its terror at natural phenomena into the only form he knows, giving nature human form. This animism was the initial direction, with the religious intuition being a product of the lower forces of the mind and not resulting from a "divine spark." Religion to Hume was a natural consequence of primitive reaction to environment. But polytheism, however unenlightened, was at least a natural reaction to life, Hume thought, as opposed to Christianity.[6]

In this view Hume was concerned less with the potential content of the savage "fables" than with the mind that created them and its relationship to the environment. This marked a considerable change from the ideas of Grotius, Pufendorf, and the earlier national historians, who, when they thought about the environment of their ancestors at all, settled for a vague Arcadia. This change of focus was a part of the general broadening of interest during the Enlightenment from the phenomenal world to its psychological effects.[7]

Initially, however, the concern for the environment of the primitive in the explanation of his fictions often led to a description of the milieu in such a way as to let the reader recreate the experience for his own still-impressionable senses; this technique came to be of importance in the re-creation of the past, both in theoretical works and in formal literature. For example, Nicholas-Antoine Boulanger's concern is not with the "chimera" of myth, but with a real human being in a real environment, and in his *Antiquity Unveiled through Its Mores (L'An-*

tiquité dévoilé par ses usages, 1766) he attributes the origin of idolatry to the terror of the Flood. Instead of relying upon an abstract assertion, however, Boulanger conjures up for the reader's mind the psychological effect the Flood must have had on the postdiluvians. He describes in detail the storms, earthquakes, and other "alien convulsions," and often lapses into present tense in his recounting, thus allowing the destruction to happen as the reader reads: "To all these strange convulsions, fire once more adds its fury—it leaves the bosom of the earth, with a horrendous sound proclaiming its strainings, it explodes across the mountains and the plains. Volcanoes kindled in a thousand places vomit at the same time water, fire, incendiary rivers and torrents of lava which consume what the waters have left."[8] The memory of the catastrophe, says Boulanger, is responsible for what he calls "this profound and universal sadness."[9]

An approach such as Boulanger's marked a major innovation in the attitude toward mythology. "Fables" now became more than examples of priestly chicanery—they were attempts to cope with reality. Boulanger did not go so far as Vico, who maintained that there was truth in mythology, nor did he attribute any poetic merit to the fables, but he did imply that there was an inner necessity to idolatry, as opposed to conscious invention. He also saw a continuity from the initial trauma to the present "universal sadness," a psychological explanation of the fact that mankind, in the days of the sentimental novel, enjoyed melancholy.

This new approach to mythology has implications for the later development of the literary consciousness in its modern form. The descriptive technique is a common one in the works of J. G. Herder, whose attitude toward empiricism was basically different from that of Boulanger. In his *On the Origin of Language* (*Abhandlung über den Ursprung der Sprache,* 1770), for instance, Herder goes from a generality based upon the assumption of a universal human nature to a re-creation in the present tense of the poetic experience of nature by the primitive, then to a generalization based upon this experience, and finally to a scientific documentation of the thought from contemporary anthropology:

> Since all of nature sounds, nothing is more natural to a sensuous human being than to think that it lives, that it speaks, that it acts. That savage saw the tall tree with its

mighty crown and sensed the wonder of it: the crown rustled! There the godhead moves and stirs! The savage falls down in adoration! Behold, that is the story of sensuous man, the dark link by which nouns are fashioned from verbs—and a faint move toward abstraction! With the savages of North America, for instance, everything is still animated: Every object has its genius, its spirit.[10]

Although this is a development of Hume's version of the fear theory, Herder's accent is quite different: he has let the reader participate (by switching to the present tense) for a good reason, in that he saw the creations of the primitive mind not as the origin of idolatry but as a poetic means of expressing *truth* in those sense impressions transformed by the passions. Herder was in many ways breaking new ground in the extant ideas about the nature of the primitive mind, primitive language, and primitive society.[11] Where progressivists such as Condorcet looked forward to the day when language would become as mathematics and shed its depressing ambiguity, Herder saw in the "wild fabling" representations of truth, of a now lost relationship with nature.

Herder's theory of the mythic mind was a generalization and synthesis of more specific theories on the nature of primitive imagery. In discussing the imagery of the Bible, for instance, Bishop Lowth had noted that the untutored mind does not describe reality but "wonderfully magnifies" it through the passions. But Lowth was only able to say that the passions are "naturally inclined to amplification"; he could not describe the creative process, for he could not conceive of nature in nonmechanistic terms. Herder's technique, though, of making the reader a *part* of the process shows that he saw that the nature of the mind was something less mechanical than a passive recorder of sense impressions.

The analysis of the primitive experience of reality was put in a more literary context by Schiller (1795), who distinguished between the prelogical "naive" poet and the modern "sentimental" poet. The former experienced nature somewhat as Herder had described—immediately, spontaneously—and his poetry, Schiller argued, thus attained an objectivity and correspondence to nature lacking in the modern rational mind, to which nature is mediated by reflection.[12]

Schiller saw this "naive" poet as part of a historical stage in man's development. The relationship of the modern poet to this naive experience was, however, another (and complex) problem, particularly when couched in terms of a nonclassical esthetics.

The new concern with the veracity of primitive emotion established a theoretical, quasi-factual basis for the creation of a heroic northern past, much as Tacitus had done for the German humanists. In this context, eighteenth-century primitivists often drew a moral distinction between the primitive emotion and the modern intellect, a distinction which ultimately resulted in a view that the "runic rhyme" was not barbaric, but true poetry. This turnabout in taste involved an expansion of the earlier, limited role allowed the "marvelous" in formal literature; the stage was then set for the primitivists' creation of the myth of a golden age of a Nordic muse, which myth was to provide the temporal setting for the figure of the noble Nordic as literary myth.

The responsibility of the poet to represent reality in empirical terms when dealing with historical subjects was a fundamental tenet of Enlightenment esthetics. But in expanding Enlightenment psychology into the theory of mythology and the mythic imagination, the concern with the *effects* of the phenomenal world upon the senses of the beholder resulted in a general interest in the nature of the poetic process as distinct from its product,[13] either in the semidivine nature of the poet-as-creator (Shaftesbury) or in its effect upon the *sentiment* of the reader (Dubos).[14] In his role as creator the poet can make new worlds, Bodmer maintained, and is not confined to representing empirical reality. In this sense—within the creation of the poet—the nonempirical elements were not "falsehood" but truth.

When consideration was given to how the reader experienced the irrational, the question arose whether the modern, enlightened mind could feel empathy with the mentality which produced the heathen fables. Hobbes had admitted that at one time the strange fictions were believed but was glad to note that man had irrevocably progressed beyond such delusions.[15] Later critics such as Breitinger, however, suggested that "through an effort of the Imagination we can remove ourselves to the past" and experience the marvelous almost as the heathens did.[16]

Fundamental to both these acceptances of nonreal elements in literature, however, was Leibniz's concept of "possible worlds," where probability was the criterion for truth and the poet was the creator of those worlds. The range of representation allowed the poet in his document was thus considerably extended. The "marvelous," both in the poet's act of creation and the reader's experience, must be subordinate to the probable, and this distinction—as Wolff and Baumgarten maintained—was made according to the earlier empirical distinction between true and false.[17]

The concept of "possible worlds" elaborated the earlier distinction in the acceptable use of the irrational according to whether the subject matter was actual (historical) or fanciful.[18] Among those critics who allowed the possibility that the poet could employ the marvelous or the reader experience the marvelous as real, the emphasis was upon the author's fidelity to the heathen customs he represented—his "realism," as it were.[19] The "fables" of the Germanic past, as they had been restored in the social myth of the antiquarian scholars, came to play a role in this discussion, for since Germanic mythology had been established by scholars as originally monotheistic and nonidolatrous, later writers of literature were able to use these "facts" as a pleasing contrast to the rationally offensive classical "superstitions," for which the modern mind had to make a greater suspension of disbelief. Johann Christoph Gottsched, the legislator of neoclassical taste in Germany, discussed the use of the Germanic marvelous in his preface to Schönaich's epic *Hermann* (1751), saying that in presenting subjects from Germanic history the Germanic poet need not run the danger of violating verisimilitude, for even though Varus and his idolatrous Romans believed in the ancient fables "Herman and his Germans were free of such superstitions. They worshiped one god only, as the Originator of all things." Thus the modern poet, Gottsched continues with pleasure, can freely employ Germanic beliefs, because they correspond surprisingly with "contemporary verisimilitude, and with the beliefs of the poet."[20]

To provide an empirical justification for the Nordic past as literary myth in which the mythic consciousness could validate the ideas of the nature of "true poetry" in empirical terms, the cultural disparagement of the "Goths" not only had to be at least partially replaced by a positive evaluation of their historical role, but the poetic merit of the "runic odes" and their superabundance of the barbaric marvelous had to be proved—proved in the sense that they were not only not barbaric but were documents of supreme creative genius, as the eighteenth century imagined it to be.

Such an idea was unacceptable to Shaftesbury, who did not see "romances" as falling within the realm of the probable but as "false, monstrous, and Gothick; quite out of the way of Nature."[21] Bishop Hurd, however, who shared some of Shaftesbury's ideas about the creative imagination, said that the primitive state in which the "Goths" lived was the source of the high poetic worth of their mythology and suggested that the northern literature did not present falsehood but reality: "What we hear censured in their writings, as false, incredible, and fantastic, was frequently but a just copy of life, and that there was more of truth and reality in their representations, than we are apt to imagine."[22] Hurd's idea of the "superior solemnity" of the Gothic superstitions has much in common with the psychological theories of myth mentioned above and the theories of primitive language as expressed by Bishop Lowth and Herder, but it was Hurd who, by arguing that "Gothic" poetry expressed fact, was chiefly responsible for freeing the term *Gothic* from its negative connotation.[23]

Applying the method by which Montesquieu had incorporated the myth of northern freedom into Enlightenment thought, critics such as Thomas Warton began to explain the character of a peculiarly Nordic poetic genius. Warton based his theory upon the facticity of the legend of the migration of the historical Odin from Asia, saying that since "in the infancy of society, the passions and the imaginations are alike uncontrolled," the Asian people naturally had a "certain capricious spirit of extravagance," and a natural warmth of fancy. But the warmth (and he appears to mean this literally) persisted after the migration into the North, and the senses of the "Asiatics" were presented with the Nordic landscape, the "piny precipices, the frozen mountains, and the gloomy forests," and it was this that gave "a tincture of horror to their imagery."[24] What is emerging here is a "factual" explanation for the "wild horror" that eighteenth-century gentlemen believed they found in the primitive poetry of their barbaric ancestors: such "explanations" ultimately provided the necessary base in empirical truth for the Nordic past to express mythic truth in formal literature.

Other writers concerned with explaining the Nordic muse in terms of Locke and Montesquieu allowed the reader to experience the assault on the senses along with the northern primitive by the technique of recreating the environment. James Beattie, in his essay "On Fable and Romance" (1764), gives a long description of how in the North "the demon yelled in the storm, the spectre walked in darkness," and how in the castles "the howling of winds through the crevices of old walls . . . the grating of heavy doors on rusty hinges of iron; the shrieking of bats" and other natural causes would "multiply their superstitions, and increase their credulity; and . . . would encourage a passion for wild adventure."[25] Although Beattie appears to have taken his data concerning the Nordic environment from *The Castle of Otranto,* he is applying the same method of explaining the Nordic poetic process as did Boulanger in finding myth to be a result of the trauma of the Flood. The idea and description of the Nordic muse (although "Nordic" was a concoction of whatever the particular critic wished to consider wild and savage) was kept acceptable to the empiricist through an increasingly sophisticated series of explanations, based upon Lockean psychology, notions about the "wild" Nordic landscape stemming from the previous century, and the generally unquestioned notion of a migration by a historical Odin from Asia.[26]

With an empirically satisfactory explanation of barbaric imagery established, some critics (though not many) elaborated the explanation of Nordic poetry into its consequences of esthetic relativism, and allowed the possibility of true poetic inspiration occurring not just in the classical South but also in the chill, forbidding North, and expressed this view with images of the mythic time of a Nordic golden age. In 1769 William Duff had written that genius consists of original creation (familiar ground from Addison and others) and cited as principal evidence of original genius "the whole system of heathen mythology." Duff unites genius, mythology, and imagination, separating his admiration for myth's creative nature from his condemnation of it as religion; Bishop Hurd and Thomas Warton had expressed similar views in terms of the "Gothic mythology," but Duff, like Herder a year or so later, goes farther and says that imagination is at its perfection in the rudest form of social life when the imagination has not been troubled by reflection: "As [the primitive poet] is not familiarised by previous description to the scenes he contemplates, these strike upon his mind with their full force; and the Imagination astonished . . . spontaneously expresses its vivid ideas in bold and glowing metaphors."[27] This was a turning point in the view of primitive poetry, as the psychologizing of myth had been one for the theory of the mythic imagination. It was recognized that poetic inspiration was not confined to the South—as Hugh Blair put it, "warmth of fancy is the characteristic of an age, not of a people."[28]

With the acceptance of the reality of a primitive Nordic golden age, the central problem for the literary consciousness was whether this moment of creative innocence when the "marvelous" was real could be recovered by the modern poet and experienced (as probable) by the modern reader.[29]

In Scandinavia there were suggestions that the peculiarly Nordic naive experience could be recaptured. It has been indicated that the general method employed by Montesquieu to explain the northern idea of freedom on the basis of sense impressions had been extended into the explanation of the "wild" character alleged to be the essence of the vigorous Norse literature. Gerhard Schøning, in his *History of the Kingdom of Norway* (*Norges riiges historie, 1771–1783*), says that to elaborate upon the profundity and odelike character of the Norse poems is beyond him, but he asks the readers to note in the wild poems "the exactitude of the poet, by observing what must be the soul and life in the ancient heroic songs, their arousing of the sense and setting it afire with images of the tumult of war and sound of the weapons."[30] Implied in Schøning's analysis is that the modern reader can also participate in this excitement.

Could this naive experience also be recaptured and imitated by the eighteenth-century poet? In other words, could the standards of eighteenth-century poetic values be extended to incorporate as "true" a "Gothic" style which for years had been dismissed as barbaric and tasteless? This implied conflict between literary standards was documented in the case of the Swedish poet Frans Michaël Franzén. In 1797 Franzén wrote "A Song to Gustav Philip Creutz" ("Sång öfver grefue Gustaf Philip Creutz"), in which he discusses at length the possibility of a Gothic (Swedish) muse, independent of Greece and Rome. He considers this historically, saying that at one time (in the golden age) this existed. The significance of Franzén is that he applies the theory of the effect of the Nordic landscape on the poet by demonstrating it in formal literature. Franzén's description of the particular nature of the Nordic setting came to be standard in poetry, taking the Norse environment out of the realm of piny Arcadias.[31] He sees the landscape, with its gloom, its mountains, its glaciers and cliffs, in animate terms: "Lovely is the cliff itself, which nods / In the gleaming light." In this environment, Franzén describes the Gothic Bard, whose song was an immediate expression of Nordic nature: "Like the north wind, sharp / Stormed his song." This song was—in the poem's first stanza—"Chilling-beautiful in Scandia's dark," and Franzén maintained that it was possible for the modern northern poet to recover this indigenous inspiration, described as singing of the stars that swing around the peaks in the Great Bear, of ghosts that rise up like the north wind from the grave's shadow and of elves dancing in the moonlight.

This version of the poem ran afoul of the Swedish academy (principally Carl Gustaf Leopold) and some revisions were suggested; these Franzén followed. The second version explicitly renounces the possibility of an independent Nordic genius, saying that only in the South, "Where Nature carefree laughs, / Was Beauty born—and was born no more" (p. 53). Furthermore, the Gothic song which in the earlier version was "chilling-beautiful" is described as "just a scream / Of the barbarian, who, possessed, / Expressed his feeling with anger" (p. 51). In short, not only did Franzén, under pressure by the Swedish neoclassical establishment, reject the idea of a golden age of northern inspiration, but he also denied the possibility of achieving in the present a separate northern poetic identity.

But it is Franzén's first version of "Creutz" that understandably attracted the most critical attention and has been called a turning point in Swedish literary history. [32] In terms of the mythic consciousness and the Nordic past, the controversy over Franzén's poem dramatizes the beginning of the assertion of the mythic-literary consciousness as opposed to a previous view of literature in which myth was not only a "shriek of the barbarian" but, in more general terms, false.

But both the vision of the Nordic past adumbrated in "Creutz" and the academy's criticism of the first version were resting upon ostensibly sound empirical foundations. The deeper analysis of the nature of the primitive mind, although still on a Lockean basis, enabled a minority of "primitivists" to interpret contemporary anthropological data in Rousseauistic terms and to advance as a "fact" a theory of original genius which basically had its roots not in Enlightenment empiricism but in the mythic consciousness.

Although the creation of the modern mythic consciousness of a Nordic golden age of poetic expression had been given quasi-historical status, as a myth it had to reintegrate the historical present with this genesis, recapture in an acceptable way this primitive oneness with nature. There were many effusions about the relationship of the "sensitive heart" to nature, but nature was still regarded as an objective order in the eighteenth century. Thus, as W. K. Wimsatt observes, there was in formal literature "an absence of poetic quality—that is, of a poetic structure adequate to embody or objectify the new feeling." [33]

Creating the illusion of a spontaneous apprehension of nature and the simultaneous attachment to empiricism is a formal problem of imagery and technique. In terms of imagery, Martin Lamm has suggested that the vogue of *ut pictura poesis* poetry in the eighteenth century was an attempt to bridge the gap between man and nature. [34] That is, poets felt, either consciously or unconsciously, that by describing nature, recreating the visual impressions of the uncorrupted environment of the golden age, it would be possible for the reader to experience through sense perception the primitive intuition.

Another means by which poets attempted to establish this immediate relationship was also dominated by scientific principles, and this was to allow nature to speak through mechanical response, such as echo. For example, the Norwegian poet Christian Braunmann Tullin in his poem "The May-Day" ("Maidagen," 1758), of which Lessing thought quite highly, [35] uses the device rather effectively to drive home the point that, unlike in the city, God expresses himself directly in the "wild" Norwegian nature. The poet, enraptured, asks a singing bird:

> O sweet little flautist!
> Who made you such a creator?
> I shouted over toward a mountain,
> And Echo answered: "—a Creator."

In general, however, the descriptive technique and tricks such as echo proved to be blind alleys, for the poet or narrator still only perceived nature through the senses, i.e., passively. But when the setting of the poem was temporalized (that is, the golden age is put into the past), the result proved more successful. This was perhaps because of the latitude given the poet by allowing his poem to take place in an age before the separation of mind from nature; it will be recalled that the use of the "marvelous" had been extended to include possible worlds, and one of these was the historical golden age, when man still experienced nature naively.

As a literary example of this setting, we may consider the Danish poet and dramatist Johannes Ewald's musical drama *The Death of Balder* (*Balders død,* 1773).[36] Though pedestrian in some ways, the play is an illustration of how a good poet can rise above the conventions of sentimental drama through poetic techniques and place a banal conflict into a more discerning context of man in a cosmic process, a view less optimistic than that usually found in the eighteenth century. This discrepancy between theme and action seriously mars the plot, but Ewald's intuitions about the complexity of human experience have high value as poetry.

Olof Dalin, in his interpretation of Norse mythology, dated the end of the golden age in the North from the death of the god Balder, and this is the dramatic moment of Ewald's drama, the literary high point of the "Nordic Renaissance" in the eighteenth century. Ewald does not escape the problem of characterization (characters animated either by virtue or by vice) nor does he make any radical breakthrough in imagery to express the naive experience of a Nordic golden age; rather, he is able by manipulating the convention to tie the sentimental love triangle into the larger course of Norse mythology. Through a skillful handling of imagery Ewald is able to imply cosmic consequences to Balder's love for the mortal girl Nanna. Balder in this play is portrayed as half-man, half-god, and Ewald emphasizes his human side, but through Balder's friend Thor and the nature imagery, the gravity of Balder's actions at the divine level is implied.

The play need not be described in detail, but Thor reminds Balder of the prophecy that should he fall in love with a mortal, a spear will be made and tempered in the fires of Nastrond (which Ewald makes into the source of fire at the creation of the Norse cosmos) and this spear will not only mean the death of Balder but the beginning of Ragnarök.

The other member of the triangle is the mortal Hother, "King of the Danes," who like Nanna and Balder is a paragon of virtue. Nanna's moral excellence is so unimpeachable that she is virtually incapable of doing anything but defending it, and the contest between the virtues of Balder and Hother is so balanced that Ewald is obliged to use a clumsy deus ex machina to effect Balder's killing by the spear, lest Hother's virtue be compromised.[37]

Although the love triangle is almost pedestrian and poorly handled, through imagery Ewald links it to a sense that something larger is happening, that a turning point in the history of creation has been reached. Primarily, this is done not through new techniques but by taking what was a static device—the echo effect—and integrating it into a developing complex of imagery which involves nature with the development of the theme.

The setting of the first scene is the typical Nordic landscape: "steep and jagged cliffs." The first line of the play is Balder's: "The land, as though proud of mountains secure, / Calmly defies the Heavens." Balder's second speech begins a development of imagery through a "Nordic" kenning which will become thematic: "Odin's red arrow [lightning] will / Slip from your hard sides; / The sun will not melt your snow." The red-fire image and the idea of melting develop into the main themes of the play: fire is both internalized into the fires of passion, which Balder cannot extinguish, and also into wrath. It is linked to the motif of the spear (again presented in terms of nature) by the Valkyries: "The red of dawn shone / Ten thousand gleaming spears on Scotland's mountains" (p. 37). The center of the play is the vision of the fatal spear in fiery Nastrond: "the entrance of a large cave is visible, illuminated only by the flames . . . on each side a little round altar. On the first burns a fire, where the fatal spear lies" (p. 64).

Another developing image pattern is the involvement of nature as a sentient entity in the tragedy. Thor says the cliffs echo Balder's woe (the echo effect), and that this will be the sign of the catastrophe. Nature, originally described as "calm," becomes steadily less so; ominous thunder rolls as Loke mentions the spear to Hother (p. 33). The same sort of imagery amplifies Hother's despair at the beginning of Act III; sitting on a cliff, he sings:

> Let the cliffs tremble,
> When the storm roars
> And thunder crackles—
> My soul is light!
> Ah, what I feel
> Is more than thunder,
> More than Northern storms,
> More than fright!

Hother is to signal Loke by a horn, and when he comes across it, it gives a "gruesome echo" in the cliffs (p. 60). The imagery is connected

to the Norse creation by Loke; telling Hother how the Valkyrie Rota
found the fateful branch which will kill Balder, Loke says:

> I heard a sound, like the storm's
> When it uproots the oak on the cliff; then I heard
> The voice of Rota, and thick, black drops
> Of Giant-blood, of they that Odin slew
> Dripped through the cracks in the cliff—Then I knew
> By all the signs, she had found the branch. (p. 63)

On the next page, Hother sees the vision of Nastrond in the cliffs.

When Hother, armed with the spear, meets Balder, "nature is still"
as Balder notices; the cliffs will not answer Nanna's despair. When
Nanna finally kills Balder's false hope, Rota appears behind Balder
and after Balder's death, Hother says, "He is dead, the great Balder!"

> —(*A voice, far away in the forest*):
>> He is dead, the great Balder!
> —(*Many voices, who answer each other among the cliffs*):
>> The great Balder is dead.
> —(*Chorus*):
>> Thunder, roll! Storm rage!
>>> Scream, heaven, earth and sea!
>> Scream, men and gods,
>>> At the great Balder's grave!

And the play ends.

Although Ewald does not develop the fire image past the Nastrond
scene, he uses the echo effect and other forms of imagery not just as
nature description (as Haller and Tullin), but as a thematic device to
integrate nature into the mythological aspect of the play. Ewald extends the subject into nature, through sympathetic imagery.[38] This is
not pantheism; in terms of the mythic consciousness, what is seen in
The Death of Balder is a rudimentary, sometimes crude depiction of a
nature not exhausted by empirical description but existing also as an
extension of the mind.

It is perhaps too venturesome to conclude that the development of
sympathetic imagery as a technical device expressing the sense of
immediacy with nature has a nostalgia for a prerational apprehension
of nature as an unconscious cause; yet there is a striking similarity

between this technical means of amplifying emotion or theme by projecting it into nature and what Cassirer calls "the mythical consciousness of the object." In *An Essay on Man* Cassirer summarizes this consciousness of nature as being "sympathetic," in that myth is a product not of the intellect but of emotion. The mythic consciousness of the primitive, Cassirer says, "by no means lacks the ability to grasp the empirical differences of things. But in his conception of nature and life all these differences are obliterated by a stronger feeling: the deep conviction of a fundamental and indelible *solidarity of life* that bridges over the multiplicity and variety of its single forms."[39] It may be that the device of sympathetic imagery as a technique in formal literature and the mythic principle of identity have something in common; at least, the use of sympathetic imagery was able to express an involvement between the subject and his environment through emotion, something empirical nature description was unable to achieve save through an announcement by the narrator.

Since the conscious use of myth was generally restricted to decorative, intellectual allegory, the neoclassical lyric poet had difficulty in objectifying the animate or divine "soul" or nature. When the setting of the poem was temporalized, however, and the narration placed before or at the end of the golden age, it was possible to simulate the naive experience of nature for the reader by giving him the impression that the poem is being spontaneously created by a *Volksdichter* as he reads it. Northrop Frye calls this technical device "poem-as-process." There has been ample indication of the theoretical interest in the late eighteenth century in the creative process of the prescientific mind; Mr. Frye takes this one step further and describes the attempts made by the authors to give the effect that the poem is "spontaneous."[40] This technique has been encountered before in the discussions of the psychological theories of the mythic imagination; in formal literature, the "poem-as-process" illusion was used to take the reader back in time through the manipulation of the narrative point of view.

Thomas Gray, for instance, in his ode "The Bard" (1757) allows the reader to participate in the "Celtic" past by just such a manipulation. Strophe I begins with a direct address by the Bard to the churlish (modern) Edward I, who has ordered the Bards to be put to death; then the narrator interrupts briefly. The first antistrophe sets the scene, which became standard for the oracular poems conveying the idea of poem-as-process in the Nordic past:[41]

> On a rock, whose haughty brow
> Frowns o'er old Conway's foaming flood,
> Robed in the sable garb of woe,
> With haggard eyes the Poet stood;
> (Loose his beard, and hoary hair
> Stream'd like a meteor, to the troubled air)
> And with a Master's hand, and the Prophet's fire,
> Struck the deep sorrows of his lyre.

Then follows the Bard's curse on Edward, spoken in the first person by the Bard, and the narrator breaks in to end the poem: "He spoke, and headlong from the mountain's height / Deep in the roaring tide he plung'd to endless night."

Most of the poem is narrated by the Bard through Gray's handling of the point of view. This technique had been employed in theory by Herder and Duff in letting the reader experience the primitive creative moment by shifting to first person; with Gray, the technique became a common means of expressing the Nordic past in formal literature. "Where there is a sense of literature as process," writes Mr. Frye, "pity and fear become states of mind without objects, moods which are common to the work of art and the reader, and which bind them together psychologically instead of separating them esthetically."[42] In theory, therefore, there is a direct communication between the narrated speech and the reader-listener, an effect analogous to that intended by sympathetic imagery.

The techniques of sympathetic imagery and poem-as-process may be regarded, then, as devices by which the poet could express directly to his reader a "naive" apprehension of nature, at least as he conceived it to be. When put into the past, ostensibly narrated by the "natural" and oracular figure of the Bard or Skald, the modern reflective reader could have the illusion of sharing immediately an intuition of nature denied him in the historical present, where true, false, and probable were determined by empirical distinctions.

The figure of the Bard (or Skald) as formulated by Gray[43] was essential to implement the transition from the historical present to the mythic past. The Bard, existing at Rousseau's "mythical instant," is of two eras: he is both the end of the golden age and the beginning of the modern. Furthermore, as myth, his quasi-sacred status in the literary consciousness of sentimental primitivism objectified not only the new theories of the mythic imagination but the use of the "naive" poetic techniques. With the narration of the Bard, the reader is taken back to the golden age; with the death of the Bard at the end of the poem, it is implied that this golden age is gone, and demythologized historical time has begun. Once again the "time" of the narrative is poised between two worlds: the unfallen sacred world and the fallen world of the historical present, usually represented by a philistine such as Edward I in Gray's ode.

The formulation of the Bard as historical fact (necessary to his symbolic function as myth) was made by Bishop Percy in his *Reliques of Ancient English Poetry* (1765). The Bard is characterized as a strolling personification of the lyric. [44] (Bishop Lowth had described the Hebrew poet in essentially the same way, though emphasizing his role as *vates*.) In literature, Gray and Frans Michaël Franzén served as mythmakers, Franzén depicting the Skald in his stormy primeval landscape, with Gray's frame device becoming standard to implement the change in time and point of view.

Again and again, however, the poets claim that their portrayal can be justified historically, that the Bard figure is not just creating but also representing the Nordic past: Walter Scott, in introducing "The Lay of the Last Minstrel" (1805), says that the poem "is intended to illustrate the customs and manners, which anciently prevailed on the Borders of England and Scotland. The inhabitants, living in a state partly pastoral, and partly warlike . . . were often engaged in scenes, highly susceptible of poetical ornament."[45]

That Scott was unaware of the incongruity in his warlike pastoral primitive is evident from the poem. Scott also says that the "machinery also, adopted from popular belief, would have seemed puerile in a Poem, which did not partake of the rudeness of the old Ballad, or Metrical Romance." Hence, Scott uses the technique of poem-as-process, for the Minstrel, as the last of his race, lived in the mythical borderline of the historical golden age, and "might have caught somewhat of the refinement of modern poetry, without losing the simplicity of his original model."[46]

In this chapter we have seen the gradual development of an *illud tempus* of northern literary value, an elaboration of Rousseau's mythic instant in literary terms. The vague constellation of primitivist imagery and wish dreams of the golden age was objectified in the mythic symbol of the Bard, who as the last of the original geniuses (in the past, at least) was in the golden age but not of it. In the next chapter we will see how the temporal bond to the mythic universe was given its empirical verification to complement the mythic fantasy: Ossian.

(7)

OSSIAN AND THE NORDIC BARD
AS LITERARY MYTH:
THE SENTIMENTAL NAIVE

Few now tremble at the dauntless heroism of Fingal, and none are now tempted to don Werther's yellow vest to share the misty sighs of Temora, but the focal point for establishing the objective veracity of the myth of the noble Nordic in the eighteenth century and for reestablishing a sense of continuity with a mythic genesis was Ossian. Though Ossian is no longer read, much less admired, writers still are read and admired who, convinced of his authenticity, imitated him in the conviction that they were recapturing the synthesis of vigor and sentiment their ancestors possessed in a Nordic golden age. In the various forms of the myth of the Nordic past, Ossian was second only to Tacitus in documentary importance, for not only did he "prove" the current theories of the sentimental primitivists, but he also provided the central reference for later discussions and literary limitations.

Macpherson's fabrications were at first generally regarded as historical documents, thus serving primitivists as a corroboration for their esthetic and psychological views. As the Ossian poems were largely created from these primitivist theories concerning the naive poetic genius, it is not surprising that they functioned admirably to legitimize them. Whatever the ostensible revolt against earlier empiricism, the principal significance of Ossian was that he was believed to demonstrate the historical truth of sentimental primitivism, and so provided a temporal genesis for a modern literary myth: that is, objectifying the world of value, but in quasi-empirical terms. Not only did the epics *Fingal* and *Temora* serve as objective correlatives for primitivist values, but their mythic objectivity lent "authenticity" to the so-called Bardic movement in Germany.

The Ossianic poems began to appear in 1760, with the central poems being the "ancient epics" *Fingal* and *Temora*. Part of Macpherson's success as mythmaker was due to his structuring of these poems, for through a fairly complex handling of point of view, he managed to create the illusion that the reader was experiencing directly the raw nature and noble passion of his ancestors. Ossian, near death, sings most of the songs to Malvina, who was in love with Ossian's dead son Oscar. Ossian, consistent with the archetype of the Bard, is the last of his race, and "The Songs of Selma" ends with Ossian narrating his own impending death. Since Ossian as a son of Fingal was a major character in some of the actions, Macpherson was able to break the narrative by switching to present tense and letting Ossian speak in first person to keep the illusion of poem-as-process: "Dark as the swelling wave of ocean before the rising winds, when it bends its head near the coast, came on the host of Cairbar.—Daughter of Toscar! why that tear? He is not fallen yet. Many were the deaths from his arm before my hero fell!—Behold they fall before my son like the groves in the desert, when an angry ghost rushes through night, and takes their green heads in his hand!" (*Temora,* I, 13).[1] We participate in the golden age through the naive songs of the Bard, yet we are aware that it is coming to an end, and our own unheroic historical time is beginning with his death. As technique, this is far more subtle than that used by the writers for whom Ossian functioned as a mythic expression.

Not only did poem-as-process receive legitimacy as a "natural" technique from Ossian's poems, but those "wild images" of the primitive environment which were asserted to be the catalyst for primitive creativity were depicted by Ossian, who describes nature and its effect on his own imagination: "The bards had ceased; and meteors came, red-winding with their ghosts.—The sky grew dark: the forms of the dead were blended with the clouds" (*Temora,* VI, 113). Ossian as poet does not explain the workings of the primitive mind as did many of his imitators, for Macpherson took care of this in his copious notes to his "translations," thus separating the empirical analysis from the poem; rather, he demonstrates the creative process of the mind of the golden age. Herder and William Duff had done this in theory, but Ossian put the theory into a narrative context: the belief in Ossian's authenticity showed that sympathetic imagery and the relationship to nature such imagery implied were in fact a technique of the primitive northern poet.

Indeed, one of the merits of Ossian, and one of the inadequacies of his imitators, was just this use of sympathetic imagery to integrate nature into the action. For instance, when things are going badly for the noble Cuchullin, Macpherson's use of nature both amplifies the impending disaster and isolates the hapless warrior by focusing down upon him:

> The winds came down on the woods. The torrents rushed
> from the rocks. Rain gathered round the head of Cromla.
> And the red stars trembled between the flying clouds. Sad,
> by the side of a stream whose sound was echoed by a tree,
> sad by the side of a stream the chief of Erin sat. (*Fingal*, II,
> 30)

(One of the facts that had filtered out of antiquarian editing was that Nordic poetry alliterated.)

Fingal, on the other hand, is contrasted with Cuchullin again through nature imagery, but unlike Cuchullin he is introduced as a part of nature, the contrast being set up in terms of water versus land, light versus dark:

> Dark Cuchullin stands alone like a rock in a sandy vale. The
> sea comes with its waves, and roars on its hardened sides. Its
> head is covered with foam, and the hills are ecchoing
> around.—Now from the gray mist of the ocean, the white-
> sailed ships of Fingal appear. High is the grove of their masts
> as they nod, by turns, on the rolling wave. (*Fingal*, III,
> 40–41)

In *Temora,* Macpherson avoided what some critics thought to be a problem in Homer, his southern counterpart: the moral ambivalence in character.[2] Since the time of the humanists, history and its characters had been seen in terms of a struggle between virtue and vice. Such a view makes balanced conflict difficult to portray literarily, as it is in any esthetics where psychology is governed by moral absolutes. This is particularly true in battle scenes, where a polemic position of one sort or another is often involved. In *Temora* the villain is killed in the first book, and his noble brother is obliged by honor to oppose Fingal. Macpherson was then able to sustain his narrative by more than token opposition to Fingal's moral (hence martial) invincibility.

The Nordic hero as established by Fingal-Ossian provided a sentimental counterpart to the skull-drinking barbarian as exemplified by Ragnar Lodbrog. It has been indicated that a duality in characterization had been implicit (and explicit) in the social myths of Germania and Gothicism, and this continued into the literary myth. Although Ragnar's laughing intransigence in the face of death attracted general approbation, before the appearance of the Ossianic poems, the Norseman's "nobler qualities of the mind" had to be supplied by conjecture. In 1763, the year of *Temora*'s appearance, Bishop Percy had complained in his *Five Pieces of Runic Poetry* that the antiquarians had only concerned themselves with one side of the Nordic character: "we are not to suppose that the northern bards never addressed themselves to the softer passions, or that they did not leave behind them many pieces on the gentler subjects of love or friendship. The misfortune has been, that those compositions have fallen into the hands of none but professed antiquarians, and these have only selected such poems for publication as confirmed some fact in history, or served to throw light on the antiquities of their country."[3]

The difficulty in harmonizing the Christian *bellum iustum* and the Gothic warlike propensities noted above in Johannes Magnus and the myth of Swedish Gothicism was solved in Ossian, for the desired harmony existed as "fact" in the historical document, and there was no need for interpolation, apologies, or conjecture. Fingal himself, admonishing Oscar to "bend the strong in arm: but spare the feeble hand," voices the idea Johannes Magnus was only able to assert indirectly—his wars are either defensive (*Fingal*) or in the cause of social justice (*Temora*); "My arm was the support of the injured," he says, but "the weak rested behind the lightning of my steel" (*Fingal*, III, 45). Fingal thus functioned paradigmatically in legitimizing one of the great governing myths of the Enlightenment: that enlightened valor must triumph over tyranny and idolatry. This Fingal invariably does.

Yet the requisite barbaric half of the Nordic character does appear in the Ossianic poems. As did Lohenstein, Macpherson assigns this role to the Scandinavians. Starno in the poem "Cath-Loda" is a repository for all the pejorative connotations of "Gothic." Macpherson makes it quite clear in the notes that this duality was not confined to Ossian's narratives: "From this contrast, which Fingal draws, between his own nation, and the inhabitants of Scandinavia, we may learn, that the former were much less barbarous than the latter. . . . There can be no doubt, that he followed the real manners of both nations in his own time" ("Cath-Loda," in *Temora,* p. 187).

Macpherson's "Caledonians," although they believe in spirits, are neither idolaters nor obnoxiously superstitious, as Fingal's defeat of the Scandinavian god "Cruth-Loda" shows. Even the Caledonian spirits are less offensive than the "wild horror" of the barbaric Scandinavian poets, for Macpherson tells his reader that Ossian's descriptions of Odin's hall are "more picturesque and descriptive, than any in the Edda, or other works of the northern Scalders" ("Cath-Loda," in *Temora,* p. 189). Furthermore, Macpherson, owing to his manipulation of point of view and the judicious insertion of informative notes, was able to incorporate the "marvelous" by showing it to be a "natural" aspect of the primitive creative process.

In providing a constant commentary in terms acceptable to the enlightened reader, Macpherson's notes were as important as the narrative structure in maintaining Ossian's mythic adequacy, in that they assure the empirical "objectivity" necessary for modern myth. They (1) emphasize the historicity and verisimilitude of the poems, thus establishing them as true (*Fingal,* p. ix); (2) provide empirical historical explanations for the supernatural in the poems; (3) set up Ossian as a folk epic by comparisons to Homer, Virgil, and Milton and demonstrating that, though "Gothic" in a sense, Ossian is a true epic poet. Although Macpherson allowed that neoclassic precepts should not be enforced upon a Celtic Bard, he did say that there are general rules concerning the epic "which as they are natural, are, likewise, universal. In these the two poets exactly correspond" (*Temora,* pp. 137–138). Considered as myth, the copious notes and parallels pointing out Ossian's merits serve as a constant reminder to the eighteenth-century reader that the literary and social values he holds in the present were implicit in the very origins of the northern poetry of his ancestors; his taste was, in a manner of speaking, "as old as Creation." In Denis's translation of Ossian into German hexameters (1768–1769), which in its elegant edition was more accessible on the Continent than the English original, a German translation of the commentary of Cesarotti was added to that of Macpherson and Hugh Blair's long, laudatory essay, and Ossian's supporting apparatus came to have an aggregate character.

Ossian's initial function was to provide by analogy a reference point for all the conjectures concerning the hypothetical poetry of the various national pasts.[4] Second, by providing a northern counterpart to Homer, Ossian appeared to express the quintessence of the naive northern literary genius and thus unified the idea of a northern literature in comparison to the southern, a literary demonstration of Montesquieu. Madame de Staël, for example, commented that it seemed to her that there are two entirely distinct literatures, one from the South and one from the North, the one stemming from Homer, and the other from Ossian. In the literature of the North she classes English, German, and some Danish and Swedish works which embody the "Nordic" spirit as she extracts it from Ossian.[5]

Ossian's mythic function as the objectification of the northern muse also helped break down the stigma of northern barbarity, in that he either modified the view of the Nordic past or shaped initial reactions to it. Madame de Staël explains the sentimental melancholy of Ossian (it is an indication of Ossian's consolidating power in the myth that she assigns this trait to all northern literature) as being an extension of the "dark and moody" climate;[6] the Swedish critic Neikter used Ossian to reverse the barbarity theme, much as the humanists, inspired by Tacitus, had come to ask "Quis dicatur barbarus?". Neikter applied familiar psychology in suggesting that "Southern peoples, who have more lively passions, are more vengeful than the Northern, therefore the Homeric heroes are more fierce in their battles than the Ossianic."[7]

There were those, however, who could not accept any form of a Nordic style, even with Ossian as a touchstone. Though Carl Gustaf Leopold had used the freedom myth as the basis for his tragedy *Oden* (1790), he was also behind the Swedish Academy's rejection of Franzén's idea of a Nordic muse in the "Song to Creutz." In his essay *On Taste and Its Universal Laws* (*Om smaken och dess allmänna lagar*, 1801), Leopold maintained that those who value Ossian over Voltaire are in the same position as those who prefer the raw sense impressions of Gothic architecture over Greek sublimity: "it is impossible to unify these higher qualities with the wild, semiliterate Ossianic sort of poet."[8]

Leopold's immediate target in this and other essays was the poet Thomas Thorild, for few poets built their "spectrum of imagery" around Ossian more than he. If modern writers lack myth, Thorild had the opposite problem: he constantly invokes the mythic power of the

Bard and the Nordic landscape, for example, to give credibility to his passionate love for "Hildur":

> from dizzying mountains
> among jagged cliffs
> In the storm laments
> your lover, Hildur!

To Thorild, for whom poetry was identical with unmediated emotion—the more, the better—Ossian provided the model in the mythic past for the spontaneous genius he felt himself to be. Thorild sensed a unity in nature which transcended empirical description, but he did not express this in Neoplatonic or pantheistic terms.[9] Though he feels himself to be a reincarnation of Ossian's golden age ("You should have seen me . . . when I first saw the sun set in Glysisvall, when with Ossian I can feel the shades of heroes about me!"), Thorild conveys his apprehension of nature through the lens of an Ossian-constituted sympathetic imagery:

> From thy bosom, Nature, let in ethereal waves
> Stream pleasure and touch beauty over my song.
> Stream exultation! Thou, alas thou, immortal, gentle,
> All-enlivening, thou, Nature, my trembling harp
> Is turned. Silently weave about me, spirit of Ossian![10]

Though Thorild is a good deal more readable than most Ossianic poets, this passage illustrates a point made by Herder: as soon as modern man tried to imitate primitive poetry, the naive / sentimental problem immediately intrudes, destroying the attempt, in that the "I" of the poet is always there. Though Thorild is attempting to experience nature through Ossian's eyes, his creativity is limited to mere incantation.

Thorild is symptomatic of Ossian's reality as literary myth. The failure of the wave of Ossianic imitations shows that Macpherson was able to function in a relationship to the *illud tempus* that modern poets were not: as a kind of folk poet, transmitting a quasi-oracular form, not creating.

The Ossianic muse came to dubious fruition in Germany with the so-called Bardic movement, a group of mediocre poets inspired by a bowdlerized version of Herder's concept of *Volkspoesie* and galvanized into imitation by the paradigms of Ossian, the Bard, and Germania.[11] Most of these poets exist today only in literary histories and dissertations, for they were unable to absorb and express in their own lyrics either the quality of Ossian or the rapidly developing theories of the primitive imagination. Nor did they understand Herder's concept of *Volksdichtung* (his essay *On the Origin of Language* [*Über den Ursprung der Sprache*] appeared in 1771). Their poetry functioned as myth for a few years in the 1760s[12] during the first Ossianic craze and it was particularly vulnerable to the dialectic that ultimately overtook Ossian himself. Since the "Bards" both objectified contemporary literary values and depended upon the illusion of historicity, they fell victims not only to the revolutionary effects of Herder's conjectures on the literary imagination but also to philological scholarship as well.

The reality of their mythic touchstone was central to the "poetics" of the Bards, in that they were apparently convinced that their position as poets and their literary products were historical recreations of the position and inspiration of the Bards of the days of Thuiskon. The modern reader, on perusing their poetry, might well ask, "How is this possible?" but if Ossian's role as myth be recalled, some of the absurdities of these neoprimitivists become intelligible.

The "reality" of the Bardic esthetics stemmed from a debasement of Herder's concept of the *Volkslied*. Herder viewed the *Volkslied* as the spontaneous, unreflecting crystallization of primitive emotion, an act of creation which objectified the whole national character.[13] To Herder, Ossian was the prime example of such a *Volksdichter,* a Bard who sang "Lieder, Lieder of the People, Lieder of a simple passionate People."[14] But as the concepts of *Volkslied* and *Volksdichter* spread in the late eighteenth century, they became absorbed into more traditional literary values, yet still maintained their "natural," primitive connotations.[15] For instance, Herder was described as saying that Ossian wrote "Lieder *for* the People," not "*of* the People," a misunderstanding which incorporated the *Volksdichter* into the familiar *utile dulci* didactic tradition, and made the *Volkslied* into a free creation with predetermined intent, as opposed to a spontaneous expression of feeling. Percy, in his translations in the *Reliques of Ancient English Poetry* (1765), helped further this by "atoning for the rudeness of the more obsolete poems" in translating, but his translations were accepted as literal.[16]

Just as the reports of primitive life and the noble savage were couched in terms stemming from classical descriptions of an Arcadian golden age, so too the "wild" songs of the Germanic forebears were generally rendered in pastoral conventions—for example in Jacobi's poems in *Iris*. He has cleaned up the already purified *Volkslieder* for the "Damenwelt," but still describes his ditties historically as "the Lieder our good ancestors sang in the evening on the green hill under the ancestral linden by the waterfall," and "the Lieder our grandmothers sang as girls, fresh and pink and gay, artless as the bird toning its wild song."[17] The rubric of *Volksdichter* in the eighteenth century came to include Gellert, famed for his moral pastorals, and Gleim, the writer of didactic and patriotic lyrics.[18] As an indication of the dilution of the *Volkslied* concept, Lessing considered Gleim's verse and that of the Skalds and Bards to be essentially the same sort of poetry, for not only were Gleim's *Songs of a Prussian Grenadier* of the lower class (hence of the *Volk*) but more importantly, "all his images are sublime, and all his sublime is naive."[19]

In short, the concept of *Volkspoesie* was no longer being determined by the material, but by (a priori) values of the eighteenth century: patriotism, "passion," and the like. The linking of the original genius of sentimental primitivism, "the esthetic significance of the passionate man," with this lack of understanding of Herder's theory of *Volkspoesie* was the basis of the Bardic program.[20] Denis, Ossian's translator, who was as well versed in the primary and secondary literature of Germanic antiquities as anybody of his day, also evaluated the essence of the Nordic muse and its imitations in terms of whether it was "a daughter of Nature," "a voice of the heart," and "a product of the Natural," and used Ossian as his guide.[21]

Common to the Bards was a conscious rejection of any decadent non-Nordic elements, for only in this way could German poetry be reprimitivized and recover its historic "natural" quality. This was best expressed by Denis, who in his essay "Preface Concerning the Ancient National Poetics" ("Vorbericht von der alten vaterlaendischen Dichtkunst," 1784) outlines the poetics of the Bardic lyric and, unwittingly, the reason for their ultimate failure. Commenting that such a poetics based upon the Nordic poetry could only be a gain for the nation and enable it to recover its primal identity ("ursprünglichen Charakter"), Denis declares that this Nordic poetics must be historically based, a dependable rendering of "the virtues, manners and deeds of our forefathers."[22] This illusion of historicity was both the animating force of the Bardic theory and its fatal weakness, for the historic ideals to which the Bards (and with some exceptions the poets of the Nordic Renaissance as a whole) thought they were being faithful were creations of their own time, reifications existing as social and literary myth.

The attempts to put these vague and self-contradictory criteria into poetic practice in a Nordic universe made up the Bardic movement, which at the time was a venturesome technical effort to integrate the concept of the naive poet with the myth of the Nordic past as documented by Ossian. To illustrate the function of myth in the modern literary consciousness, we will consider some of the works of Gerstenberg, Klopstock, Denis, and Kretschmann.

The high point of the Bardic poems was the first of them, Gerstenberg's "Poem of a Skald" ("Gedicht eines Skalden," 1766).[23] As was the case with Ossian, the principal achievement in this poem is the author's handling of time, and the relationship of the barbaric past to the enlightened present. In the course of the five *Gesänge* the Skald Thorlaugr awakes from death and recalls the death of his friend and fellow Skald Hallvard; a flashback tells the tale of how the two saw the goddess Blaukullr bathing and swore eternal friendship, vowing that neither would survive the other. Subsequently, Thorlaugr kills another Skald who wants Hallvard's harp, but in doing so slips in the blood; at that moment, Hallvard returns from the wars, thinks Thorlaugr is dead, and kills himself. Thorlaugr grieves, builds a pyre for Hallvard and sacrifices himself.

The fourth *Gesang* ends the flashback and has an admiring description by the Skald of the present state of Denmark and a praise of Gerstenberg's friend Cramer, upon whose estate the Skald's burial mound lies; Thorlaugr notices, however, that the old gods are gone, and the fifth *Gesang* is a recounting of Ragnarök, with the last six lines returning the reader to the present:

> Distanced to new regions,
> My enthused eyes look around, see
> The image of a higher Divinity, its world
> And these heavens, such a canopy!
> My feeble spirit, bowed with dust,
> Grasps not their miracle, and falls silent. (p. 302)

Some readers (Goethe among them) thought the elements in "Poems of a Skald" too heterogeneous, but the poem has unity of a sort. The reawakening of Thorlaugr in the first Gesang is a motif from the "Völuspá," which prepares for the Ragnarök description in the fifth Gesang; although the voyeur incident of Blaukullr's bath is strictly from Thompson,[24] and is rather out of place, it is the sight of the divine which ostensibly motivates the friendship.

Gerstenberg, though not the first to refer to the change in religion in the Germanic countries in literature, nonetheless was the first to do so in the sense of Schiller's "The Gods of Greece"—that is, to say that the pagan outlook had a value of its own, which was forever lost. Yet Gerstenberg's employing of the poem-as-process technique allows the reader to experience this "pagan" view through the Skald narrator. The recounting of Ragnarök, with the downfall of the old gods and the coming of the "higher divinity," unified the time scheme in the poem; Thorlaugr in the fourth *Gesang* is astounded at how much more beautiful things have become since his time:

> How charming, how enchanting laugh
> The regions serene! How replete with gentle glory!
> In majesty more lovely, in beams more mellow
> Gleams this sun! (pp. 299–300)

But even though Gerstenberg, through his handling of time and point of view, asserts the independent value and identity of the Nordic past, he avoided the conflict posed by the social myth of progress and the moral ambiguity of paganism by allowing the narration of the primitive poet to take place in the present, and Thorlaugr to remark on how much better things have become. As the critic Nicolai noted in his review of the poem, Gerstenberg presents the "raw" barbaric past, but without offending modern sensibilities or the idea of progress.[25]

The paragon of the Bards was Klopstock, who unlike Gerstenberg, read Ossian before reading about Odin and Thor, and his "Nordic" poems and dramas are predicated upon the superiority of an Ossian-constituted Teutonic muse to that of the artificial South.[26] Klopstock was the first major German poet to attempt the use of the Nordic gods in his poems, and nowhere are the inadequacies of the eighteenth-century assumptions concerning mythology more evident than in these attempts. In "The Mound and the Grove" ("Der Hügel und der Hain,"

1767) the North-South polarity stemming from the Hermann myth forms the basis of the poem: in the battle for a modern poet's soul, a southern poet is defeated by a Nordic Bard, whose "Telyn" (an instrument apparently invented by Klopstock) sings of "souled Nature," and of itself chords this as "Fatherland!"[27]

Klopstock attempted to carry out the programmatic implications of "The Mound and the Grove" in some of his poems, but his method of doing this was singular: in attempting to replace decadent southern mythology with the virile Germanic pantheon, he merely removed Apollo and substituted Braga. For example, in rewriting "To the Poet's Friends" ("An des Dichters Freunde")—which he later retitled "Wingolf"—Klopstock replaced these stanzas from 1747[28]

> As Hebe, bold and youthfully fiery,
> As with the golden quiver of Latona's son,
> Eternal, so sing I, my friends
> Celebrating in mighty dithyrambs.
>
> Would you be verses, O song? Or,
> Unsubmissive, like Pindar's songs,
> Like Zeus' noble, intoxicated son,
> Whirl free from the creating soul?

with these appearing in 1771:

> Like Gna in flight, youthful, fiery,
> And proud, as if the gods gave to me
> From Iduna's gold, so sing I, my friends
> Celebrating in bold Bardic song.
>
> Would you be verses, O heroic song?
> Would you soar lawless, like Ossian's flight,
> Like Uller's dance upon sea-crystal,
> Free from the poet's soul?

Though Klopstock is widely cited as the inaugurator in German poetry of the new sensibility of nature, his handling of mythology illustrates Wimsatt's point that the late eighteenth century lacked the poetic structures to objectify this new attitude. The sterile view of the nature of mythology is illustrated by Gerstenberg's reaction, for he thought that the Teutonic mythology had "completely supplanted" the classical in Klopstock's poetry. It is thus evident that Klopstock was unable to alter the classical formal conventions in his odes in order to assimilate any subject matter intrinsically "Teutonic,"[29] even with Ossian as a literary complement to Hermann as a symbolic genesis.

But such was the momentary power of this myth to constitute reality that Lessing could praise lines like this from the drama *Hermanns Schlacht* (1769) as being "completely in the ancient German manner": [Hermann speaks] "Noble lady of my youth! Yes, I live, my Thusnelda! Arise you free princess of Germany! I have not loved you before, as today! Has my Thusnelda brought me flowers?"[30] Klopstock, too, was apparently convinced that this was fairly accurate, and footnotes the morality of his Teutons. If Klopstock's lyrics point out the inability to harmonize classical convention with an ostensibly Nordic inspiration, his "Bardieten" are now almost unreadable attempts to create (or, Klopstock thought, recreate) a Nordic dramatic genre. In the preface to the *Hermanns Schlacht* Klopstock notes that the historical "Bardiet" as a genre kept closely to fact and was exact in portraying the manners of the age.[31]

Yet the "realism" was not just a figment of Klopstock's or Lessing's imagination, for when Hermann's father Siegmar calls upon "Wodan," Klopstock feels obliged to employ philology to legitimize the morality of his mythic Teutons. He scrupulously notes (citing Cluverius) that the Germans were not idolaters but revered one god; "their colonies in Europe altered the belief in the Supreme Being through additions, although not as much as did those worshippers of Zeus or Jupiter."[32] But the realism of the *Hermanns Schlacht* was not just based upon an updating of humanist social myth; the poetic element in the "spontaneous" choral songs of the Bards and Druids also had their base in historical fact, largely in Ossian. Compare, for example, the Bards' often repeated chant in the play, "Hear deeds of the ancient times!" ("Höret Thaten der vorigen zeit!"), with Ossian's invocations effecting the temporal transition, "A song of the days of old!"

Klopstock, however, became the idol of the Bards—if Ossian had proved that the picture the eighteenth century held of the noble Nordic was historically true, Klopstock in their eyes demonstrated that the imagined moral and literary virtues of the Teutonic *Urzeit* could be successfully revived in the present by the creative genius of the self-conscious artist. In "Preface Concerning the Ancient National Poetics" Denis asserts that to recreate the magnificence of the original Germanic muse the modern Bard must not betray his muse through anachronism. Yet it is a singular commentary on the expressiveness of the myth that Denis, who was the most philologically oriented of any of the Bards, cites the works of Klopstock and K. F. Kretschmann as exemplary for those who wished to write a "natural" Nordic poetry and effect a "complete transition of oneself into other times."[33] Ironically, Denis was more to the point than he knew, for the mythic world given symbolic form by Klopstock and Kretschmann was for a time *more real* than empirical fact.

In our discussion of Thorild we saw how the presence of the self-conscious modern poet deflated the attempt to revive the style of the primitive narrative; this "psychological self-identification" was the most common effect of the Ossianized Nordic muse. As an example, we may consider the otherwise forgettable masterpiece of K. F. Kretschmann, *The Song of Ringulph the Bard, When Varus was Defeated (Gesang Ringulphs des Bardens, als Varus geschlagen war,* 1768).[34] Ringulph was ostensibly the Bard during the battle of Teutoburg Forest, and technically the poem is an attempt to recount the battle by combining the devices employed by Macpherson and Gerstenberg. In order to make the experience direct, Kretschmann makes Ringulph the narrator using the poem-as-process technique.

Kretschmann's ability to visualize was so poor, however, that *Ringulphs Gesang* illustrates blatantly a contradiction between the concept of primitive poetry and literary convention, indeed, the fundamental contradiction in the sentimental poets' attempt to recapture the naive: unlike his model Ossian the supposedly naive Rungulph seems incapable of narrating an objective event, and although the poem begins by Ringulph being commanded to stop a love poem to his sweetheart Irmgard and tell of Hermann and Varus ("wie Allvater schuf"), most of Ringulph's song is about himself and not epic at all. The actual battle takes up a small part of the fourth *Gesang* (out of five), and Hermann is mentioned only in passing.

Kretschmann intends to take his reader back in time to let him experience the event as process, with the Ossianic Bard implementing the transition to the sacred time. "Ha!" Ringulph begins, recalling the scene in present tense, "There they lie, yes, / The legions lie slain!" and "Ha's" and "Ach's" dot the narrative to maintain the illusion of process, passion, and spontaneity, but the contradiction in the Bardic myth becomes painfully obvious: Ringulph can only sing about himself.

Although "Ringulph" never gets around to much of a description of the actual battle, Kretschmann employs the values symbolized by the event and the Hermann myth to unify the otherwise trivial anecdotes in his poem. The moral polarity of freedom-tyranny in the struggle between North and South turns the actions in the poem into a victory of virtue over vice;

> Thus must they all fall to ruin.
> Those who would oppress our freedom! . . .
> The chains, triumph! rent asunder;
> That was the battle divine! (vv. 32–40).

The North-South contrast governs the most minute details of the poem, from Ringulph's account of his own initiation into bardsmanship, where his song is to be "wild," unbound, not like the ossified southern creations, to the dramatic action, such as it is. The polarization even extends to the landscape.[35] The poem ends with a prophecy, where the victory of Hermann is expanded to the symbolic victory of freedom over tyranny in general, with Rome a barbaric grave: "Now I see atop the wreckage-heap / Proud priests there, sitting: / Horrid the gleam of the sacrificial knife" (vv. 245–247). The "Bard" is overly sensitive to the values of a later era, in that he sees the event as a symbolic genesis. The Roman barbarity is in contrast to the "natural" religion of the Germans—"Then he celebrated the Father of Nature: / He is Druid, and altar is the flowers" (II, 67–68).

The German Bards explicitly used the technique of sympathetic imagery and the echo effect as an index of the "naturalness" of their poetry: "The sacred Grove hears the songs, and in the fields / Sounds the echo."[36] Still, the participation of nature in the poem, a merit of Ossian's, is largely absent in the Bardic lyrics, with the ecstatic nature description usually only spliced onto the poem by exclamation points.[37] Also, the Ossianic balance between the subjectivity of the poet and the objectivity of the action is seldom if ever reached by any of the Bards: although Denis says that the proper subject matter of the Bardic poems should be "deeds of Heroes" (*Heldenthaten*), his poems by the Bard Sined tend to be about Sined himself, as did Ringulph's.

Concerning Denis, Gleim wrote to Jacobi in 1768: "How my Herder, who has long sighed deeply for such a bard. will rejoice."[38] But Herder, although unaware of Ossian's role as myth, sensed the great discrepancy between the lyrics of the Bardic movement and those of his idol, as well as the key to their mediocrity: they are not *Volkspoesie* but *about Volkspoesie*. If Herder had provided some of the impetus to the Bardic movement, his thought was also instrumental in the dialectic which implemented its demise.

It will be remembered that Herder had attempted to describe the workings of the primitive imagination but did not explain how it worked; the Bards occasionally try the same description, but in the first-person narration of their "primitive" poet. Thus the ostensibly naive poet is sometimes found describing the workings of his own imagination. In the following excerpt from Kretschmann's "Ringulph's Lament,"[39] the poet through the technique of poem-as-process attempts to let the reader experience the genesis of myth but at the same time cannot resist "explaining" it as the reaction of the credulous primitive mind to an escalation of sense impressions:

> I crept in the forest
> By the light of stars;
> I heard what
> The owls sang,
> And rendered their sorrows' woe
> Upon my delicate lyre.
> In the high peaks roared
> The spirits of airy night;
> Then a chill broke out upon my brow,
> And strongly beat my heart.
> And look, it seemed to me
> As though there stood a man... Are you a man? An elf
> of midnight?

A literary myth predicated upon the assumption that this was realistic could not (and did not) withstand empirical scrutiny for long. In view of Herder's insights into the nature of the mythic imagination, his reaction to the ostensible historicity of such creations is predictable. Though partly responsible for catalyzing the vogue of *Volkslied* imitations in the eighteenth century, Herder saw that the literary myth of the Bardic poets failed in its necessary historical underpinnings: "Ringulph," he noted, has "no Germanic language and nerve of song"; "where Ringulph, the bard, sings well, he always sings modern, just in the manner of our century; sings only a modern song on an old Skaldic harp."[40] Herder sensed the "psychological self-identification" as Frye terms it, of the Bardic attempts at "natural" poetry.[41]

Herder also realized that the harmony of Ossian, his ideal of a natural poet, was not to be recovered in the fashion of the Bards by attempting to reanimate dead forms; Ossian, he said, who sang so well of his world, teaches us to do the same for ours, and not to rob another century. "The language of the Bards, then," Herder remarks, "remains language in the broadest sense, as poetry, superfluous as a framework, and therefore is subject to the old laws given to 'mythology'. It is a means to an end, but never the end itself."[42]

Herder and some others—notably Thorild—were close to a theory of the mythic imagination which could be applied programmatically; that is, a development of the fear theory as formulated by Hume into a positive appreciation of the nature of myth in poetry: "We construe the essence of the world after our own essence."[43] Herder was nearer to the truth than he knew, for in adopting Ossian as the objective correlative for their theories, Herder and other sentimental primitivists lacking Herder's insight construed the past in their own image, but they were of necessity convinced that the reality of the golden age of the Ossian Nordic past lay in the realm of historical truth and not in the realm of myth. In a sense, *Fingal* and *Temora* were indeed folk epics,—of the eighteenth-century primitivists. With the Ossian poems the theories and values of sentimental primitivism attained the quality of the sacred by projection into mythic time, and this projection formed the cornerstone for the creation of a mythic universe of a Bardic never-never land in which the Northern original genius existed as fact, and to which the modern poet could "translate" himself (to use Denis's term).

Yet because of their pretense to historicity, both the Bardic movement and Ossian were vulnerable to the dialectic between the mythic consciousness and empirical thought. As had been true with the social myth of Swedish Gothicism, the criteria for validating truth evolved from under the mythic structure, but the dialectic was more complex in this case. Though Herder believed in Ossian's authenticity, ironically his insights into the nature of myth adumbrated a new view of the imagination which would render Ossian symbolically inadequate. But

Herder's theoretical criticism of the Bards was also taken up by philologists, who approached with sharpened methodology the myth's claim to objectivity—its historical base. In 1800 Kretschmann wrote an article asking "Did the Ancient Germanic Peoples Have Bards and Druids or Not?"[44] Bards and Druids had been integral accessories to both the social and literary myths of the Nordic past since the days of the humanists, and Kretschmann, using traditional sources dating from those days, answers his question in the affirmative. The following month H. Anton replied to Kretschmann by proving that "The Germanic Peoples Had No Bards and No Druids," attacking not only the methodology (argument by analogy) but the veracity of Kretschmann's sources. Citing recent advances in historiography, he notes that "these critiques taught us that there were no Bards and Druids in the Northern countries, for nowhere is there a historical proof." "I assumed," he says, "that we in our criticism at the end of the century must be more advanced than we were at the beginning."[45] This was the twilight of the Bards.

The Bardic movement was an attempt to put into poetic practice the theories of the imagination, the primitive mind and poetry, and the expression, the passions, which, when projected into the Nordic past, served as a guarantee of the spontaneity of the creative act. Herder's comments also exposed the fatal weaknesses of the literary myth: partly, that the contemporary poetic conventions and concepts of character were incapable of assimilating the more profound ideas of the mythic imagination of the primitive in a way distinctively "Nordic"; partly, that what many of the Bards thought to be empirical truths were value truths, expressed as social and literary myth.[46]

The fate of the Bardic movement is the fate of all modern myth: when its objectivity was disproved it lost its ontological base and could no longer validate mythic truth. Herder and others were able to dispatch the Bardic lyrics by exposing them, but the theoretical criticism of the Bards was taken up by philologists who approached with sharpened methodology the cornerstone of the myth: Ossian himself. As myth, Ossian was seriously undermined late in the eighteenth century and by the same empirical method, though the dream of his authenticity lasted well into the nineteenth century. In general, Ossian's literary merit was conditional upon his historicity,[47] and when the latter disappeared, so did the former.

The course of the Ossianic controversy has been traced many times; Hume, for example, basing his suspicions upon his distaste for the barbaric (a distaste he found confirmed in the figure of Ragnar Lodbrog) raised the question of the dissimilarity and contradiction between these two halves of the archetype of the Nordic character. This, to Hume, contradicted the fact of a universal primitive mentality.

But Hume's investigation was based on earlier esthetic criteria; later in the century, the empiricist attack was better armed and took the form of philology. John Pinkerton, for instance, in his *Inquiry into the History of Scotland* (1789) and his *Dissertation on the Origin and Progress of the Scythians or Goths* (1787). concentrated what he termed the "fierce light of science" upon Nordic history and found error wherever he looked. His criteria were not based upon revulsion at the very idea of the Goths, for he used the humanist social myth in his admiration for "the sacred name of our fathers" and their annihilation of southern tyranny; his delight is in the mathematical pleasure resulting from discerning fact. Conversant with the recent Scandinavian scholarship of Suhm, Schøning, and others. Pinkerton relies solely upon fact in attacking Ossian's "costume."[48] The exposure of anachronism was mortal: "Eternal ladies in mail, where no mail was known, sicken one at every turn."[49] As Ossian objectified the chivalric dreamworld of the sentimental primitivists, the analysis using empirical time as a criterion for truth destroyed the temporal link to the *illud tempus:* "here is a total confusion of all history, chronology, and geography, and costume; a radical and ruinous defect, unknown in any poetry that has hitherto found continual applause. and indeed affording a disgust sufficient to obliterate all pleasure. in pursuing so ignorant and insane a mass of fiction."[50]

Even Pinkerton's sources were not immune to his criticism. An earlier generation of Scandinavian historians had seized upon the legends of the historical Odin's migration from Asia in their effort to connect the present to the heroic past: Pinkerton demolishes this myth with the same technique he used on Ossian. Scholars such as Suhm, operating under the assumptions of euhemerism, had been obliged to posit two or more historical Odins in order to establish an empirical connection between the present and the heroic past through the migration. and this methodology had been sufficient to support the myth. Pinkerton shows, however, that there is no trace of this migration in all the "hundred martial nations of Germany" that Odin would have had to have passed through, and follows this reasoning to the conclusion that Scandinavians "still confound the *mythologic* with the *historic* period." "Odin is wholly a mythologic personage; and has nothing to do with history . . . the tales about him, and his Æsir, are all poetical allegories; and have no more to do with history than Greek mythology."[51]

In 1817 the Swedish poet and critic Erik Gustaf Geijer could look back on this period as a closed book, and describe it as an unsuccessful attempt to "return to ourselves." His comments upon the ineffectiveness of the Klopstock method of studding manuscripts with "By Thor!"[52] show the increased sophistication with which a new generation viewed the Nordic past. Though there were a few who attempted to prolong the Bardic myth, by this time the implicit dialectic had rendered it symbolically inadequate, and Gräter and Ling became embarrassments to the generation of the Grimms and Geijer.

The assault on Ossian was symptomatic of a larger calling-into-question of the whole moral universe of sentimental primitivism, for Geijer and others saw that the simple structure of good versus evil, virtue versus vice was inadequate to explain the colliding contraries of experience. William Blake had sensed that a new symbolic orientation was needed to explain the often contradictory images of moral experience; this was to be put onto a more theoretical plane by the speculative mythologers of the romantic movement, and several poets, such as Oehlenschläger and the young Grundtvig in Denmark, Geijer and Atterbom in Sweden, approached the Nordic past with a sense that it may have given a more profound understanding of life than did Christianity. It is also true that most of these poets turned away from the Nordic past, unable to synthesize their vision of the Nordic past with Christianity to achieve the "new mythology" demanded by Friedrich Schlegel.

(8)

THE MYTH OF SYNTHESIS

With the demise of the Ossianic universe the latter decades of the eighteenth century had no satisfactory images to express a myth of northern origins. The recently discovered *Nibelungenlied* would not function mythically until Wagner, and *Beowulf* had not yet been translated. To be sure, the sentimental world of Ossian continued to have its proponents, most notably F. D. Gräter in Germany and Pehr Henrik Ling in Sweden, two men who, though they were not alone in attempting to remythologize the North, became comic anachronisms in their own time because of their advocacy of outdated myth forms. Gräter was a firm believer in Ossian as late as 1812 and fanatically attempted to prolong the era of Klopstock and the Bards. Ling, called the incarnation of the *Sturm und Drang,* though fifty years too late,[1] matched Gräter in his enthusiasm for the Nordic past, and wrote not one but two mastodontic epics of Swedish genesis. His inability to keep up with the intellectual times made him a constant embarrassment to Nordic enthusiasts of the romantic movement, however.[2]

Even by the time Ling confessed the gospel of transcendental idealism in the 1830s,[3] his contemporaries, once inspired by a Gothic vision, had turned to other areas. It is to the rise and fall of this idealism-inspired vision we now turn. In this chapter we will consider the development of an understanding of human history which was satisfying on both a mythic and an intellectual level; mythic, in that there evolved a symbolically adequate formulation of the accessibility of the golden age; intellectual, in that man was not asked to uneat the apple. The tension between unreason and reason, so vexing to the Enlightenment, was shown to be only apparent, subordinate to a process of synthesizing, suprahuman reason. In the concluding chapter we will deal with the role played by this "myth of synthesis" in the literary consciousness of the Nordic past.

On a conscious level, the possibility of synthesizing the perception of the "Ancients" with that of the "Moderns" had seldom been raised in the eighteenth century. Two great controlling myths, primitivism

and progress, each assumed a temporal gulf between the present and
the past. As myth, however, Ossian had served as just such a bridge.
To primitivists, Ossian served as a link between a naive golden age of
the North and modern historical time in that the accretion of empirical apparatus—notes, introductory essays, and commentaries—
demonstrated to the primitivists that this mode of cognition was intelligible and acceptable to the modern mind. Partaking of both worlds,
the Bard was thought to exist empirically at the ideal point of the
Rousseauistic golden age, between the "rude essays of uncorrected
fancy and the modern refinements," as Hurd put it. The death of the
Bard symbolized, in Eliade's terms, the fall into historicity.[4] The
figure of the last of the Bards survived Ossian's demise, however, and
continued to embody this fall, most notably in the works of Walter
Scott, Victor Hugo, and Erik Gustaf Geijer, but as myth he expressed
an apprehension of time vastly different from that of the Bards of the
eighteenth century.

In the previous chapters we have seen that these attempts to reestab-
lish such a resonance were largely unconscious, for the conceptual
schemata supporting these mythic universes were fundamentally incapable of integrating a dualistic epistemology. In this chapter we will
see how idealism, which viewed historical time in terms of the evolution of reason itself, viewed mythology in dramatic terms, and offered
as reality a vision of realizing this interplay of myth and history in
formal art.

We have met the poetry of Erik Gustaf Geijer before, in the discussion of the handling of time in "Odalbonden." In Geijer's companion
poem "The Last of the Skalds" ("Den siste skalden," 1811)[5] we can
see this new sense of identification with the golden age. Though the
narrative framework of the poem stems from Thomas Gray's
mythmaking,[6] Geijer's relatively sophisticated handling of point of
view suggests an understanding of history and symbol far more profound than that of Klopstock and the Bards. Informing the smooth
integration of empirical present and mythic past is an awareness of
history as a process, a conscious apprehension of historical time which
not only appreciated the mythic past as an aboriginal analogue to the
historical present but incorporated the golden age and historical time
into a unified drama, a dynamic unfolding of truth. In this context the
Nordic past was not seen as "monstrous fictions" or as disguised

empirical truth but as a higher form of truth, a poetic apprehension of reality from which modern man has fallen, and to which he must return. In Sweden the "Gothic Society," of which Geijer was one of the founders, was dedicated to just such a reawakening of the slumbering Nordic spirit, a "remythologizing" in Gothic images. "The Last of the Skalds" was one of several Nordic poems appearing in *Iduna*, the journal of the society,[7] and will serve here as an introduction to the complex attempt to create a "new mythology" based on transcendental idealism.

As Geijer's poem "Odalbonden," "The Last of the Skalds" does not immediately state a location in time; there is none of Ossian's announcing "A song of the days of old!" It begins with a description in third person—"His stature was heroic"—and only then it is said that the old Skald is an anachronism, "a guest from gray days of old," before "new laws" (Christianity) had changed the northern world. The Skald goes to the royal hall, and gradually the scene is made present, first through direct speech, then through a switch to present tense in the narration ("Who are you, stranger?" the king asks), and the Skald tells of his youth and travels in the decadent South. "where sin ripens in the blaze of sun." The king agrees to hear the Skald. whereupon the narrator says the Skald "sang the last song."

At this point the meter changes from pentameter to dimeter, and the middle part of the poem is the poem-as-process, the abrupt, unrhymed song of the Nordic poet of heathen days, who is singing the "last song" of his age in an alien, Christian era. The degenerate conduct of the diners implies that the North has lost something in virtue as a result of the transplanted southern religion. During the Skald's song, however, the scene rolls back still further in time, and the Skald tells of the Nordic golden age when Skalds "sang their songs / better than I." He narrates a vision (in past tense) of "bygone days," when the poet was not scorned, as in the present (by implication, the present of both the Skald and Geijer). At that time, the Skald says, song worked immediately upon men's souls. At the heart of the Skald's narration, a sudden switch to present tense recreates this direct effect for the listeners (both the readers and those in the king's hall).

Time then becomes fluid again, as the Skald reverts immediately to the preterite and begins his narration of the symbolic event which marked the beginning of the Christian era and the beginning of the end for the golden age, of which the Skald is the last survivor: the destruction of the pagan temple at Uppsala. The audience (again, Geijer's readers in the historical present of 1811 and in the present of the poem) have the destruction described for them. Suddenly a change to direct address makes the time of this event present to all, as the witnesses shout, *"Now they are leaving, / The ancient gods!"*

After the experience of the symbolic event, the scene returns to the hall, where the Skald continues, "Then I was baptized...," but says that his heart was still with the old gods. The true Christian God, he suggests, since he is so mighty and gentle, will not be so unkind as to avenge himself upon an old pagan Skald, and the song concludes with the old man saying he will soon go to Odin's hall.

A shift from past to present tense and from the dimeter of the Skald's song to the pentameter of the narration moves time forward to the present of the king's hall: "the king stands, wrathful in mind." In a philistine reaction to the Skald's song, the king moves to kill the heathen dog, an ironic contrast to the Skald's comment about the true nature of Christianity, but he is too late, for the poet is dead, his soul blending with the sound of the harp. In the last four lines Geijer manipulates time one last time, bringing the poem up to the world of 1811:

> And sometimes even here in our times
> you hear that sound in evening's hour:
> then children whisper soft, and run to bed:
> "The last of the skalds is wandering the meadows."

Geijer handles time in the poem in such a way as to take the reader back gradually through stages not only to the golden age of Nordic poetry but also to the event which symbolized the abandonment of the native Norse myth for the imported southern Christianity. He does this by a series of switches in point of view, accomplished through changes in tense and verse form. The reader is transported to the time of the king's banquet, which is gradually made present, then through the technique of poem-as-process back to the golden age, which is again made present by a tense change. After the destruction of the Uppsala temple, Geijer reverts to the pentameter of his frame, the banquet hall, the "time" of the Skald's death. The point of view shifts once more in the last lines, when Geijer brings the poem up to his own time.

Geijer's handling of time is a means of expressing value by indirectly describing the relationship of later eras to the golden age. The degeneracy which has crept into northern society since the introduction of the nonnative faith and the resultant decay of the Nordic muse are established as "truth" not only in terms of the era of the Christian Middle Ages but also as being true of Geijer's era as well. Owing to the fluidity of time in the poem, statements which, logically, are bound to the age of the Skald become truths independent of historical time, valid for all eras subsequent to the end of the Nordic golden age. Yet this is done without Geijer's being blatantly didactic: it is the Skald who says in his song

> Do I not know
> mighty Sweden's
> royal hall?
> Where braver men
> sat in the high-seat,
> king, prior to you
> and poets of old
> sang their song
> better than I. . . .
> Honorable then were
> the rewards of song.

Geijer has skillfully avoided the egregious self-identification that made the Ossianic imitations so shallow; the result is a much more effective sense of congruence with the golden age. It might also be suggested that the mythic identity with the Skald and his "last song" of genuine Nordic poetry implies that the modern incarnation has recaptured the inspiration, and the era characterized by a swinish debasement of true religion might be coming to an end. Regarded in this manner, then, Geijer's successful symbolic representation of the "Last of the Skalds" might indicate that he considers it one of the first of the attempts to remythologize the Nordic muse.

The assumption of such a congruence implies not only a radically different view of myth but a different apprehension of time than had been held in the Enlightenment. We have noted above that a constant problem in the myths of the Nordic past was their dissimilarity to the present: to see the present as a moral analogue of the past involved the questions of reconstructing paganism as a proto-Christianity, the duality of warlike heroism versus sentimentality in the Nordic character, and the larger conflict with the social myth of progress. Geijer has dealt with the pagan-Christian problem, and has assigned an independent truth to the pagan religion but has assumed a unifying deity transcending the social institutions of paganism and Christianity. It is just this faith in the philosophical synthesis of contraries that formed both the basis of the romantic proclamation of the necessity of a "new mythology" and the failure of this vision. We have touched upon the program of the "Gothic Society." To P. D. A. Atterbom in Sweden, for instance (one of Schelling's most ardent disciples), the "Gothicizing" of art would be a reincarnation, a necessary step to the bridging of myth and history, and initially this was the program of Atterbom and "Aurora Society" in the early 1800s.[8] Though this schema provided a symbolic universe which gave an ontological status to poetry, and hence a hitherto unprecedented validity to the literary imagination, the attempt to draw the Nordic warriors from their graves failed as myth, though occasionally it succeeded as art. To understand this, we must first outline the development of the faith in a new concept of reason and a new understanding of human history as process.

As Eliade suggests, the mythic consciousness "annihilates" historical time in that profane time only attains reality when transformed by mythic paradigms. In a rite, the present and the *illud tempus* are fused; on a larger scale, historical time is seen as a transitional period between two sacred timeless realms, genesis and apocalypse; the reality of the empirical event is apprehended as incarnating genesis and prefiguring apocalypse. But any understanding of history depends for its symbolic adequacy upon the tenability of its assumptions,[9] and as we saw with the myths of Swedish Gothicism and Ossian, the criteria for truth evolved, exposing the symbols as factually untrue. Although the general concept of history in the Enlightenment had dynamic aspects,[10] history was seen as a static display of eternal verities.[11]

The distinction between the mythical structures of idealism and those based upon Enlightenment empiricism cannot be one of emotion versus reason; actually, Friedrich Schlegel in his "Discourse on Mythology" ("Rede über die Mythologie," 1800) proclaimed that Western culture lacks a midpoint and needs a new mythology, but that this mythology must be consciously synthesized, "forged from the deepest depths of the spirit," regaining its objectivity by reuniting art and science. Schlegel considers idealism and the "magic wand of philosophy" to be the key to this new understanding; it is a faith in reason, but a "higher" reason than mere Enlightenment empiricism. As in the Middle Ages, the verities of faith were held to complement the verities of reason, but while the Middle Ages could subordinate the facts of reason to the facts of myth, idealism attempted a synthesis subordinating the facts of faith to the facts of rational inquiry, and for a while succeeded in synthesizing a modern myth.

The distinction to be drawn is in a new definition of reason, a definition recognizing the inadequacy of empirical thought to give symbols sufficient for the understanding of historical process, while at the same time maintaining a faith in the ultimate rationality of creation. It was the higher reason of poetic symbol that expressed reality.[12] This new concept of reason sees the empirical fact as an illustration of what Frye calls a "higher energy"[13]: in short, while the rationally ordered world was not rejected, it was seen as but a symbol of a higher, unifying process. Reason was understood as an element of this cosmic process, and the rational insights of man in historical time are stages in the development of the higher reason of a new golden age.

Although we have discussed the dialectic between mythic symbols and rational symbols in previous chapters, the dialectic of modern myth takes its present form with the development of the modern consciousness of symbol. If the symbol exists as a mediating lens between the eternal and the empirical, it is understandable that mythologizers could extract eternal truths from primal constructs recognized to be symbolic. Ironically, despite the conscious manipulation of symbol and the awareness of the symbolic nature of myth, not only did the romantic period fail to synthesize its "new mythology" in Gothic terms but at the same time created several myths which, once again, were thought to be objectively and not symbolically real.

Although the development of the modern view of symbol distinguishes the romantics of whatever camp from the Enlightenment,[14] and although this new understanding of symbol resulted in a respect for the irrational and a new interpretation of mythology, the idealists based their faith in philosophy upon the fundamental assumption of rational inquiry that nature (space) and history (time) are in themselves rationally constituted, that philosophical inquiry produces knowledge which is not in itself symbolic but is true of the universe in itself.[15] This assumption was latent in the antimetaphysical Enlightenment, but it was a confessed metaphysical axiom among the idealists, with "mere empiricism" held to be a lower form of reason than the reason animating the cosmic process of synthesis.

Though Newton's mathematical time provided the ostensible basis for the eighteenth-century conception, we saw above that there were two insights into the meaning of history, both with some mythical elements: first was the myth of progress, second was the myth of sentimental primitivism. The myth of progress had its sacred aspect in a coming age of reason, the primitivist had its sacred aspect in a departed age of intuition of sentiment. Bury maintained that these insights of progress and providence are mutually exclusive.[16] This is perhaps the underlying tension in the idealist myth of history, for in a movement beginning with Kant and culminating with Schelling and Hegel, the underlying faith is in the possibility of a reconciliation with the fallen state of spontaneous intuition: the higher reason of a lost but recoverable golden age.[17]

On a more immediate level, this tension involved the medieval problem of reason and revelation, with the assumption that they are ultimately reconcilable under one aegis or another. The basis for the idealist myth is the idea that truth develops. Lessing, for instance, in *The Education of the Human Race (Die Erziehung des Menschenge-schlechts,* 1780), put Christianity in a historical context—a transition to a third kingdom, which will harmonize reason and revelation. But in suggesting that "real" Christianity was not bound to scripture, Lessing anticipates the later rejection of the idealist drama of history and the return to orthodoxy on the part of romantic "Gothicists."[18] Kant, however, put the question of history-as-process in terms of fundamental oppositions, and saw the drama of history as the development of rational freedom.[19] While nature is now Newtonian, apprehended as the realm of necessity, history is the realm of freedom. The fall from the naive state into reason is only an apparent schism of consciousness, argues Kant, for the perfection of the race necessitates a full development of moral reason before the millennial return to nature. The resolution of the antinomies of man's historical existence is thus the goal of the drama of history.

Significant is the developing new idea concerning what history is a history *of*. For Kant history was the development of reason through a dramatic encounter with unreason and an eventual supremacy of man's rational will. Schiller also saw history as a dramatic process, but in his essay *The Nature and Goals of Universal History* (*Was heisst und zu welchem Ende studiert man Universalgeschichte,* 1789) he expands the range of study from politics to cultural history; avoiding Kant's millennium of reason, Schiller emphasized that the past was an ancestor of the present and an integral part of our knowledge.

In discussing the idea of history-as-process, we must reconsider Herder, who as we have seen synthesized ideas of sentimental primitive perception. This insight into the nature of language and myth implies a cultural relativism, in that for Herder, mythical symbols are not "merely" allegories of an empirical content but are poetic and absolutely true.[20] In place of the Newtonian model of eternal, rational laws, then, Herder of necessity sees that there are no unvarying laws in cultural history.[21] Though Herder was a mythmaker in several respects, he failed, as did Kant and Schiller, to explain the *genesis* of the historical process through which the Cartesian dualism was being resolved. While he established the truth of nonrational perception, he could not provide an explanation of *why* reason emerged from unreason.[22]

Though it was Schelling who was to provide the schema for the understanding of history which would make it possible to see the "new mythology" in Gothic images, it was Fichte who gave concepts by which a reconstituted freedom myth could be couched in Nordic terms.[23] Fichte's emphasis on the creative power of the will and the striving hero who creates reality, though it led to a subjectivism alien to the communal power of the myth of the Nordic past, found an image in the Viking archetype of the Nordic hero. Furthermore, Fichte described this striving as moving toward a return of a golden age. The present moment, then, gains significance with Fichte in that it is part of a falling-away from the golden age and a simultaneous return to it. Here was the basis for a conceptual schema needing only mythic images.

Though Kant and Fichte saw history as a dynamic process, a drama in which the Cartesian dualism was being resolved as an evolution of rational freedom, they had not been able to establish this intuition mythically: that is, they could not give it a narrative form, explaining the genesis of reason and providing a character for the dramatic process.[24] Although Fichte was partially successful as mythmaker in that he explained historical time both in terms of a genesis in a golden age and a prefiguration of a coming higher synthesis of reason and intuition, he too found no way to account for the genesis of change in culturally acceptable terms, to say *why* the golden age came to an end and why reason replaced intuition. It is the moral explanation of change which is characteristic of myths of origins, and it is in this context that we will consider Schelling.

The first element of Schelling's mythmaking was a rejection of the subjectivism of Fichte: the structures of *Naturphilosophie* were asserted to be objectively real, truths about objective nature.[25] Though Fichte had dramatically portrayed the progressive striving of the ego toward freedom, the subjective consequences of Fichte's heroic struggle left this freedom with no values. Schelling, however, claimed an absolute knowledge gained through what he called philosophy, supporting his mythic insights by reference to physical nature: Schelling established his symbols as facts.[26]

This conception of symbol enabled Schelling to succeed where his Enlightenment predecessors had failed. Though Kant, Schiller, and Fichte had all attempted to explain the relationship between reason and unreason in terms of cultural metamorphosis, it was Schelling who provided for his generation a mythical understanding of the relationship between intuition and reason as being part of a cosmic process. The fall was not absolute, but for Schelling and his followers, time is both progressing and reversing. In other words, we are simultaneously journeying from the golden age and returning to it, our apogee being man's conception of self as an entity alienated from nature and God.[27] Schelling uses the metaphors of the Iliad and the Odyssey to describe this journey and return.

Though he later modified his views Schelling saw three major phases of history: the Absolute appears as fate. nature. and providence. Fate and providence correspond to necessity and freedom, Greek and Christian worlds, while nature is the Absolute seen as mechanism. He elaborates upon this in the eighth *Lecture on Academic Studies,* saying that with the fall from the innocence of the golden age, necessity appears as fate, in apparent conflict with freedom. Nature has no such strife, but the process of history is a reconciliation (*Versöhnung*) of this illusory antinomy into a higher identity where symbols are no longer finite.[28] The event in historical time has symbolic significance, a consequence of the Fall and presaging of reconciliation with the Absolute in a new golden age.[29]

Although this view of history culminates with the mythmaking edifice of Hegel's logical categories,[30] Schelling functioned as mythmaker so far as the role the Nordic past played in the mythic consciousness of transcendental idealism is concerned. Schelling knew nothing of Norse mythology, but his great achievement was to provide for a time a schema for understanding historical time in terms of suprahistorical values, process in terms of permanence, thus giving a satisfactory explanation in philosophical concepts of creation myths' fundamental concern—the change from the timeless golden age into historicity. Furthermore, an integral part of Schelling's mythmaking was the incorporation of a coming golden age into this schema, a higher synthesis of apparently contradictory faculties. This synthesis can only be expressed by a new poetry, which will once more use the archetypal language of mythology to integrate thought and reality.[31] Some poets saw themselves in this role, and for a time attempted to fuse private and communal symbols in Nordic imagery.

The elevation of reason from empiricism to idealism was partially due to a continuity of scientific triumph and partly due to a distrust of the sentimental reliance upon feeling and subjectivity in defiance of reason. Friedrich Schlegel gave the definitive formulation of the lack of a world model in his "Discourse on Mythology," culminating in his declaration that "we have no mythology." But in saying that the modern culture must create a mythology, synthesizing reason and the symbol-making potential to transform the apprehension of the objective world, Schlegel anticipates the dilemma of the romantic mythologers: although recognizing the symbolic nature of myth, neither he nor Schelling could accept that the mythic symbol did not conceal a unified conceptual content, rational and philosophic in essence. In Schelling, this assumption of the rational essence of the symbol led to the subordination of the value truths of faith to the conceptual truths of philosophy. Though Schelling's formulation of this expressed as myth the insights of some romantics, (not all romantics, of course, were animated by transcendental idealism) the assumption that religion is but a stage in the development of a higher reason proved to be the key to Schelling's demise as mythmaker.

Schelling's faith in philosophy to provide absolute knowledge led him to a satisfactory (for a time) handling of the problem of reason and intuition: *Gefühl* was subordinated to logical categories. The fall was not from intuition to reason, good to evil; in the golden age, philosophy was expressed in mythic symbols, Schelling maintained, and evil was an interaction of order with a latent chaos. Evil, then, was not the opposite of good, but a product of the conflict between order and chaos.[32] Mankind is evolving in historical time both away from the age of mythology and back to it: as the Absolute reveals itself in time, the rational nature of the Absolute asserts itself over chaos and mankind is to bridge the illusory gap between necessity (nature) and freedom (history) with a higher form of reason, sensing the unity in all creation.[33] The event in historical time was a symbol of the Absolute, but Schelling insists on the reality of the symbol.[34] This was the gospel of *Naturphilosophie,* at least until the 1820s.

The faith in the transcendental unity of reason and unreason and the ability of philosophy to attain in a higher form the knowledge of the Absolute once revealed in mythology resulted in what one might call a "mythologizing" of philosophy: that is, a faith among the idealists that Schelling's formulation of the essence of nature, history, and mythology was a means of reattaining the immediate knowledge of the golden age, but in a higher, modern form. Here is Schelling's real accomplishment, while it lasted—to allay the rejection of reason as bankrupt by claiming a transcendental unity of the rational and the irrational.

The respect for mythology as philosophical truth, a part of the Absolute's self-revelation, made the study of mythology relevant to the present (and, in mythical terms, to the reattainment of a higher form of this philosophy in the coming golden age). This will be developed in more detail later, but to the students of mythology following Schelling, especially Creutzer and Görres, the mythological symbol was real: real, that is, as a revelation of cosmic process. Fundamental to the mythic aspect of idealism, however, was the assumption of a transcendental unity of both the rational and the nonrational symbol which proved to be the ultimate undoing of its mythic adequacy.

But to approach the complex development of the Nordic past as a mythic symbol in the Scandinavian romantic movement requires more analysis of this new view of mythology-as-symbol. As shown above, the symbolic interpretation of mythology played a central role in the mythologizing of philosophy and was an integral part of idealism's understanding of its own values. The tension latent in all modern myths, however, was soon to be the serpent disrupting the faith in the cohabitation of mythology and philosophy.

The attempt to establish contact with a golden age through what Schelling called a "rightly understood" approach to mythology was not unprecedented.[35] As we have seen, scholars of the Renaissance and humanists decoded classical mythology in this manner, finding empirical connections to the mythic world of innocence and origins. In Nordic terms, we saw the creation of a social myth by using mythological data in the Swedish great power era, and later, a typical Enlightenment approach by P. F. Suhm, who showed that the present was historically descended from Odin.[36]

The urge for a factually based myth continued with the German mythologers, notably Kanne, Görres, and Creutzer. The editing of Sanskrit texts and research such as Friedrich Schlegel's *On the Language and Wisdom of India* (*Über die Sprache und Weisheit der Indier*, 1808) formed the basis of the conjecture that Western civilization had its genesis in the East. With the spatial projection of the golden age into India, the mythologers for a time handled a central problem for the myth of transcendental idealism: the religious primacy of Christianity versus the assumption of unity and universalism. Lessing had suggested that Christianity was not bound to scripture, and the new consciousness of symbol led mythologers to assert that Christianity was but a symbolic expression of a higher, archetypal revelation which took place farther to East.[37] All mythologies, Görres showed, including Christianity, had the same basic forms and the drama of history had its golden age and primal revelation in India.[38]

The key to the romantic view of mythology may be found in Herder, for Herder popularized the idea that mythology is not a conscious product, a deliberate allegory or disguised historical event, but a symbolic expression of a spontaneous perception of nature.[39] Though Herder did not have the vocabulary to express it, his implication was that the structures of mythology were not rational in nature but poetically symbolic. With Hamann and Heyne, Herder maintained that the coherence in mythic narrative was an inner necessity, a living expression of man's relationship with the world. We noted above that Herder objected to the Bardic imitations of Germanic myth, and the reason is clear: for Herder, mythology must be living, spontaneously believed, and a new mythology can only be attained on this basis. It is this insistence Friedrich Schlegel attempts to transcend when he maintains that the new mythology will be a synthesis of the ancient and the modern, but it is to this idea that later critics such as Erik Gustaf Geijer return when analyzing the failure of the early romantics to mythologize the Western consciousness.[40]

Friedrich Schlegel, although of peripheral importance to the specifically Nordic aspects of the myth of history-as-process, must be mentioned briefly here, for it was he who formulated the romantic demand for a new mythology, and in this sense he was central to the symbolic world of the romantics. Early in his career Schlegel viewed the estrangement of modern man from nature as irreconcilable, with irony being the only attitude possible for the modern poet. Around 1800, however, his writing changed tone, and an eschatological element creeps in. In the "Discourse on Mythology" he turns from the idea of inevitable estrangement to the necessity of a "matrix," a firm foundation, a "new mythology." History, to Schlegel, is a process of ever-increasing self-consciousness, culminating with the ideas of Fichte. The drama of historical process will, says Schlegel, produce the opposite of subjectivity, a new objectivity, a synthesis of ancient objectivity and modern subjectivity where philosophy will yield its place to poetry, and art, science, and philosophy will be unified in a higher objectivity, a new golden age.

This new mythology is not pantheism, though there are elements of Spinoza. Rather, it is a transformation of the objective world, a presentation of the sublime in images, myths, or (as he calls it in the second edition of the "Lectures") symbols. The consciousness of symbol enables Schlegel to handle for a time the potentially explosive problem of Christianity: the new mythology will be a synthesis of the universal revelation and the particular national myths, which are "rays" of the primal Eastern revelation. More specifically, it will be a "representation of Christianity in the garb of national myths."[41] There are some familiar elements here, for the national aspect included the northern sense of nature, elevated by Christianity's higher light.

Schlegel had wondered whether this new vision would remain forever abstract and unrealized;[42] in this context, it is curious that the Nordic past did not play a larger role in the historical research of the German mythologers than it did, for we noted above that the false etymology of Æsir-Asia had been an integral part of the myth of Nordic origins for a hundred years. The euhemeristic "fact" of the historical Odin's migration from Asia had been the basis for Leopold's *Oden,* Suhm's conjectures, and Ling's epics. It is just that, in spite of the Asian credentials of the Nordic past, the Germans did not apparently consider Norse mythology part of their golden age, and in general reconstituted the Catholic Middle Ages as a mythic symbol.[43]

It was particularly in the Scandinavian countries that the Nordic past functioned as a golden age during this period. Though Fichte's emphasis on the heroic striving of the ego played a central role in the romantic vision of the Nordic past,[44] the extreme subjectivism of Fichte and Schlegel—culminating in the "Magical Idealism" of Novalis[45]—generally drew the northern countries to Schelling as a base for the idealist images of the Nordic past as myth. Schelling's objections to Fichte's lack of sense for nature and science has been mentioned above; as early as 1800 Schelling took issue with Schlegel's subordination of reason (philosophy) to poetry, and from then on they were in different camps.[46] For Schelling, the new myth of synthesis was to be philosophically based; indeed, Schelling's faith in the ontological status of philosophical inquiry justifies the suggestion that he "mythologizes" philosophy, for it is his insistence upon the objective reality of the symbolic construct that distinguishes his mythmaking from Schlegel's.[47]

The myth of synthesis was frequently couched in theoretical terms with Nordic images in Scandinavia. Oehlenschläger's defense of his drama *Hakon Jarl the Mighty* (*Hakon Jarl hiin Rige,* 1805) is typical in this regard. *Hakon Jarl* is a powerful drama concerning the downfall of Nordic paganism with the death of Hakon and the advent of Christianity, and in a sophisticated defense of his characterization, Oehlenschläger links the degeneracy in the human world (symbolized by Hakon's willingness to sacrifice his son) to the loss of Balder on the mythic plane. Balder, "the good principle," was the moral keystone to the Norse mythic world; with his death, the gods not only began their decline, but the violence in the Nordic archetype gained the upper hand, and paganism became fanaticism. Though the excellence of *Hakon Jarl* is the Schilleresque conflict between two antithetical world views, personally Oehlenschläger longs for a synthesis his drama in no way suggests: that "the holy Cross might fuse and become one with

Thor's mighty Hammer! That the man Action might find the lovely maid Perception (*Erkiendelse*)!"[48]

Though Oehlenschläger's views on synthesis and the relationship between the mythic world and the human world are typical, he was not part of a collective movement to remythologize his country. In Sweden, however, there were three attempts to Nordicize Sweden, the last vestiges of whose Baltic empire disappeared when Finland was lost in the Russo-Finnish war of 1809. Though all of these saw poetry as the way to the "new mythology," it is important to distinguish between the theoretical pronouncements of the groups and the writings of individual poets within the groups, which will be considered in the concluding chapter.

The most eager disciples of Schelling were the "Phosphorists," or the Aurora Society, led by Per Daniel Amadeus Atterbom. In 1810 Atterbom introduced a note of nationalism into his criticism, suggesting that Norse mythology is the true expression of Swedish genius. He also maintains that Norse mythology is not dead but still lives in oral tradition.[49] In 1811 Atterbom attempted to put his theory into practice with the poem "Skaldarmal," and appended one of his lengthy commentaries.[50] The commentary is a combination of Dalin, who it will be recalled had seen a trinity in the Nordic pantheon (Allfather, a Middle-god, and a World-soul) and Schelling's concept of synthesis-reconciliation. Thor is the savior figure.

In the "Skaldarmal" commentary, Norse mythology is interpreted as religion (which to Atterbom meant philosophy), less pure than Christianity but anticipating it. In the commentary, Atterbom does not think out the nature of the "new mythology," but in the same year in a review of the "Gothic Society's" organ *Iduna* Atterbom says that for a state to recover its identity the mythological age must return.[51] It is not just return, however, for as Holger Frykenstedt has shown in detail, Atterbom saw the ultimate stage of knowledge as being philosophy.[52] The "new mythology" will be both the recovering of ancient wisdom and the understanding of this through idealism.[53] It is significant in this context that the Nordic gods in the *poem* are not seen as religious but only nature gods.

A more specific concern with the Nordic past was shown by the Gothic Society, whose charter depicts the archetypal Nordic in terms of the freedom myth, with the deterioration from the golden age being caused by southern influences. For most of the members, the new age was to be a recovery of the old, and the problem of the new era's relationship to Christianity was not touched upon. Erik Gustaf Geijer, however (a much deeper thinker than his Gothic comrades, and Atterbom too, for that matter), came to see the problems involved revitalizing national pagan myths. In a talk to the society in 1811, he advocates as necessary a synthesis of the wildness of pagan Nordic freedom with later concepts of law: the journey backward must be forward as well.[54] In the first issue of *Iduna* (1811) Geijer goes deeper into the nature of Norse mythology, seeing it essentially in terms of Schelling's *Philosophy and Religion:* from a world-historical point of view, as idealistic, a spiritual principle breaking into history. Actually Geijer was the first to put Norse mythology into Schelling's schema, by comparing the Norse revelation of the Eternal as fate to the Christian revelation as providence (*Försyn*). Again it might be noted in passing that Geijer's poems in *Iduna* have a different view of the relationship between paganism and Christianity, and the sense of unity and continuity between pagan and Christian which animates the myth of synthesis does not animate Geijer's Nordic poems.

Geijer and his fellow "Goth," Esaias Tegnér, both outgrew the fraternal aspect of the Gothic Society and eventually abandoned its vision. In *Fritiofs Saga* (1825) Tegnér was to write the most lasting expression of the romantic vision of the Nordic past, but he saw from the beginning the gulf between pagan and Christian, and though with Geijer he could admire the ideals of the Gothic Society, he made no attempt to Schellingize Norse mythology and found the images one-sided. By 1812 Geijer and Tegnér agreed that *Iduna* should expand its scope and include non-Gothic poems; the national past was being replaced by a view of universal humanity.

The third attempt to remythologize Sweden was the "Manhem Society," under the leadership of C. J. L. Almquist. Greta Hedin notes that Almquist was in many ways inspired by Schelling, but Almquist from the beginning did not share the faith in philosophy as he planned this secret society. The process of development culminates in a Swedenborgian mysticism ("amor-chaos"), not intellect,[55] and the goal was God, not Gothicism. The members of this society were to pass through nine grades (described in Hedin, pp. 140–154) symbolic of the stages of human development. Grades 3 to 5 were degrees of Æsir-life: free, natural, happy, from gods to heroes. The Christian counterpart to these stages was that of the medieval knight, animated by love for woman. The final stages were developmental and synthesizing: love of God, and return to the fatherland.

Though diverse in many respects, the Aurora, Gothic, and Manhem societies may be regarded as conscious attempts to synthesize social myth according to the idealist program of a "new mythology," to awaken through poetry dormant virtues for the new era through images of the golden age. To a certain extent we can regard the eschatological aspect of the myth of synthesis as a displaced Christian myth:[56] the journey (to use one of Schelling and Hegel's favorite metaphors) forward is also a return to innocence. History did not bear out the hope for a new era of synthesis, however, whether couched in images of Catholic chivalry or Gothicism. In dealing with the reason for the failure, we touch upon the central problem of myth in the modern consciousness: can myth be synthesized consciously? We conclude *The Golden Horns* with an analysis of the role of the myth of synthesis in particular works of poets involved in forming these "new mythologies," for the tension between an intellectual commitment to a synthetic social myth and the myths informing their private symbolic worlds constituted the romantic dilemma.

(9)

THE GOLDEN HORNS

Though the myth of synthesis was but one of the constitutive myths of romanticism, its role in formal literature illustrates a central problem in the modern mythic consciousness. The call for a "new mythology" had been worked out on theoretical grounds and, in Scandinavia at least, a generation of gifted poets received the gospel of Schelling with the faith that here was their touchstone to guarantee the reality of their inspiration.[1] In Denmark and Sweden the times were to be particularly ripe for a reinvigorating of the national spirit: Sweden was to lose Finland and the last vestige of its Baltic empire in the Russo-Finnish war in 1809; Denmark was to lose Norway after the Napoleonic wars and be in the throes of national bankruptcy. Surely a Nordic eschaton must be at hand, with the power of poetry reawakening the slumbering might of Asa-Thor.

In spite of the sincerity and intensity of attempts, however, rebirth did not materialize. The previous chapter mentioned three attempts to create social myth on the basis of idealism: the Aurora Society, the Gothic Society, and the Manhem Society. In this chapter we will analyze the failure to synthesize a Nordic myth of origins in terms of particular texts and writers. One of the truths of the myth of synthesis was that of an underlying unity in apparent antinomies, and the poets informed by this myth had to cope with the fundamental dualism in the vision of the Nordic past: the split archetype of the Nordic hero, or, fundamentally, the nationalist nostalgia for vigorous Nordic paganism versus the values of the Christian present. The awareness of the nature of symbolic perception produced a heightened awareness of the problem and produced some art of high dramatic worth (writers such as Oehlenschläger employed the split archetype and let it express the mythic conflict), but this same awareness sharpened the dilemma of individual poets.

The tidings of philosophy were brought to Scandinavia by Henrik Steffens, whose *Introduction to Philosophic Lectures* (*Indledning til philosophiske Forelæsninger,* 1803) proclaimed that "the mark of the

Eternal which reveals itself in the rhythmic march of History must be recognized with a vision that, independent of Time, recognizes the Eternal as its midpoint. To find this is the problem of Philosophy."[2] He announced that there was indeed a plan to history—the progressive self-revelation of the Eternal. Through our longing back to the golden age when word was the same as deed, we are beginning to look into the essence of nature, and to realize the stamp of the Eternal in the phenomenal world.

Steffens used no Nordic images in his galvanic lectures, but several of his auditors, among them Adam Oehlenschläger, did in their poetry. After his conversation with Steffens in 1803, Oehlenschläger (whose previous Nordic output had been *Eric and Roller,* a sentimental tale in the Ossianic mode)[3] wrote the poem "The Golden Horns" ("Guldhornene," 1803), which may be said to have begun the romantic movement in Scandinavia. The poem is a veritable alembic of the motifs we have outlined, and couched the symbolic view of history in Nordic images.

The empirical events were the finding (one in the seventeenth, the other in the nineteenth century) of two drinking horns, one inscribed with runes, from the period of the migrations; in the poem, however, Oehlenschläger understands the events in mythic terms, "in terms of the whole," as Steffens would put it. Antiquarians, sensing the lost drama of the days "when it shone from the North, / When heaven was on earth," pray for insight.[4] The Norse gods, "with star-glancing eyes," answer the plea, with a gift of the first golden horn. It is not to be those who look with empirical minds who find it, however, but a lass with lily-white hands, thinking of love (to Schlegel, the feminine equivalent of masculine genius). As she removes the horn, sympathetic imagery announces the importance of the act, but not even modern innocence can bring back the golden age. Modern materialism sees the horn only as gold, and a century passes. Steffens had said, though, that the poetic apprehension of reality is never quite extinguished, and for the "few" who understood the gift, "who sense the High / In nature's eye," the gods will once more give man a sign.

This time, though, the finder is "the son of Nature," and once again sympathetic imagery underscores the higher meaning of the action. Honor these signs from Eternity, say the gods, "for Fate is capricious; / Perhaps soon they will vanish." Man has a chance, however, to achieve the great synthesis of mythologies: "Jesus' blood on the Lord's altar / Fill them, as Blood of the Grove." Here, presumably, is the opportunity to effect the reconciliation between a fate-dominated myth (paganism) and one governed by providence (Christianity),[5] for the gods' acts have been providential, and it is man who must respond.

But man did not. The horns had been stolen in 1803; at the time of the writing of the poem, Oehlenschläger did not know that the horns had been melted down for their gold. To the poet, living in the symbolic universe constituted by Schelling and Steffens, the causality is mythic: "What they gave, they then rescinded. / Divinity disappeared for evermore."

"The Golden Horns" brings into sharp focus the central problem in remythologizing the Nordic past: the relationship to Christianity. It is clear that for Oehlenschläger the Norse gods are "eternal symbols of an eternal, living principle in the world of nature and the spirit."[6] In *Balder the Good (Baldur hiin Gode,* 1806), Balder for the first time is seen as adumbrating Christ, in that Balder symbolizes the good principle, which can never be annihilated.[7] Yet practically Oehlenschläger sees that the two institutions are fundamentally alien, not complementary.[8] Though the gods in "The Golden Horns" decree the synthesis, Oehlenschläger did not see this actually coming about, neither in the poem nor in his drama *Hakon Jarl the Mighty (Hakon Jarl hiin Rige,* 1807). In theory Oehlenschläger adopts the tolerance of Lessing's *Nathan the Wise (Nathan der Weise,* 1779); particularly at the beginning of Act III of *Hakon Jarl,* the encounter between paganism and Christianity still is dramatized as an either/or.

Though the romantic Christianity of Novalis was alien to Oehlenschläger, and he underwent no religious crisis, as an artist he created a myth world that was somewhat ambivalent. The original development of the myth of Nordic origins was as a moral contrast to the South, and Oehlenschläger is very much in this tradition, adding elements of Herder and Schelling, who emphasized the role of myth in national identity. Though in his defense of *Hakon Jarl* Oehlenschläger says he would like for the cross and the hammer to fuse,[9] he was too much under the power of the freedom myth to replace it with the myth of synthesis.

Oehlenschläger's sense of history as process and mythology as symbol allowed him to employ the freedom myth in a deeper, much less monolithic manner than had been done previously. Oehlenschläger saw Norse mythology itself as a process, and with the death of the good principle in Balder, destruction was inevitable. He allows Hakon to symbolize this deterioration, and though in theory the author declares that the "good principle was reborn in Christ," the artistic excellence lies in the portrayal of Hakon, embodying the tragedy of Norse paganism.

Oehlenschläger's estheticism helped him avoid a spiritual crisis in his handling of the Nordic past, but the political crisis of 1814 produced a major attempt to synthesize the diverse archetypes of the hero in *Helge*. Helge is the personification of the wildness and potential disaster the author saw in the Nordic character, while his brother Hroar is less heroic but of a milder nature. The drama is essentially a refining and synthesis of dualism in Helge's son Hrolf Krake. The sense of refinement as process is expressed in Oehlenschläger's use of the demonic: Helge consorts with mythical personifications of the demonic, and his running afoul of the mermaid Tangkiær begets the vengeful daughter Skuld, who causes Helge to be humiliated by Queen Oluf, implements his falling in love with his own daughter Yrsa, and ultimately causes the death of their son Hrolf Krake.

This process is developed in a trilogy, *Helge* being the first part, *Hroars Saga* (1817) the second, *Hrolf Krake* (1828) the third part. The milieu becomes increasingly historical and less mythical as the trilogy progresses, with the demonic world of *Helge* giving way to the less mythological "Saga" which is in turn replaced by the "heroic poem" *Hrolf Krake*. The theme of refinement and synthesis is suggested even within *Helge*, for the first section is a "Drapa," an Old Norse poetic form identified by Oehlenschläger with murder (*drab*); the second part is an "Eventyr" (folk tale); while the third is a formal imitation of a Greek tragedy with Nordic content.

The characters are the best expressions of this theme: the female characters progress from the supernatural Tangkiær to the demonic Skuld to the more human but still brutal Queen Oluf (modeled on the *Nibelungenlied's* Brynhild) and finally the modern sentimental daughter Yrsa. Yrsa was baptized in whale's blood but overcomes her lineage of hate at the end of *Helge* through love, in the personage of Freia (who appears as a *dea ex machina*). Freia orders her to replace thoughts of suicide with mother love for her unborn son, who will be named Hrolf and will be the best symbol of "Nordic strength's un-bendable loyalty." Presumably, he will unite the heroism of Helge with the virtues of Hroar.

Oehlenschläger developed a sophisticated analysis of his own world of literary myth and attempted to employ its fundamental schism in a unified artistic program. But the appeal of violence in Nordic origins was too strong: only *Helge* is read today, and the synthesis remained theoretical. Tangkiær is an effective projection of the wild-ness in Helge, but Hroar is uninteresting; as Sven Møller Kristensen has observed in his study of romantic dualism, the synthesis is persua-sive intellectually, but Helge is the only character to come alive.[10]

The problem was much more acute for Oehlenschläger's contem-porary N. F. S. Grundtvig, for Grundtvig took seriously Schelling's identification of myth, poetry, and religion, and the failure to synthe-size the religious dualism produced a profound religious crisis. At first glance, Grundtvig, also an auditor of Steffens and a deeper thinker than Oehlenschläger, appears more optimistic than Oehlenschläger does in "The Golden Horns." Certainly he was initially more a part of the idealist mythic world in his handling of the Nordic past. For Grundtvig, however, the problem of "The Golden Horns" surfaced, but in a personally shattering way.

Oehlenschläger saw the problem was ultimately an esthetic one, a handling of ideas with which he identified as an artist but over which he had control. For Grundtvig the mythic roots went deeper, in that the problem of belief was involved, and he moved from an initial faith in the myth of synthesis to a religious renunciation of his earlier position as blasphemous. In 1806, after reading a pedestrian adaptation of "Skirnir's Journey" by Jens Møller, Grundtvig was awakened from rationalism and entered what he called a "Nordic intoxication" (Asarus). In "Masked Ball in Denmark" ("Maskeradeballet i Dan-mark," 1808) Grundtvig proclaims that at this low point in history the time for synthesis was at hand:

> Great Odin! White Christ!
> Erased now is your strife.
> Both sons of Allfather.
> With our cross and our sword
> Is hallowed here our pyre:
> Both you loved our Father.[11]

"Masked Ball" is a slight work, however, compared to the monumental vision of *Scandinavia's Mythology* (*Nordens Mytologi,* 1808). Grundtvig had earlier sensed a dramatic principle unifying Norse mythology, and in *Scandinavia's Mythology* he explicates Norse mythology in terms which on one level are in the Schelling-constituted universe. The power of Schelling as mythmaker for Grundtvig can be seen in the assertion that the poetic vision, which he says he is recapturing, has priority over his material. He edits, alters, and omits material to make it fit what he says was the original insight of the Norse imagination. Here, of course, is a convergence not only of the conscious faith in the reality of the poetic symbol but of the unconscious assumption of the objectivity of mythic constructs.

In contrast to the sentimental universe of Ossian, Grundtvig sees the Norse creation as innately one of conflict and history as five-act drama. Creation's fundamental tension is between the eternal Allfather and Mass. Mass developed into the giants and the gods (power) were created by Allfather to do battle. The gods fall away from Allfather by creating independently and make alliances with Loke (wisdom, as Grundtvig interpreted him) and the giants, resulting in a "sinful peace."[12] Allfather then sends the Norns (fate) to lead creation to Ragnarök, where the sinful individuality will be purged.

The battle between the gods and the giants has several phases. The Norns lead Loke away from the gods, and he begets the monsters who will attack them. With the death of Balder (goodness), the last tie to the Eternal is broken, though through the acquisition of Sutting's Mead (poetry), Odin can raise himself at times to Allfather.

Earthly life is an analogue to the divine, with the heroes engaging in essentially the same strife as the gods. It is all a preparation for Ragnarök, the final conflict between power and mass. After Ragnarök the Eternal again dominates creation, and there will be a new order, governed by Balder (goodness) and Hother (blind power).

As mentioned, Grundtvig asserts that he is seeing the Eddas "with their own light,"[13] save that he clothes in philosophical language the essence of the ancient poetic symbols. At this point in his career, Grundtvig says he views the Nordic past religiously,[14] but it is just this intensity of commitment that caused him some problems, and in turn indicates the dilemma in the mythic structures of idealism.

I. A. Scharling has shown that although much of the impetus for the vision of *Scandinavia's Mythology* came from Schelling, Grundtvig was unable to overcome his fundamentally dualistic concept of experience and assimilate Schelling's monistic synthesis.[15] Flemming Lundgreen-Nielsen refines this point and says that the real impulse was Grundtvig's Christianity.[16] In *Scandinavia's Mythology* Grundtvig could not accept the idea of common revelation. He sees Norse mythology as a supreme *human* construction, and there is no direct prophecy of Christianity.

In 1810 the imperatives of Christian myth asserted themselves against Grundtvig's philosophically constituted poetic vision, and the resultant crisis led him to give up the faith in the Nordic past as a blasphemous idolatry. The problem was not just on the level of religious myth, for even the appeal of the Nordic self-willed hero (with will given philosophic status by Fichte) caused spiritual problems for Grundtvig. Oehlenschläger could modernize the concept of blind fate and subordinate its workings to human will,[17] but Grundtvig could not with a clear conscience let his hero Palnatoke declare in Fichtean rhetoric "What the man wills, can man and gods / Hinder, thwart, true enough; / But the man cannot cease to will," for in Grundtvig's Christian world this is rebellion.[18] Though he maintained in 1811 that *Scandinavia's Mythology* was objective, and not a free creation,[19] he renounced the possibility of synthesis (particularly the "Masked Ball"),[20] and having rejected the myth of higher reason, he returned to the animistic faith in Christian myth. Though in 1812 in *The World's Chronicle (Verdens Krønike)* Grundtvig subordinates will and power to faith, he has lost the concept of history as drama and sees it merely as a chronicle.[21]

Atterbom, the leader of the Swedish "Phosphorists," also had a Fichtean concept of the hero similar to Grundtvig's. His commentary to "Skaldarmal" emphasizes the point made earlier in his review of the journal *Iduna,* that struggle and combat are "the basis of virtue,"[22] but this heroic assertion is nowhere present in the poem. This part of the program was to remain theory, for as Wallén notes, violence was basically alien to Atterbom's poetic inspiration.[23]

Atterbom too failed to incorporate the theory into his poetic production, although in "The Advice of Mimer" ("Mimers Råd," 1839) he attacked the depersonalizing aspects of liberalism in Nordic images.[24] In general, though, he was unable to remythologize his own poetry, much less transform contemporary Sweden. In Atterbom's case, poetic imagery went more in the subjective direction of Novalis, while the communal myths remained in the realm of theory.

Geijer, though under the regulating influence of idealism in his youth,[25] was much less ethereal than Atterbom, and had a much closer poetic relationship to the myth of the Nordic past. While in the Gothic Society, he could subscribe to the idealist view that myth symbolized the transcendental unity of all revelations,[26] though his historical sense gave him reservations concerning the society's program.[27] Geijer, however, was unable to assimilate the freedom myth to idealism's synthesis in his writings, but in the 1811 issue of *Iduna* he wrote five poems of generally high quality which more clearly than any other works delineate the constitutive elements of the myth of the Nordic past. In his lectures, Geijer portrayed the Nordic character dualistically,[28] but in the *Iduna* poems he displays an awareness of both the social and the literary aspects of his dual mythic world. Again, though, the drama comes not from synthesis but from contrast.

We have considered two of these poems above, "The Odalbonde" and "The Last of the Skalds." Both, it will be recalled, subtly manipulate tense and point of view to involve the reader in timeless Gothic virtues; the first, the social myth of "The Odalbonde"; the second, the deterioration of the Nordic muse under the influence of Christianity, as well as the possibility of reactualizing it. The necessity to reactualize primal Nordic vigor is put in abstract, programmatic terms in the first poem of the series, "Manhem." When one considers the remaining poems, however, then the acuteness of Geijer's awareness of his own mythic world becomes evident.

The five poems present two versions of the dual archetype: the solid historical figure of "The Odalbonde" is paired with the restless, violent historical figure of "The Viking" ("Vikingen"), while the sensitive literary figure of "The Last of the Skalds" is paired with the violent literary figure of "The Last of the Warriors" ("Den siste Kämpen"). Both sets of poems are complementary contrasts: if "The Odalbonde" is an outgrowth of the Nordic landscape (in a sense both of Montesquieu and of Schelling)[29] "The Viking" is an expression of the northern ocean, as the imagery suggests.[30]

The literary pairs of the Skald and the Warrior employ the manipulative device of poem-as-process rather than the direct address used in

"Odalbonden" and "The Viking." "The Last of the Skalds" was discussed in the previous chapter as an introduction to the attempt to bridge two ages; "The Last of the Warriors" employs the technique of process twice in the attempt to convey the nostalgia for the pagan era. There is no hint of synthesis. The first change in point of view comes when the warrior hears the "distant bells" of the cloister, while "from the deeps there sang / A song, to his liking more." His naive verse expresses the truths of the earth:

> They live yet
> The ancient gods,
> And Thor in the cart
> Faintly journeys—

Though the gods live for the warrior, their root is gone for him; he recalls the Skald, who sang in his turn "of days gone by / of warriors' sport," and the narrator is now using kennings in a quasi-Nordic style. Through the lens of the Skald the warrior has returned to his golden age and reexperiences his genesis in present tense, "through the realm of the eternal night."

No evolution transforms his pagan past, though, and the warrior breaks his nostalgia to realize that he cannot assimilate the new Christian order. As in "The Golden Horns," the Norse gods are dormant in the earth but the warrior's strength is broken with the loss of his mythic world, as the narrator makes clear to his readers. In orthodox Schelling imagery, the longing of the warrior is eased, and he dies to his origin. As in "The Last of the Skalds," however, the message is didactic, though unstated: both aspects of the Nordic spirit have lost contact with their origins, but since the poems are presented in present tense the drama is actual (hopefully recoverable) for the reader: "Hail he who comes to be with Odin!"

In his lectures Geijer treated history as a regenerative process, and if we see "The Odalbonde"/"The Viking" and "The Last of the Skalds"/"The Last of the Warriors," together with the fifth poem, "Manhem," as an aggregate archetype, the eschatological vision and messianic program of the Gothicists becomes clear. With its abstraction and explicit didactic tone, "Manhem" is the least of the five poems, and may be mentioned but briefly. It begins with the folk formula for temporal transition, "Once upon a time" ("Det var en tid"), and sketches a familiar picture of the Nordic-Gothic-Swedish past: the *odalbonde,* in his Rousseauistic instant before property; the warrior, and the unselfish valor of the Nordic-Gothic-Swedish past. At that time collective unity prevailed: the *odalbonde* had no concept of mine/thine; and the warrior's heroism was unselfish. The price of individuality, however, was the loss of both aspects of the golden age: "You are gone, time of virtue and power!"

As a poet and as a historian Geijer could not bring himself to announce as detailed a reintegration with Nordic origins as had Rudbeck. Indeed, in the context of humiliating national setbacks, both Atterbom and the Gothic Society viewed the unbroken social myth of the *stormaktstid* as a golden age in itself: more a light than a shadow for this sophisticated generation. Much as Herder's historical sense could not ingest the Bardic movement, Geijer could not proclaim, but only imply, the regeneration of "the ancient virtues' temple," and "Manhem" concludes with an appeal to reincarnate the slumbering virtues of "honor, power and faith," so that Manhem/Sweden might rise again.

Objectively speaking, we may consider Geijer's *Iduna* poems as delineating the paradigms of the myth of Nordic origins. Geijer, though, one of the most thoughtful and intelligent writers on the Nordic past, soon abandoned the Nordic past as a literary myth. The objection was once again primarily religious, though in Geijer's case it was connected with a thorough critique of the monistic and rationalistic assumptions underlying the myth of idealism.[31]

The other leading "Goth," Esaias Tegnér, also had reservations about the myth of Gothicism. In a letter, Tegnér expressed concern over *Fritiofs Saga,* completed in 1825. Sagas, he says, may well be poetic in themselves, but their world is not ours. Poetry, on the other hand, must be modern; in consciously modernizing an ancient story, Tegnér fears he has fallen between two stools and anticipates little success.[32] Although there is a lack of unity in the work, *Fritiofs Saga* is by far the most popular work to come out of the romantic concern with the Nordic past, and it is precisely Tegnér's success at reconciling ancient and modern that made it so.

The basic tension in the story again stems from the dual archetype of the Nordic past: Fritiof is the son of an *odalbonde* and is in love with Ingeborg, whose Viking lineage goes back to Odin. They are eventually united, but only after Tegnér has effectively dealt with his own world of poetic myth in a way far superior to Oehlenschläger (whose *Helge* Tegnér said was his inspiration).

Tegnér accomplishes the metamorphosis of the Nordic hero partly through a substructure of light/dark imagery. Initially, fire is a catalyst for violence: Ingeborg's brothers burn Fritiof's house, whereupon the peaceful *odalbonde* changes into a revenge-driven viking. In a key scene at Balder's temple (chap. 13) the sun is blood red, neither day nor night (stanza 1). The fire in the temple should bring on a new day, but Fritiof's violence in the temple of the god of light causes it to be burned to the ground. The dawn comes, but there is no rebirth for Fritiof.

Fritiof transcends the dualities in his character in the concluding scene, "Reconciliation." Again, the setting is Balder's temple, now rebuilt. The priest of Balder tells Fritiof that once there was peace both in the world of the gods and in the human world, and even in Fritiof himself (ll. 116–128), but this state can only be reattained in both worlds by giving up the hate; strength without piety is self-destructive (l. 84). The priest says that the world of the gods is moving toward this "new light" (l. 229) with a new Balder from the South, sent by "Allfather." The world of the gods is an image of the human world (ll. 145–146), and if Fritiof can evolve, reconciliation is possible.

This evolution has taken place in the course of the poem, for at the beginning, where the duality is emphasized, Odin is identified with "Allfather" (chap. 1, "Fritiof and Ingeborg," verses 32 and 33). At the end, the priest makes clear that both the Norse gods and man are "quiet thoughts of Allfather" (l. 147). The old gods can develop, for "*One* is Allfather, though many his messengers" (l. 234).

Though this view of myth and religion was common coin in idealism, Tegnér makes Fritiof's evolution convincing. To be sure, Fritiof does not become a Kantian, but in giving up his hate and making peace with his enemy Halvdan, he is able to love Ingeborg, and the saga closes with two clasping hands over the new altar. Fritiof is symbolically reconciled with his enemy and with himself; symbolically, of course, the closing scene is the uniting of the dual view of the *odalbonde* and the Viking archetypes, which Tegnér makes plausible by letting Ingeborg represent the Viking half and expressing the synthesis through a love story.[33]

Though *Fritiofs Saga* was immensely popular as art, Tegnér joined

Atterbom, Grundtvig, and Geijer in abandoning the Schellingized Nordic past as a poetic myth. Though Tegnér was a bishop, his use of the Nordic past as myth did not produce a spiritual crisis in him as it did with Grundtvig, perhaps owing to the view of paganism as part of an evolutionary process anticipating Christianity, which Grundtvig could not accept. Tegnér's crisis was of another nature, for shortly after publishing *Fritiofs Saga* he developed a fit of Byronic melancholy, gradually culminating in insanity.

In conclusion, idealism succeeded in developing profound understanding of the mythic consciousness (Cassirer acknowledges his debt to Schelling), but the respect and status accorded to mythology as a form of cognition did not include a recognition that the truths of a mythic universe are not primarily validated by reason. Grundtvig, Atterbom, and Geijer could not accept the necessary consequences of the myth of synthesis, that the truths of Scripture were "merely symbolic," a state in the synthesizing energy of a higher reason's self-revelation. They were unwilling to pay the price of a broken myth.[34]

In the rejection of the idealist myth of the Nordic past we see that modern man's values consist of contradictory imperatives, and though he may assimilate what Berdyaev calls the "shock of colliding contraries" through an organization of values which may be symbolically adequate for a time, the dialectic of eventual inadequacy is innate in the disparate constitution of the mythic symbol and the rational symbol.

We have tried to indicate in this study the reason behind the dialectic innate in modern myths: while symbolic universes are basically formed by mythic symbols, values are assumed to be rationally organized and are so validated. The distinction made by Robert Tucker in discussing Marxism is broadly true of all modern myth: "Whereas philosophy had once arisen against a background of myth, here myth arose against a background of philosophy."[35] Idealist mythologers contributed the basis of a profound understanding of a basic symbolic mode of human consciousness, and though the idealist vision of synthesizing a "new mythology" foundered on the golden horns of modern myth, their recognition of the symbolic nature of human perception has had a darker legacy. As one of our theses here has been that the study of myth cannot be confined to one period in human history or one academic discipline, in the Conclusion we will attempt to outline some of the implications of contemporary myths.

CONCLUSION:
THE PROBLEM OF MYTH
AND FUTURE SHOCK

As a conclusion, let us return to the problem of myth. We have seen the power of images of origins to regulate man's social and literary consciousness. The various forms of the myth of Nordic origins reconciled to some extent the contradictory evidence of human experience in a world increasingly hostile to mythology. The saga texts, themselves displacements, subsequently took on a sacred character as revelations of heroic paradigms.

Though the language of mythic narrative became increasingly displaced from the sacred world, the power of myth to provide an absolute for human choice in an increasingly relativistic world remained. Nonetheless, as we have seen, the displacement of mythic language from the sacred to the secular and the consequent blurring of the distinction between the sacred and the profane left these modern myths open to assault and critical scrutiny. Furthermore, the pace of this scrutiny accelerated. Henrik Ibsen, who began his dramatic career under the literary myth of the saga era, wrote in *An Enemy of the People* that truths last at most twenty years. In our time the pace of obsolescence has increased still more to the point of "future shock."

In the ridicule surrounding the collapse of the social myth of Swedish Gothicism and the scorn accompanying the exposure of Ossian as a literary myth we see adumbrated the more complex problem of myth in the contemporary Western world. The problem is not just the absence of the sacred as a declared reality. The romantic awareness of symbol has introduced a tool for self-scrutiny, making possible the disciplines of sociology of knowledge, semiology, structuralism, and myth criticism. Unfortunately Novalis, himself a mathematician as well as a poet, had a belief we do not: that the symbol was a means of perceiving ultimate reality, permanence amidst change, and was not just an organizing instrument.

While I am aware of the sweeping nature of this generalization, let me suggest that a semiologist studying the structure of the romantic imagination would find a richer scope in it than in ours, for all the freedom demythologizing has allegedly brought us. If, with Goethe, we accept the symbol as a mediating lens between the unformed world of transcendental verities and the morally neutral phenomenal world, some of the details of the romantic perception of the world as drama, touched upon above, become clearer, as well as the nature of our own imagination.

The romantic perception of reality as having multiple dimensions of reality, unified by the symbol, produced a potential for perception, the darker side of which we have inherited. In romantic narrative, the reality of the transcendent world can be benign or demonic, depending upon the response of the protagonist in the human world. Consider, for instance, Goethe's poem "The Erl-King." During a ride, a child (oracular, in romantic convention) perceives the incursion of the demonic, but the father sees the event in demythologized terms as "only a storm." The child repeats the warning, and the father continues to ignore it; the child dies.

From a structuralist point of view, we may see the dynamics of the romantic imagination working thusly: if the human world ignores the manifestations of the transcendent or sees them in empirical terms (which is saying the same thing), the transcendent becomes demonic, to the peril of the human world. Though the demonic is accepted as real, it only becomes inimical when the middle, human, world lets it through ignoring the voice of benign transcendental inspiration. In Goethe's case, the voice is the child; in the case of the protagonist of Poe's "Ulalume," the ignored voice is "Psyche." This is not the place to develop this thesis in full, but with some ramifications it could be applied to the works of E. T. A. Hoffmann, Mary Shelley, Mikhail Lermontov and others as an underlying structure of the imagination stemming from the belief in the symbol. Some poets conceptualized this in neoplatonic terms, while others developed the pose of the Byronic hero, one of the dominant romantic myths.

We have, as I suggested, inherited a darker side of this structure, and from this legacy stems our problem of myth and, ultimately, "future shock." We have continued to recognize the importance of the symbol but have lost the faith in its transcendence. Consequently, the symbol loses its status as a necessary, though temporal, perception of transcendence and becomes "merely symbolic." Art consequently loses its communal character with the decline of communal myth and becomes expressions of private myth worlds, internally coherent perhaps, but the structures have lost their objectivity. Myth in art loses its sacred quality, even as displaced myth. This point is perhaps the root of Ricoeur's criticism of structuralism: structuralism through its moral neutrality can make no distinction between the sacred and the profane and must of necessity lose the reality of the sacred in its analyses. Even the influential Emile Durkheim in his *Elementary Forms of Religious Life*[1] sees the perceptions of space and time as being socially conditioned. It is important to see how myth symbolizes, but a language which does not recognize the sacred as a reality cannot measure it successfully. Indeed, deterministic assumptions make discussion of symbols of feeling sound like Voltaire's discussions of the *je ne sais quoi*.

With all the relativistic implications of our study of modern myth, we have noted the constancy of imagination, and the inevitability but ultimate futility of demythologizing must be part of our conclusion. Recently, a group of Christian thinkers of as diverse a cloth as Jesuit Avery Dulles and Yale Chaplain William Sloane Coffin expressed a consensus deploring the displacement of sacred concepts to secular ideologies, one of these "false theses" being that liberation from the past is required for "authentic existence and authentic religion."[2] The translation of the Episcopal Book of Common Prayer has met with similar charges of reductionism: the language implied in replacing "all things visible and invisible" with "all that is seen and unseen" suggests just the loss of dimension we have described. Karl Jaspers anticipated this situation in 1931 when he described the "melting away of historical interconnexions" as resulting in an attitude where "the unconditioned is regarded as a merely unconcrete emotionalism." But, Jaspers continues, "genuine times cannot be artificially established; they must be freely engendered by the individual in community life. If the demand for ties is nothing more than a demand for an artificial order in obedience to authority and written law, the real task is evaded, the upshot being that the unconditioned becomes impossible and freedom is paralysed."[3]

Gerardus van der Leeuw and others, most notably Paul Ricoeur and Kees Bolle, have sensed the problem in the reductionist approach to myth. Can a discussion of the sacred employ language which is not in itself sacred? Is a phenomenology of the mythic imagination and its displacements into social and literary myth possible? Certainly, the collapse of the romantic faith in the transcendental reality of the symbol poses a problem for myth in any discipline, a problem recognized most keenly by Ricoeur and Bolle. Neither of these has as his primary concern myth not employing sacred language, though both recognize the existence of such symbolic forms. Semiology, the social context of signs, is essentially a study of displaced myth, in that it makes the dual distinction that the image differs from the object, and that the reality of the image depends upon the belief in it. Semiology is, in a sense, a hermeneutics of displaced myth.

We mentioned at the outset of this enterprise that myth as a term is a problem in several disciplines, though as we have suggested myth permeates most of these. Curiously, the problem of myth is less severe in the area of social myth than in the study of literature, though few scholars in sociology seem inclined to use the term. The problem in discussing literary myth stems in part from a distrust of language; myth, after all, declares its objectivity in whatever degree of displacement from the sacred to the profane. The faith in the very possibility of objective knowledge, however, had begun to be undermined even in the physical sciences as early as the mid-nineteenth century, when James Clerk Maxwell discovered that magnetic fields were just as "real" as physical objects and their behavior could be described by equations.

The more subtle assault on language came in the 1880s with the failure of the Michelson-Morley experiment to detect the ether. The language of common sense demanded that a light wave must of necessity wave something, but the experiment which should have detected it failed to do so. The price for this failure? Thomas Kuhn in *The Structure of Scientific Revolutions* suggests that at this point a new science, a new set of paradigms for understanding phenomena, was needed to explain the facts, much as Galilean physics was needed to explain the shortcomings in Ptolemaic cosmology. To employ our terminology, the problem of light was a marginal experience for the common sense world of the nineteenth century. One response to these experiences was the revival of mysticism, Swedenborg and the interest in the occult, much as the generation of Novalis had responded to the poetic inadequacies of Newtonian mechanics with "magical idealism."

The principal result, however, of the failure of the union of science with common sense was a realization that literature was not alone in employing metaphor. One result of the Copenhagen interpretation of the quantum theory in the 1920s was a recognition that there are ultimate barriers to our knowledge of the physical world, and our representations of this knowledge are just that: re-presentations. The reality beyond its representation is unintelligible; as the biologist J. B. S. Haldane put it, "The world is not only queerer than we imagine, it is queerer than we can imagine." Einstein, of course, had a monistic drive, but it was he and not Joyce who declared that as far as fundamental principles went, "There is no logical path to these laws; only intuition, resting on sympathetic understanding of experience, can reach them."

Civilization is a seamless web, and scant wonder that Hesse, Kafka, Kandinsky, Faulkner, Schönberg, Woolf, Eliot, Joyce, and others could respond to the freeing of the symbol from mimesis in the twenties. Indeed, it should be remembered that Durkheim's seminal work first appeared in 1919. Einstein would not have carried the assumptions of relativity as far as did Durkheim, who said "there are no religions which are false."

While the arts responded to this liberation with a startling explosion of new expressive techniques, some voices have been raised asserting that the freedom gained in the liberation from nineteenth-century assumptions of objectivity in the perception of space-time are but superficial compared to the freedom lost in the devaluation of myth. Yeats, in "The Second Coming," echoes Friedrich Schlegel's assertion that "we have no mythology," but declares the permanence of the mythmaking impulse in describing the rough beast slouching toward its millennium of power.

The beast of Yeats, remember, is political, and Yeats's prophecies have been correct, for it has been in the area of social myths that myth has had its greatest significance. If myth depends for its power upon its objectivity, modern myth must claim a rational, not sacred, validation. The success and appeal of the mythic elements in modern totalitarian movements is the combination of chiliasm and rational methodology.

As Plato knew, myth is a problem to the republic, to be eradicated and replaced by art and speculation anchored in pragmatically defined "realism." We touched upon a now-comic illustration of this in discussing Sweden's Great Power Era. What Plato did not recognize is that myth enters the republic not in its art but in its facts.

While myth poses a terminological problem for scholars and artists, myth has its primary impact now in the political world, not the artistic, for the artistic symbol has lost its dimension of reality. Man's conscience now, as Thomas Mann observed, is defined in political terms. Modern political myths, however, are much less innocent than those of Rudbeck's Atlantis. Granted, chiliastic myths animated staggering cruelty and "megadeaths" during the Thirty Years' War, but modern myths combine several legacies we have discussed to add an element of cynicism. Primarily, the legacy is romantic: irony lets us study myths and their operation, and the study of symbol allows the observer to analyze them in their structure and social context. But the lack of faith in the transcendent, coupled with techniques of manipulation and conditioning, has resulted in the cynicism adumbrated in Giambattista Vico and fulfilled in Georges Sorel, who declared the necessity of manipulating social myth to implement socialism. History, as Sorel sees it, should be that myth which brings about revolution.

Since the time of Sorel, myths no longer have to be manipulated, they can be synthesized and manufactured to be used as tools for conditioning. Social signs, as Roland Barthes notes, are simultaneously expressions of popular culture and conditioning elements of it, much as we discussed the Ossianic craze. Now, however, these images can be analytically synthesized, and, indeed, it is suggested that such images are necessary to promote social doctrine or political power. Myth is fundamentally conservative, telling of things *in illo tempore* and stabilizing the present. Many of our synthetic myths are designed to advertise images of national origins. Other modern myths, however, deny tradition for doctrines of social progress or revolution. Textbooks, we learn, should be written to reflect society as it should be in the eyes of the planners, not as it is, or was. In passing, however, we should note that Eliade, Pettazoni, and others have asserted the importance of creation myths (though disagreeing about their primacy). Even contemporary myths of liberation tend to concern themselves with their beginnings and founders to stabilize the present.

The goals of this kind of modern mythmaking may be laudable; after all, if there is nothing to life but human will, human happiness is all that is worth attaining. Indeed, B. F. Skinner tells us, freedom and dignity are romantic illusions impeding the development of a science of behavior which will finally banish these "occult qualities," much as Newton wished to in his *Principia*, and finally solve the problem of man's discontent. It should be mentioned, however, that Newton never quite knew what to do about explaining force-at-a-distance; gravity turned out to be a latent marginal experience in the Newtonian world. If man needs myth for security, myths can and should be merchandised.

A conclusion should properly address the question "So what?" to an excursus, and much of the foregoing opinion has been a conjecture based upon our initial posing of "the problem of myth." I suggest that the problem is a dual one: in the arts, the absence of myth makes possible new techniques for communication, while impoverishing the store of subject matter to communicate; myth, we have argued, makes heroism possible. Social myth, on the other hand, presents a picture of synthetic images of reality warring for dominance in men's minds, affecting life from the purchase of cigarettes to political allegiances. Myth's objectivity also posits exclusive truth; as we saw in the conversion of the Germanic tribes, in a conflict of myths the power of the loser is demonized. The real loser, however, is the liberal ideal of tolerance. Both aspects of the problem of myth stem from the lack of faith in transcendence; let us hope the romantics were wrong, and that negation of the transcendent does not allow the demonic to define the human world.

BIBLIOGRAPHY

All scholarship is synthesis, this work perhaps more than most. The following bibliography gives an index to some of the scholarly antecedents of the central problem instead of listing all works cited. I have arranged it by what will hopefully be useful rubrics.

I

On the "Nordic Renaissance," i.e., the refurbishing of the Nordic past as acceptable material for origins, see:

Andersson, Theodore M. *The Problem of Icelandic Saga Origins*. New Haven, 1964.

Batka, Richard. "Altnordische Stoffe und Studien in Deutschland. Von Gottfried Schütze bis Klopstock." *Euphorion*, 3, zweites Ergänzungsheft (1896), 1–70.

———. "Altnordische Stoffe und Studien in Deutschland: II. Klopstock und die Barden." *Euphorion*, 6 (1899), 67–83.

Benson, Adolph B. *The Old Norse Element in Swedish Romanticism*. Columbia University Germanic Studies, New York, 1914.

Blanck, Anton. *Den nordiska Renässansen i sjuttonhundratalets litteratur*. Stockholm, 1911.

Castrén, Gunnar. *Norden i den franska litteraturen*. Helsingfors, 1910.

Eaton, John W. *The German Influence in Danish Literature in the Eighteenth Century*. Cambridge, Eng., 1929.

Falbe-Hansen, Ida. *Øhlenschlægers nordiske digtning og andre afhandlinger*. Copenhagen, 1921.

Hubasch, Walter. *Die Deutschen und der Norden. Ein Beitrag zur politischen Ideengeschichte vom Humanismus bis zur Gegenwart in Dokumenten*. Göttingen, 1951.

Körner, Josef. "Die Renaissance des germanischen Altertums: Eine literarhistorische Skizze." *Zeitschrift für den deutschen Unterricht* 27 (1913), 1–29.

Magon, Leopold. *Ein Jahrhundert geistiger und literarischer Beziehungen zwischen Deutschland und Skandinavien 1750–1850*. Vol. 1. *Die Klopstockzeit in Dänemark: Johannes Ewald*. Dortmund, 1926.

Mitchell, P. M. "Old Norse-Icelandic Literature in Germany 1789–1849, with a Critical Bibliography." Doctoral dissertation, University of Illinois, 1942.

Mjöberg, Jöran. *Drömmen om Sagatiden*. 2 vols. Stockholm, 1969, 1970.
Niessen, Carl. "Der 'Norden' auf dem Theater." in *Märchen, Mythos, Dichtung*, ed. Hugo Kuhn and Kurt Schier. Munich, 1963.
Nordby, Conrad Hjalmar. *The Influence of Old Norse Literature upon English Literature*. New York, 1901.
Oppel, Horst. "Studien zur Auffassung des Nordischen in der Goethezeit." *Deutsche Vierteljahrsschrift für Literaturwissenschaft und Geistesgeschichte*, Buchreihe, 28. Halle, 1944.
Robson-Scott, W. D. *The Literary Background of the Gothic Revival in Germany*. Oxford, 1965.
Rubow, Paul V. *Saga og pastiche*. Copenhagen, 1923.
Springer, Otto. *Die nordische Renaissance in Skandinavien*. Stuttgart, 1936.
Wallén, Erik. *Nordisk mythologi i svensk romantik*. Stockholm, 1918.

II. THE PROBLEM OF MYTH

A. The theoretical foundations of *The Golden Horns* come from: Cassirer, Ernst. *The Philosophy of Symbolic Forms*, trans. Ralph Manheim. New Haven, 1953. Vol. 1: *Language;* Vol. 2: *Mythical Thought;* Vol. 3, *The Phenomenology of Knowledge*. Also: Ricoeur, Paul. *The Symbolism of Evil*, trans. Emerson Buchanan. New York, 1967. Ricoeur's concern with explicating the sacred is described by David M. Rasmussen, *Mythic-Symbolic Language and Philosophical Anthropology: A Constructive Interpretation of the Thought of Paul Ricoeur*. The Hague, 1971: "Is there a way in which mythic-symbolic language can be retained as a significant dimension of human meaning?" (p. 23), and "mythic-symbolic discourse is constitutive for the human quest for freedom" (p. 128). Further on the problem of freedom and myth, see Kees W. Bolle, *The Freedom of Man in Myth*. Nashville, 1968, and Nicholas Berdyaev, *The Meaning of History*, trans. George Reavey. Cleveland, 1962.

B. For a historical perspective on the ideas of myth, see:
Chase, Richard. *Quest for Myth*. Baton Rouge, 1949.
de Vries, Jan. *Forschungsgeschichte der Mythologie*. Munich, 1961.
Holm, Søren. *Mythe og symbol*. Copenhagen University Festskrift, 1971. Copenhagen, 1071.

C. The bibliography on the reality of myth is extensive. See:
Campbell, Joseph. *The Hero with a Thousand Faces*. New York, 1949. (Classic work on the eminence of the quest-myth.)
Castelli, Enrico, ed. *Mythe et foi*. Actes du colloque organisé par le centre

international d'études humanistiques et par l'institut d'études philosophiques de Rome. Paris, 1966. (Excellent collection of essays; among others: Raymond Panikkar, "La foi dimension constitutive de l'homme"; Geo Widengeren, "Mythe et foi à la lumière de la phénoménologie religieuse"; Alphonse de Waelhens, "Le mythe de la démythification.") Also:

Dillistone, F. W., ed. *Myth and Symbol*. Theological Collections, no. 7, London, 1966.

Durkheim, Emile. *The Elementary Forms of the Religious Life*, trans. J. W. Swain. New York, 1965.

Eliade, Mircea. *Cosmos and History: The Myth of the Eternal Return*, trans. W. R. Trask. New York, 1954.

⸻. *Patterns in Comparative Religion*, trans. R. Sheed. Cleveland, 1963.

⸻. *The Sacred and the Profane: The Nature of Religion*, trans. W. R. Trask. New York, 1959.

(See also: Altizer, Thomas J. *Mircea Eliade and the Dialectic of the Sacred*. Philadelphia, 1963.)

Holloway, John. "The Concept of Myth." In *The Story of the Night*. London, 1961. (Critique of Cassirer, p. 169.)

Malinowski, Bronislaw. "Myth in Primitive Psychology" in *Magic, Science, and Religion*. New York, 1955.

Murray, Henry A., ed. *Myth and Mythmaking*. New York, 1968.

Pettazzoni, Raffaele. "Die Wahrheit des Mythos." *Paideuma* 4 (1950),

⸻. *Essays on the History of Religions*. Leyden, 1954.

van der Leeuw, Gerardus. "Die Bedeutung der Mythen." In *Festschrift für Alfred Bertholet*, ed. W. Baumgartner. Tübingen, 1950.

⸻. *La religion dans son essence et ses manifestations*. Paris, 1948. (See especially section 60, 1–10.)

D. On the Golden Age as myth of origins, see:

Doren, Alfred. *Wunschräume und Wunschzeiten*. Vorträge der Bibliothek Warburg, ed. F. Saxl. Leipzig, 1924–1925.

Eliade, Mircea. "Kosmogonische Mythen und magische Heilungen." *Paideuma*, 6 (1956), 194–204.

Emrich, Wilhelm. "Begriff und Symbolik der 'Urgeschichte' in der romantischen Dichtung." *Deutsche Vierteljahrsschrift für Literaturwissenschaft und Geistesgeschichte* 20 (1942), 273–304.

Esnoul, Anne-Marie, ed. *La naissance du monde*. Sources Orientales, I. Paris, 1959. (See especially the concluding essay by Eliade, "Structure et fonction du mythe cosmogonique.")

Gandillac, M. de, Goldmann, L., and Piaget, J. *Entretiens sur les notions de genèse et de structure*. Paris, 1965.

Leach, E. R. "Genesis as Myth." *Discovery* 23 (1962), 30–35.

————. *Lévi-Strauss in the Garden of Eden: An Examination of Some Recent Developments in the Analysis of Myth.* Transactions of the New York Academy of Sciences, series 2. New York, 1961.

Levin, Harry. *The Myth of The Golden Age in The Renaissance.* Bloomington, 1959.

Long, Charles H. *Alpha: The Myths of Creation.* New York, 1963.

Mähl, Hans-Joachim. *Die Idee des goldenen Zeitalters im Werk des Novalis.* Probleme der Dichtung, vol. 7. Heidelberg, 1965.

Norden, Eduard. *Philosophische Ansichten über die Entstehung des Menschengeschlechts, seine kulturelle Entwicklung und das goldne Zeitalter.* Beiträge zur Geschichte der griechischen Philosophie, part 3. *Jahrbücher für classische Philologie,* 19. Supplementband. Leipzig, 1893.

Pettazzoni, Raffaele. "Myths of Origins and Myths of Creations." In *Essays on the History of Religions.* Leyden, 1954.

Svendsen, Paulus. *Gullalderdrøm og utviklingstro.* Oslo, 1940.

Tuveson, Ernest Lee. *Millennium and Utopia: A Study in the Background of the Idea of Progress.* Berkeley, 1950.

van der Leeuw, Gerardus. "Urzeit und Endzeit." In *Eranos Jahrbuch* 17: Der Mensch und die mythische Welt. Zurich, 1950.

Veit, Walter. "Studien zur Geschichte des Topos der Goldenen Zeit von der Antike bis zum 18. Jahrhundert." Dissertation, Cologne, 1961.

Vretska, Karl. *Das Goldene Zeitalter.* Mitteilungen des Vereins klassischer Philologen in Wien, vol. 10. Vienna, 1934.

E. The problem of myth in the study of literature has also received copious treatment. As mentioned, we are not primarily concerned with defining myth in terms of Jungian archetypes, although Maud Bodkin's *Archetypal Patterns in Poetry* is a seminal example of this approach.

Douglas, Wallace W. "The Meanings of Myth in Modern Criticism." *Modern Philology,* 50 (1952–1953), 232–242.

Frye, Northrop. *The Anatomy of Criticism: Four Essays.* Princeton, 1957. For a foreign assessment of Frye, see Robert Weimann, "Northrop Frye und das Ende des New Criticism." *Sinn und Form* 17 (1965), 621–630.

Frye, Northrop. *Fables of Identity.* New York, 1963. (See especially "Myth, Fiction and Displacement.")

Grassi, Ernesto. *Kunst und Mythos.* Hamburg, 1957.

Kerényi, Karl. "Romandichtung und Mythologie." In *Briefwechsel mit Thomas Mann.* Zurich, 1945.

Krieger, Murray. "Critical Historicism: The Poetic Context and the Historical Context." *Orbis litterarum,* 21 (1966), 49–60.

May, Rollo, ed. *Symbolism in Religion and Literature*. New York, 1960. (Excellent collection, including essays from Tillich, Burke, Richards, Heisenberg, and Whitehead.)

Miller, J. E., ed. *Myth and Method*. Lincoln, Neb., 1960.

Ostendorf, Bernhard. *Der Mythos in der Neuen Welt: Eine Untersuchung zum amerikanischen Myth Criticism*. Frankfurt, 1971. (Good survey.)

Poulet, Georges. *Trois essais de mythologie romantique*. Paris, 1966.

Rahv, Philip. *The Myth and the Powerhouse*. New York, 1965.

Scott, Nathan A. "The Broken Center: A Definition of the Crisis of Values in Modern Literature." In *Symbolism in Religion and Literature*, ed. Rollo May.

Sebeok, Thomas Albert, ed. *Myth: A Symposium*. Bloomington, 1955.

Slochower, Harry. *Mythopoesis: Mythic Patterns in the Literary Classics*. Detroit, 1970.

Slote, Bernice, ed. *Myth and Symbol*. Lincoln, Neb., 1963.

Vickery, John B., ed. *Myth and Literature: Contemporary Theory and Practice*. Lincoln, Neb., 1966.

Weimann, Robert. *Phantasie und Nachahmung: Drei Studien zum Verhältnis von Dichtung, Utopie und Mythos*. Halle, 1970. (See especially chap. 3: "Literaturwissenschaft und Mythologie.")

Weisinger, Herbert. *The Agony and the Triumph: Papers on the Use and Abuse of Myth*. East Lansing, Mich., 1963.

III

Structuralism, with its bases in linguistics and anthropology, has given the study of myth a new direction, particularly as a result of the work of Claude Lévi-Strauss. For a bibliography, see: Harari, Josué V. *Structuralists and Structuralisms: A Selected Bibliography of French Contemporary Thought, 1960–1970*. Ithaca, 1973. Further:

Barthes, Roland. "An Introduction to the Structural Analysis of Narrative," *New Literary History*, 6 (1975), 237–272.

Boon, James A. *From Symbolism to Structuralism: Lévi-Strauss in a Literary Tradition*. New York, 1972. (Good bibliography.)

Ehrmann, Jacques, ed. *Structuralism*. Garden City, 1970. (Extensive bibliographies on linguistics, anthropology, literary criticism, and structuralism in general.)

Goldmann, Lucien. *Pour une sociologie du roman*. Paris, 1964.

Lane, Michael. *Introduction to Structuralism*. New York, 1970. (Excellent introduction.)

Leach, Edmund. *Claude Lévi-Strauss*. Rev. ed. New York, 1974.

Lévi-Strauss, Claude. *The Savage Mind.* Chicago, 1966.

———. *Structural Anthropology.* New York, 1963.

———. "The Structural Study of Myth." *Journal of American Folklore,* 68 (1955), 428–444.

Ricoeur, Paul. "The Hermeneutics of Symbols and Philosophical Reflection." *International Philosophical Quarterly,* 2 (1963), 191–218. ("Reflective thought is essentially demythologizing, it interprets mythology by reducing it to allegory," p. 204.)

———. " 'La pensée sauvage' et le structuralisme." *Esprit* 31 (1963), 596–627. (This issue of *Esprit* is given over to a discussion of *The Savage Mind* and structuralism.)

Schiwy, Günther. *Neue Aspekte des Strukturalismus.* Munich, 1971. (Good critical overview from a Marxist point of view.)

———. *Strukturalismus und Christentum.* Freiburg, 1969.

———. *Strukturalismus und Zeichensysteme.* Munich, 1973.

Scholes, Robert. *Structuralism in Literature: An Introduction.* New Haven, 1974. (Critical bibliography; fine introduction.)

Sebag, L. "Le mythe, code, et message." *Les temps modernes,* 226 (1965), 1607–1623.

Weimann, Robert. "French Structuralism and Literary History." *New Literary History,* 4 (1973), 437–469. ("The method of historical materialism and the method of structuralism are not the same," p. 469.)

IV

The extension of myth into areas other than literature was guided by:

Bastide, R., ed. *Sens et usage du terme 'structure' dans les sciences humaines.* The Hague, 1962. (Interdisciplinary collection of essays.)

Berger, Peter, and Pullberg, Stanley. "Reification and the Sociological Critique of Consciousness." *History and Theory,* 4 (1965).

Berger, Peter. *The Sacred Canopy: Elements of a Sociological Theory of Religion.* New York, 1967.

Berger, Peter, and Luckmann, Thomas. *The Social Construction of Reality.* Garden City, 1966.

Böhler, Eugen. *Der Mythus in Wirtschaft und Wissenschaft.* Beiträge zur Wirtschaftspolitik, vol. 3. Freiburg, 1965.

Cassirer, Ernst. *An Essay on Man.* New Haven, 1944.

———. *The Myth of the State.* New Haven, 1946.

Cox, Howard L. "The Place of Mythology in the Study of Culture." *American Imago,* 5 (1948), 83–94.

Luckmann, Thomas. *The Invisible Religion: The Problem of Religion in Modern Society.* New York, 1967.

Marchal, A. "L'attitude structuraliste et le concept de structure en économie politique." In Bastide, *Sens et usage*.

Niebuhr, Reinhold. *Reflections on the End of an Era*. New York, 1934. ("Meaning can be attributed to history only by a mythology. The modern empiricist does not escape mythological interpretations of history in his effort to avoid them," p. 123.)

Parámio, Ludofo. *Mito e ideologia*. Madrid, 1971.

Plamenatz, John. *Ideology*. New York, 1970. (Chap. 6: "The Political Uses of Ideology.")

Viet. J. *Les methodes structuralistes dans les sciences sociales*. Paris, 1965.

V

Our conjectures on the contemporary problem of myth stem from readings in several areas.

A. For further reading on the decline of the idea of objectivity in the physical sciences see:

Einstein, A. "Address to Max Planck." in *Albert Einstein: Essays in Science*. New York, n.d.

Gillispie, Charles Coulston. *The Edge of Objectivity: An Essay in the History of Scientific Ideas*. Princeton, 1960. (Excellent survey of the development of the idea; bibliographical essay. See especially chap. 10, "Field Physics," and the Epilogue on the modern implications.)

Heisenberg, Werner. *Physics and Philosophy: The Revolution in Modern Science*. New York, 1958. (See chap. 7, "Criticism and Counterproposals to the Copenhagen Interpretation of Quantum Theory," and chap. 11, "The Role of Modern Physics in the Present Development of Human Thinking.")

————. "Sprache und Wirklichkeit in der modernen Physik." In *Sprache und Wirklichkeit: Essays*. Munich, 1967.

Holton, Gerald. *Thematic Origins of Scientific Thought*. Cambridge, Mass., 1973. (Good discussion in chap. 9 of "Einstein, Michelson and the 'Crucial' Experiment.")

Husserl, Edmund. *The Crisis of European Sciences and Transcendental Phenomenology*. Northwestern Studies in Phenomenology and Existential Philosophy. Evanston, 1970.

Kuhn, Thomas. *The Structure of Scientific Revolutions*. 2nd ed. Chicago, 1970.

Planck, Max. *L'image du monde dans la physique moderne*. Paris, 1963.

Polanyi, Michael. *Personal Knowledge: Towards a Post-Critical Philosophy*. Chicago, 1958.

Reichenbach, Hans. *The Theory of Relativity and A Priori Knowledge*. Berkeley, 1965. ("Our intuitive geometrical images are not sufficient for the characterization of a physical state," p. 107.)

B. We discussed the problem of myth in formal art at some length; while Eliade in "Myths of the Modern World" states that "the poet discovers the world as if he were present at the world's origin" (*Myths, Dreams, and Mysteries*. New York, 1960), Nathan A. Scott is less abstract (and less optimistic) in "The Broken Center: A Definition of the Crisis of Values in Modern Literature" (in *Symbolism and Literature*, ed. Rollo May, New York, 1960). Wylie Sypher, *Loss of the Self in Modern Literature and Art* (New York, 1962), correlates the increase in depicting the private world with the decline of the belief in scientific objectivity; see chap. 4, "Existence and Entropy," and chap. 6, "The Zero Degree of Painting." On social myth and art, see:

Barthes, Roland. *Mythologies*. New York, 1972. (Contains the essay "Myth Today," where Barthes states that "myth is depoliticized speech," p. 145.)

———. *Writing Degree Zero and Elements of Semiology*. Boston, 1970.

Huaco, George A. "Ideology and Literature." *New Literary History*, 4 (1973), 421–436.

Patai, Raphael. *Myth and Modern Man*. New York, 1972.

Sauvy, Alfred. *Mythologie de notre temps*. Paris, 1966.

C. The Third Reich was, of course, the twentieth-century expression of Nordic origins as social myth. The principal document for this myth is Alfred Rosenberg, *Der Mythus des 20. Jahrhunderts* (Munich, 1935), with the methodology defended in Rosenberg's *An die Dunkelmänner unserer Zeit* (Munich, 1935). See:

Chandler, Albert R. *Rosenberg's Nazi Myth*. Ithaca, 1945.

Neurohr, Jean. *Der Mythos vom dritten Reich*. Stuttgart, 1957.

D. On contemporary social myth in general, radicalism and Marxism in particular, see:

Adelmann, Frederick J., ed. *Demythologizing Marxism*. The Boston College Studies in Philosophy, vol. 2. The Hague, 1969.

Feuer, Lewis. "Political Myths and Metaphysics." *Philosophical and Phenomenological Research*, 15 (1955), 332–350.

Godelier, Maurice. "System, Structure, and Contradiction in *Das Kapital*." Originally in *Les temps modernes*, 246 (1966), trans. in Lane, Michael, *Introduction to Structuralism*. New York, 1970.

Horowitz, Irving Louis. *Radicalism and the Revolt against Reason. The*

Social Theories of Georges Sorel, with a Translation of his Essay "On the Decomposition of Marxism". New York, 1961. (See especially chap. 5, "The Psychology of Action," pt. 1, "Political Mythology and the Higher Truths.")

Naess, Arne. *Democracy, Ideology, and Objectivity: Studies in the Semantics and Cognitive Analysis of Ideological Controversy*. Oslo, 1956.

Sebag, L. *Marxisme et structuralisme*. Paris, 1964.

Tucker, Robert. *Philosophy and Myth in Karl Marx*. Cambridge, Eng., 1971.

Tudor, Henry. *Political Myth*. New York, 1972.

Voegelin, Eric. *The New Science of Politics*, Chicago, 1952.

———. *Science, Politics and Gnosticism*. Chicago, 1968.

NOTES

CHAPTER 1

1. Reinhold Niebuhr, *Reflections on the End of an Era* (New York, 1934), p. 123.

2. René Wellek, "Philosophy and Postwar American Criticism," and "Trends of Twentieth-Century Criticism," in *Concepts of Criticism*, ed. S. G. Nichols (New Haven, 1963), pp. 336, 361; for a Marxist view, Robert Weimann, "Literaturwissenschaft und Mythologie," in *Phantasie und Nachahmung: Drei Studien zum Verhältnis von Dichtung, Utopie und Mythos* (Halle, 1970), p. 145, and "Tradition und Krise amerikanischer Literarhistorie: Zu ihrer Methodologie und Geschichte," *Weimarer Beiträge*, 3 (1965), 429–431; Philip Rahv, *The Myth and the Powerhouse* (New York, 1965), p. 4; Richard M. Dorson, "Theories of Myth and the Folklorist," in *Myth and Mythmaking*, ed. Henry A. Murray (New York, 1968), p. 68.

3. Peter L. Berger and Thomas Luckmann, *The Social Construction of Reality* (New York, 1966); Karl Mannheim, *Ideology and Utopia*, trans. Louis Wirth and Edward Shils (New York, 1936).

4. Paul Ricoeur, *The Symbolism of Evil*, trans. Emerson Buchanan (Boston, 1967), pp. 347–357.

5. Discussing "The World of Franz Kafka," Erich Heller attributes the aridity of the modern mind to not sharing Goethe's belief in the reality of the symbol (*The Disinherited Mind*, New York, 1959, p. 210).

6. Ricoeur emphasizes "the dramatic character of the primordial time" in mythic expressions of the Sacred which of necessity gives myth a dramatic form: "The myth performs its symbolic function by the specific means of the narration because what it wants to express is already a drama" (*Symbolism of Evil*, p. 170).

7. Structuralists have noted that myth deals with antinomies; Kees Bolle characterizes the freedom attained in myth as a renewal stemming from "breaking through the extreme oppositions" under which man lives; myth's totality and efficacy "destroys the oppressive finiteness of man" (*The Freedom of Man in Myth*, Nashville, 1968, pp. 87, 88).

8. Raffaele Pettazzoni, "Die Wahrheit des Mythos," *Paideuma*, 4 (1950), 4–7.

9. Text in *Ancient Near Eastern Texts Relating to the Old Testament*, ed. James B. Pritchard (Princeton, 1950; 2nd ed., 1955), pp. 60–72. In myth,

says Mircea Eliade, "every creation, every existence begins in time; *before a thing exists, its particular time could not exist.* . . . The way in which a reality came into existence is revealed by its myth" (*The Sacred and the Profane,* trans. Willard R. Trask, New York, 1959, p. 76).

10. If, as Heidel suggests, the function of *Enuma elish* was to control flooding, always a potential danger to the human world, a culture holding this text sacred could only believe reality is not neutral, but has a violent essence. See A. Heidel, *The Babylonian Genesis* (Chicago, 1942; 2nd ed., 1951), p. 17.

11. "By being thrust back into temporal distance, by being situated in the depths of the past, a particular content is not only established as sacred, as mythically and religiously significant, but also justified as such " (Ernst Cassirer, *The Philosophy of Symbolic Forms,* trans. Ralph Manheim, New Haven, 1955, 2: *Mythical Thought,* 105). Eliade has discussed this characteristic of "sacred time" in detail; in *Cosmos and History,* trans. Willard R. Trask (New York, 1959) he concludes that in myth "everything which lacks an exemplary model is 'meaningless,' " i.e., it lacks reality, but the reality of a content may be established by "the abolition of time through the imitation of archetypes" (pp. 34–35). Carl Kerényi emphasizes the importance of this "Begründung," in that authenticity is established through recounting what "originally was"; philosophy, however, has a different orientation, attempting to transcend the phenomenal world to what "really is" (*Essays on a Science of Mythology* by C. G. Jung and Carl Kerényi, trans. R. F. C. Hull, New York, 1949, pp. 7–9).

12. See Mircea Eliade, "Sacred Time and the Myth of Eternal Renewal," in *Patterns in Comparative Religion,* trans. Rosemary Sheed (Cleveland, 1963), pp. 388–408, and Cassirer, *An Essay on Man* (New Haven, 1944), p. 94, where he writes of the temporal and spatial "solidarity of life" in the mythic consciousness.

13. Cassirer, *Symbolic Forms,* 2:110–111.

14. This is a common theme in Eliade's works, but is succinctly put in *Myth and Reality,* trans. Willard R. Trask (New York, 1963), chap. 2, "Magic and Prestige of Origins," pp. 21–38.

15. Kerényi, *Essays,* p. 8; Harry Levin, *The Myth of the Golden Age in the Renaissance* (Bloomington, Ind., 1969), p. 4.

16. Eliade, *Cosmos and History,* chap. 4, "The Terror of History," pp. 141–162.

17. "Faith in reason," Whitehead observes, "is the trust that the ultimate natures of things lie together in a harmony which excludes mere arbitrariness. It is the faith that at the base of things we shall not find mere arbitrary mystery" (*Science and the Modern World,* New York, 1925, p. 24). After

such "exposure," formerly "objective" social doctrine is perceived as "mythical" (in the negative sense, to be sure). See Alphonse de Waelhens, "Le mythe de la démythification," in *Mythe et foi,* ed. Enrico Castelli (Paris, 1966), pp. 259–261.

18. Christopher Dawson, in *Progress and Religion* (New York, 1960), pp. 146–149, sees the "Religion of Progress" characteristic of the secularization of thought as beginning in the Renaissance, though, as Whitehead points out, the Scholastic faith in general principles played an integral role in the development of scientific method (*Science and the Modern World,* p. 19).

19. In modern times, Rudolf Bultmann mounted the same attack in his essay "New Testament and Mythology," saying that as the modern world has been irrevocably molded by science, "the only criticism of the New Testament is that which arises *necessarily* out of the situation of modern man" (in *Kerygma and Myth: Rudolf Bultmann and Five Critics,* ed. H. W. Bartsch, rev. ed. by R. H. Fuller, New York, 1961, p. 7). Paul Tillich, however, suggests that "wherever scientific criticism is effective, it leads not to a demonization, but rather to a profanization of the symbols" ("The Religious Symbol," in *Symbolism in Religion and Literature,* ed. Rollo May, New York, 1960, p. 95).

20. Although Heller sees the "estrangement" in modern man as stemming from the defining of symbol in rational terms (*Disinherited Mind,* pp. 264–266), the reduction of the mythic symbol to a historical or empirical content (Euhemerism and allegory) was common even in early classical culture. See Jan de Vries, *Forschungsgeschichte der Mythologie* (Munich, 1961), pp. 1–43.

21. Cassirer, *Symbolic Forms,* 2:104.

22. Ibid., 2:38, 53–59, 63.

23. Ibid., 2:40, 41, n. 13.

24. This "innate power," Tillich maintains, distinguishes the religious symbol from the sign ("The Religious Symbol," p. 76). Myth is a species of symbol; again, the knowledge of myth involves narrative. Ricoeur distinguishes between exile as a symbol of alienation and the myth of the expulsion from Paradise (*Symbolism of Evil,* p. 18). The efficacious bond formed by narrative is the basis of what Eliade calls the "ontological obsession" of myth (*Sacred and the Profane,* pp. 94–95).

25. "The Old Testament," says Bultmann, "never speculates about the purpose (telos) of creation, or inquires into the rational intelligibility of the universe.... The very fact that the world is not susceptible to rational understanding makes it an object of awe as the handiwork of God" (*Primitive Christianity in Its Contemporary Setting,* trans. R. H. Fuller, Cleveland, 1956, pp. 17–18). Perhaps the lack of paradigms is at the root of the de-

mythologizing tendencies scholars have noted in the Old Testament. The lack of coherence stems from an attenuation of the principle of concrescence; as Peter L. Berger points out, "God demanded sacrifice, but he was not dependent upon it. And, consequently, he was fundamentally immune to magical manipulation" (*The Sacred Canopy,* New York, 1967, pp. 116–117).

26. References from *The Confessions of Saint Augustine,* trans. Edward B. Pusey (New York, 1961).

27. Bronislaw Malinowski, *Magic, Science, and Religion* (New York, 1954), p. 100; The mythic narrative "is the bridge between the golden age of primeval craft and the wonder-working power of today. Hence the formulas are full of mythical allusions, which, when uttered, unchain the powers of the past and cast them into the present" (p. 83).

28. Myth is not perceived as being such until "exposed" as "untrue" (n. 17 above). Ricoeur makes the valuable distinction that "criticism of the pseudo-rational is fatal not to myth, but to gnosis. It is in gnosis that the simulacrum of reason attains realization. . . . as the word itself makes clear, gnosis tries to be 'knowledge' " (*Symbolism of Evil,* p. 164). On Plato and myth, see Ernst Cassirer, *The Myth of the State* (New Haven, 1946), pp. 69–77.

29. Mythopoesis in formal literature, asserts Harry Slochower, implies the dissent of the hero from his culture; his quest expresses "the never-ending need of the dissident hero to galvanize his state towards reshaping its tradition" (*Mythopoesis: Mythic Patterns in the Literary Classics,* Detroit, 1970, p. 25). As mentioned, artistic irony is not a concern of this study.

30. *Drömmen om Sagatiden,* 2 vols. (Stockholm, 1969, 1970).

CHAPTER 2

1. The story is in Eliade, *Patterns in Comparative Religion,* trans. R. Sheed (Cleveland, 1963), p. 394.

2. Paul Ricoeur, "Structure et herméneutique," *Esprit,* 31 (1963), 596–627.

3. Iceland was Christianized in 1000, and the events of the "saga-era" took place from ca. 930 to 1030; the sagas were written down in the thirteenth century. Hence the reliability of the sagas has been a matter of heated debate. For a useful discussion of the reliability of source material, see E. O. G. Turville-Petre, *Myth and Religion of the North* (New York, 1964), pp. 1–34.

4. *Heimskringla,* trans. Lee M. Hollander (Austin, Texas, 1964), p. 374. In these sagas the pagan gods are acknowledged as real, but asserted to be demons, lesser forms of divinity. See, for instance, *Kristni saga,* chap. 9. The Christian God was referred to increasingly in terms of light, the terror of

demons and trolls. This was formalized in the Gulathings Law: "We shall bow to the East (where the sun rises) and pray to the holy Christ" (*Norges gamle love*, Christiania, 1846, 1:3).

5. The translation cited is by H. A. Bellows, *The Poetic Edda* (New York, 1957). The standard edition is by Sigurðr Nordal, *Völuspá* (Reykjavík, 1923).

6. Kees W. Bolle, *The Freedom of Man in Myth* (Nashville, 1968), p. 61.

7. This power manifests itself in the individual or the family as *hamingja*, *gæfa* (*gipta*), terms usually translated as "luck." See Folke Ström, *Nordisk hedendom* (Göteborg, 1961), pp. 70–75.

8. Ström's contention is that this power bond, originally thought to be connected to the gods and creation—a temporal bond—gradually became divorced from mythology and was seen as being latent in the individual, a power to control (*hamingja*). It is still a mythically based principle of causality (Ström, p. 68).

9. In Snorri's *Prose Edda* Ymir is described as evil (*illr*), as are his kindred. They were slain by Odin and his two brothers, and from Ymir's body the gods "made of him the earth: of his blood the sea and the waters; the land was made of his flesh, and the crags of his bones. . . . They took his skull also, and made of it the heaven" (*The Prose Edda*, trans. A. G. Brodeur, New York, 1929, p. 20); Odin's mother is said to have been a giant (*Prose Edda*, p. 19).

10. This sense of inexorable decay is objectified in the world-tree Yggdrasil, whose roots and branches extend through all creation. Yet its trunk is rotting, and serpents are gnawing at its roots.

11. Einar Haugen finds the theory of Lévi-Strauss that myth incorporates ("neutralizes") opposites particularly applicable to Norse mythology. See "The Mythical Structure of the Ancient Scandinavians," originally in *To Honour Roman Jakobson* (The Hague, 1956), reprinted in *Introduction to Structuralism*, ed. Michael Lane (New York, 1970), pp. 170–183.

12. The strong element of fate in the sagas is obvious, but Peter Hallberg points out that the sagas are less concerned with fate per se than with the characters' reactions to it. See *The Icelandic Saga*, trans. Paul Schach (Lincoln, Neb., 1962), p. 96.

13. M. I. Steblin-Kamenskij, *The Saga Mind*, trans. Kenneth H. Ober (Odense, 1973), pp. 24–25. Although the thesis of *The Saga Mind* is congenial to the present argument—that the key to discussing saga-realism lies in a view of reality which is not ours—the author's terminology is somewhat confusing. See the review article "The Syncretic Saga Mind" by Peter Hallberg in *Mediaeval Scandinavia*, 7 (1974), 102–117.

14. Translation from *Njál's Saga*, trans. Magnus Magnusson and Hermann Pálsson (Baltimore, 1960), pp. 109–110.

15. It is not a "soul" but a mythic object: "Sie ist nicht einfach Bild, sondern das geistige Wesen an sich" (Jan de Vries, *Altgermanische Religionsgeschichte,* 2nd ed., Berlin, 1957, 1:228). The words for types of tutelary spirits developed metaphoric connotations similar to "luck, fortune" ("your *fylgjur* lie in Iceland"), but these qualities were still a part of the person and could be lent or transferred (see Turville-Petre, *Myth and Religion of the North,* p. 230).

16. See Alexander Jóhannesson, *Isländisches etymologisches Wörterbuch* (Bern, 1956), p. 558, and Turville-Petre, *Myth and Religion of the North,* p. 228.

17. Turville-Petre, pp. 269–273. Thus the continuity in the family was a physical one, for what Cassirer calls the "solidarity and unbroken unity of life" characteristic of myth's principle of concrescence means the living and the dead "form a unique and uninterrupted chain" (*Essay on Man,* New Haven, 1944, p. 83); see also de Vries, *Religionsgeschichte,* 1:197: "Die Sippe umschliesst also Tote und Lebende in einer unverbrüchlichen Gemeinschaft. Ihre Glieder sind wesensverbunden."

18. Emil Birkeli, *Fedrekult i Norge,* Skrifter utgitt av det Norske Vitenskaps-Akademi i Oslo, II. Hist. Filos. Klasse, no. 5 (Oslo, 1938), goes into great detail concerning social relationships with the dead; the persistent identification of these rites as "heathen" leads Knut Rygnestad to interpret these encounters as social—unusual, but necessarily explicitly sacred—rather than religious. See *Varsel og gravferdsskikkar,* Det Konglige Norske Vitenskabers Selskabs Skrifter, no. 6 (Trondheim, 1964), pp. 9–18, and Reidar Th. Christiansen, *The Dead and the Living* (Oslo, 1946), pp. 27, 45–46.

19. Christiansen, pp. 7–8, n. 4.

20. Turville-Petre, pp. 269–273, and H. R. Ellis, *The Road to Hel* (Cambridge, 1943), pp. 198–199.

21. C. F. Bayerschmidt, "The Supernatural in the Sagas of the Icelanders," in *Scandinavian Studies: Essays Presented to Dr. Henry Goddard Leach,* ed. C. F. Bayerschmidt and Erik J. Friis (Seattle, 1965), p. 53. While the mythically constituted supernatural is accepted as part of reality, the characters find Christian miracles fantastic (Steblin-Kamenskij, *The Saga Mind,* p. 122).

22. See W. Henzen, *Über die Träume in der altnordischen Literatur* (Leipzig, 1890), and E. O. G. Turville-Petre, "Dream Symbols in Old Icelandic Literature," in *Festschrift W. Baetke* (Weimar, 1966), pp. 334–354. Cassirer observes that "mythical thinking makes no clearer distinction between life and death than between sleeping and waking. The two are related not as being and nonbeing, but as two similar, homogeneous parts of the same being" (*Philosophy of Symbolic Forms,* trans. Ralph Manheim, New Haven, 1955, 2: *Mythical Thought,* 36–37).

23. Cassirer, *Symbolic Forms,* 2:110–111.

24. To Steblin-Kamenskij, genealogies "are not form, but content," expressing the organic character of time in the "syncretic truth" of the sagas (*Saga Mind,* p. 65). Certainly the authors of the sagas considered the relationship of a character to his past important; see the genealogies mentioned by Ellis in *The Road to Hel,* p. 142, and Keil, *Altisländische Namenwahl,* Palaestra 176 (Leipzig, 1931).

25. Richard F. Allen, *Fire and Iron: Critical Approaches to Njáls Saga* (Pittsburgh, 1971), pp. 76–94.

26. Ólafur Lárusson, "Islands forfatning og lover i Fristatstiden," in *Lov og ting,* trans. Knut Helle (Oslo, 1960), pp. 34–42.

27. Einar Ól. Sveinsson cites Nicholas of Cusa's descriptions of the world as a "coincidentia oppositorum" in emphasizing the fusing of elements in *Njála;* the author "manages to give the whole heterogeneous subject continuity" (*Njåls Saga: Kunstverket,* trans. L. Holm-Olsen, Oslo, 1959, p. 39).

28. Just as the characters find the past tightly knit to their world, the implied narrator of the saga also establishes a continuity to his present, often through the place of crucial action: "Thord wakes up with this, and seeks to avenge his brother, but Thorgrim runs the spear through him as well. The place is now called Davredal and Norwegians' Fall. Then Thorgrim goes home and fame comes from the affair" (*Gísla Saga,* chap. 7).

29. Developed in detail by Karl Lehmann and Hans von Carolsfeld, *Die Njalssage insbesondere in ihren juristischen Bestandtheilen* (Berlin, 1883).

30. This is more evident in the less displaced narratives, where the legendary heroes are announced as part god and part man (Sigurðr is an example, but Haugen's description of the hero in Lévi-Strauss's terms as a "neutralization" of the world of *vættir* and the world of *menn* applies to whatever degree of displacement: "The hero was the essence of the potency implied in the word *man* itself, borrowing from the visible as well as the invisible world" ("The Mythical Structure of the Ancient Scandinavians," pp. 180–181).

31. Following Dumézil, Haugen suggests the structural importance of the world-tree Yggdrasil, "for ever both living and dying." It objectifies and embodies the opposition of "the living" (*kvikvendi*) and "the dead" (*dautt*) (pp. 178, 182).

32. Paul Ricoeur, *The Symbolism of Evil,* trans. Emerson Buchanan (Boston, 1967), p. 226.

CHAPTER 3

1. Paul Tillich, "The Religious Symbol," in *Symbolism in Religion and Literature,* ed. Rollo May (New York, 1960), p. 87.

2. Nicholas Berdyaev, *The Meaning of History,* trans. George Reavey

(Cleveland, 1962), p. 182. As a term, *secularization* has undergone the same dilution of content as has *myth;* at least *displacement* conveys an attenuation from myth rather than a movement toward the profane. See Peter L. Berger, *The Sacred Canopy: Elements of a Sociological Theory of Religion* (New York, 1967), pp. 106–107.

3. Ernst Cassirer, *The Philosophy of Symbolic Forms*, trans. Ralph Manheim (New Haven, 1955), 3: *The Phenomenology of Knowledge*, 164.

4. Cassirer, *Symbolic Forms*, 3:165. See W. Nestle, *Vom Mythos zum Logos*, 2nd ed. (Stuttgart, 1942), and Gilles Quispel, "From Mythos to Logos" in *Eranos Jahrbuch*, 39: *Man and Speech* (Leiden, 1973), pp. 323–340.

5. The dualism of Gnosticism, where the negative, chaotic forces of the world are juxtaposed to the good, orderly (but removed) nature of the Creator, may be seen as a transitional form of displacement. See Hans Jonas, *Gnosis und spätantiker Geist* (Göttingen, 1954), shortened in English as *The Gnostic Religion*, 2nd ed. (Boston, 1963), and Berger, *Sacred Canopy*, pp. 71–72. In this context we may understand Ricoeur's point that "criticism of the pseudo-rational is fatal not to myth, but to gnosis. It is in gnosis that the simulacrum of reason attains realization" (*The Symbolism of Evil*, trans. Emerson Buchanan, Boston, 1967, p. 164).

6. In the Greek world view, Bultmann observes, man "is able to solve the riddle of his own being in discovering the rationality of the universe at large." See *Primitive Christianity in its Contemporary Setting*, trans. R. H. Fuller (Cleveland, 1956), p. 129.

7. See the discussion by Henri-Charles Peuch, "La gnose et le temps," in *Eranos Jahrbuch*, 20: *Mensch und Zeit* (Zurich, 1952), pp. 60–67.

8. Walter Baetke, "Die Aufnahme des Christentums durch die Germanen," in his *Vom Geist und Erbe Thules* (Göttingen, 1944), pp. 96–97, sees the theology of the conversion as stemming from Augustine.

9. "If then, Socrates, amid the many opinions about the gods and the generation of the universe, we are not able to give notions which are altogether and in every respect exact and consistent with one another, do not be surprised. Enough if we adduce probabilities as likely as any others; for we must remember that I who am the speaker and you who are the judges are only mortal men, and we ought to accept the tale which is probable and inquire no further" (*Timaeus*, trans. Jowett, New York, 1949, p. 29). The urgency of undisplaced myth is gone. See Peuch, "La gnose," pp. 64–67.

10. Bultmann, *Primitive Christianity*, p. 17; see also Mircea Eliade, *Cosmos and History*, trans. Willard R. Trask (New York, 1959) p. 105.

11. Bultmann, *Primitive Christianity*, p. 32.

12. On the *Crede ut intelligas* topos, see Raymond Panikkar, "La foi di-

mension constitutive de l'homme," in *Mythe et foi,* ed. Enrico Castelli (Paris, 1966), pp. 17–19. This was a common objection to early Christianity by Hellenic pagans; see A. D. Nock, *Conversion* (Oxford, 1933), p. 232.

13. Berger suggests that "secularization" is latent in the positing of a "radically transcendent" Deity. See "Sacred Canopy," pp. 115–120, and Geo Widengren, "Mythe et foi à la lumière de la phénoménologie religieuse," in *Mythe et foi,* pp. 318–320.

14. "Religious symbols represent the transcendent but do not make the transcendent immanent. They do not make God a part of the empirical world" (Tillich, "The Religious Symbol," p. 77).

15. Peuch, "La Gnose," p. 71, Berdyaev, *Meaning of History,* pp. 33–35, and Charles Norris Cochrane, *Christianity and Classical Culture* (New York, 1957), pp. 237–245, where the author outlines the bases for "the Christian theory of progress."

16. Henri-Charles Peuch, "Temps, histoire et mythe dans le christianisme des premiers siècles," in *Proceedings of the VIIth Congress for the History of Religion* (Amsterdam, 1951).

17. The date of the actual promulgation of the Creed has become a matter of debate, but the decision for "substance" rather than "essence" stemmed from the "amateurish theology" of Constantine. See Hans Lietzmann, *A History of the Early Church* trans. Bertram Lee Woolf (Cleveland, 1961), 3: *From Constantine to Julian,* 116–120; for subsequent debate, pp. 219–233.

18. Bultmann, *Primitive Christianity,* p. 187.

19. "Figura," in *Scenes from the Drama of European Literature* (New York, 1959), p. 53.

20. "Die Civitas Dei bleibt ein *Eschaton,* ein Ziel des kosmischen, geschichtlichen und individuellen Prozesses, aber es ist doch *ewiges* Leben." Gilles Quispel, "Zeit und Geschichte im antiken Christentum," in *Eranos Jahrbuch,* 20: *Mensch und Zeit,* p. 131. On figural history in Augustine, see Auerbach, "Figura," pp. 38–43.

21. *The Meaning of History,* p. 183.

22. Ibid.

23. In Gregory of Tours, *History of the Franks,* ed. O. M. Dalton (Oxford, 1927), 2:68–69. William A. Chaney, *The Cult of Kingship in Anglo-Saxon England* (Berkeley, 1970), emphasizes the sacral role of the king and its importance in conversion (pp. 156–173).

24. Baetke, "Die Aufnahme des Christentums durch die Germanen," pp. 96–97, 106–107.

25. As indicated above, diabolization is a characteristic of the religious consciousness as it breaks away from its roots in myth: in the conversion, the converts were asked "Forsachistu diabolae?" to which they replied "ec for-

sacho diabolae." Then, "end allum diobol gelde?" followed by "end allu dioboles uuercum?" with the convert renouncing as devils "uuoden ende thunaer ende Faxnote ende allem them unholdun" in the name of the Trinity. For this and other formulas, see Massmann, *Die deutschen Abschwörungs-, Glaubens-, Beicht- und Betformeln vom achten bis zum zwölften Jahrhundert* (Leipzig, 1839), p. 68.

26. A. Chr. Bang, *Den norske Kirkes historie* (Christiania, 1912), p. 72. Since conversions often proceeded from the ruler on down, the lack of observance of the conditions was a "sin" against both Church and state, fines being paid half to Christ and half to the King. See A. Taranger, *Den angelsaksiske Kirkes inflydelse paa den norske* (Christiania, 1890), p. 298.

27. See Jan de Vries, *Altgermanische Religionsgeschichte,* 2nd ed. (Berlin, 1956), 1:177–178. Baptism appeared to be a transference of power in a very real sense; in *Die Bekehrung des norwegischen Stammes zum Christenthume* (Munich, 1856), 2:279, Konrad Maurer notes six instances reported where the baptizer is alleged to have used his power to kill a backslider. See also Thomas B. Willson, *History of the Church and State in Norway* (Westminster, 1903), p. 68.

28. See Maurer, *Bekehrung,* 1:213ff. for other instances.

29. *Íslendinga sögur,* ed. Guðni Jónsson (Reykjavík, 1946), III, 353. See de Vries, *Religionsgeschichte,* 2:436.

30. The change in social customs (*siðr*) was directly connected to the decline in the forms of the pagan religion: "Für den heidnischen Germanen war mit dem Untergang des *siðr* doch auch wohl das Wesentliche seines Glaubens verloren gegangen" (de Vries, *Religionsgeschichte,* 2:444). See W. Baetke, "Die Isländersagas als Quellen der Bekehrungsgeschichte," in *Vom Geist und Erbe Thules,* pp. 78–79.

31. *Ólafs Saga Tryggvasonar,* ccxxi, in *Flateyjarbók* (Christiania, 1869), I, 267.

32. *Saga of Hákon the Good,* chap. 15, in *Heimskringla,* trans. Lee M. Hollander (Austin, 1964), p. 109.

33. *Diplomatarium Norvegicum* (Christiania, 1852–55), 1:979; 2:694, 910, 1048; 3:273. In Norway the term *heidninghaug* was used until relatively recently. See Emil Birkeli, *Fedrekult i Norge,* Skrifter utgitt av det Norske Vitenskaps-Akademi i Oslo, II. Hist. Filos. Klasse, no. 5 (Oslo, 1938), p. 166. In the Elder Gulathings Law, the giving of things to the dead is considered the equivalent of sacrificing to the gods: "Blot er oss oc kviðiat at vér scolum eigi blota heiðit guð. ne hauga. ne horga." See *Norges gamle love* (Christiania, 1846), 1:18 (hereafter cited as *NgL*). On the "trolls": Páll Jónsson Vídalin, *Skýringar* (Reykjavík, 1854), p. 227. This was evidently connected with the practice of obtaining wisdom from the dead (see de Vries, *Religionsgeschichte,* 1:328–330).

34. Borgarthings Kristenrett (*NgL*, 1:362); Gulath. I (*NgL*, 1:18); Sverres Kristenrett I (*NgL*, 1:430); Frosathingslov I (*NgL*, 1:182); Landsloven 4, (*NgL*, 2:51); Jónsbók, Mannhelgeboken 2 (*NgL*, 4:208); Gulath. Kristenrett Anh. (*NgL*, 2:326); Nyere Gulath. Kristenrett (*NgL*, 3:308).

35. *Den norske Kirkes historie*, p. 77.

36. Berkeli, *Fedrekult*, pp. 69–73, cites passages from the laws illustrating this.

37. *NgL*, 1:14. See Birkeli, *Fedrekult*, pp. 70–74.

38. *NgL*, 1:135. Also *NgL*, 1:13–14: "A body is not to remain indoors over five days without mitigating circumstances." Penalties for violations of this were severe. A similar strategy was employed in England. See Chaney, *Cult of Kingship*, pp. 101–104.

39. *Monumenta Germaniae Historica*, Epist. Tomus 3 (Berlin, 1892), 271–272. Translation in Ephraim Emerton, *The Letters of Saint Boniface* (New York, 1940), pp. 48–49.

40. K. Müllenhof and W. Scherer, *Denkmäler deutscher Poesie und Prosa* (Berlin, 1892), 1:1–2.

41. Gustav Ehrismann, *Geschichte der deutschen Literatur bis zum Ausgang des Mittelalters*, 2nd ed. (Munich, 1959), 1:145.

42. Richard Henzel, *Kleine Schriften* (Heidelberg, 1907), p. 10, and Erich Auerbach, *Mimesis*, trans. Willard R. Trask (Princeton, 1953), pp. 101–102. In the *Chanson de Roland*, for example, the protagonist is actually the Christian religion, for although the lives of the pagan knights do not differ greatly from those of the Christians, "paien unt tort et chrestiens unt dreit." More on the attempt to synthesize paganism and Christianity in Robert Levine, "Ingeld and Christ: A Medieval Problem," *Viator*, 2 (Berkeley, 1971), 105–128.

43. Text in *Deutsche National-Literatur*, ed. J. Kürschner (Berlin, 1885), 1:258–261.

44. See Lars Lönnroth, "The Noble Heathen: A Theme in the Sagas," *Scandinavian Studies*, 41 (1969), 1–29.

45. Lönnroth, "The Noble Heathen," p. 16.

46. See E. O. G. Turville-Petre, "Godless Men" in *Myth and Religion of the North* (London, 1964), pp. 263–268, and Folke Ström, *Den egna kraftens män*, Göteborgs Högskolas Årsskrift, 54 (Göteborg, 1948), no. 2.

47. Peter Berger and Thomas Luckmann, *The Social Construction of Reality* (New York, 1966), p. 100.

48. *Bonifatii epist.* 37, in *Bibliotheca rerum Germanicarum*, ed. Jaffé, 3, Monumenta Moguntina (Berlin, 1866), 104. In the first German synod (742) "God's people" are warned to "cast away the contamination of heathendom" by "foregoing offerings to the dead" (Hefele, *Conciliengeschichte*, III Freiburg, 1877, 510), but the problem appears to have continued (Birkeli, *Fedrekult*, pp. 20, 68–69), as did other manifestations of syncretism: Helge

the Lean, described as "blandinn i trú," prayed to Christ except when at sea and in difficult situations, when he called upon Thor; some kings on the Continent and in England, just to be safe, built altars both to God and to "demons" (Gregory of Tours, *Hist. Francorum,* 5:43; Bede, *Hist. Eccl. gentis Angl.,* 2:15; see de Vries, *Religionsgeschichte,* 2:429–430).

49. From the Synod of Liftinse (743 or 745); the problem was taken up again in the Council of Frankfurt (794), which discusses "de sacrificio, quod aliqui sanctorum" (Hefele, *Conciliengeschichte,* 3:510, 507). See Baetke, "Stufen und Typen in der Germanenbekehrung," in *Vom Geist und Erbe Thules,* pp. 131–133.

50. Reidar Th. Christiansen, *The Dead and the Living* (Oslo, 1946), p. 36 and elsewhere mentions survivals of these customs.

51. Christiansen, *Dead and Living,* p. 10. He mentions a story from Telemark, in which a dead brother returns on Christmas Eve and says "Bære va de på Kvålsodd vera / å sita mæ duka bor, / hell liggje i Heruvdalen / uti den svarte jor. . . . / De æ vondt å vera i Heruvdalen / gange der i den kalle vind" (in Berge, *Norskt bondeliv* (Risør, 1925), p. 1). See also Haakon Shetelig, "Folketro om gravhauger," *Maal og minne,* festskrift til H. F. Feilberg (1911), pp. 206–212.

52. Cited in Shetelig, "Folketro," p. 211. For more on survivals, see Bente Gullveig Alver, "Conceptions of the Living Human Soul in the Norwegian Tradition," *Temenos,* 7 (1971), 23–26, on the *fylgja,* and Hans-Egil Hauge, *Levande begravd eller bränd i nordisk folkmedicin,* Stockholm Studies in Comparative Religion (Stockholm, 1965), pp. 96–104, on the creation of a guardian of a place through burying an animal or person alive (English summary, pp. 133–134). On survivals in Sweden of customs regarding the dead, see Louise Hagberg, *När döden gästar* (Stockholm, 1937).

CHAPTER 4

1. A transitional stage in the development from an animistic cosmology to one governed by rational necessity—"astrobiology"— has been discussed by George Gusdorf, *Mythe et metaphysique* (Paris, 1953), pp. 106–112, and René Berthelot, *La pensée de l'Asie et l'astrobiologie* (Payot, 1949). A similar transition occurs in the development of the "new physics" in the sixteenth century when it was suggested that the retrograde motion of the planets evidenced their possessing free will.

2. In the Middle Ages, the data of science were not marginal experiences, in that empirical phenomena were classified, not measured, and understood as

symbols of a universe both animistic and rational in constitution. Even before the time of Galileo, there had been considerable precedent for accepting innovation into the myth world of the Church. See Alfred North Whitehead, *Science and the Modern World* (New York, 1925), p. 33; E. A. Burtt, *The Metaphysical Foundations of Modern Science* (Garden City, 1954), p. 16; A. C. Crombie, *Medieval and Early Modern Science* (Garden City, 1959), 2:106–119, and I. Bernard Cohen, *The Birth of a New Physics* (Garden City, 1960), pp. 108–111.

3. The thirty-four epicycles of the Copernican system (required by the mythic assumption that celestial motion was of necessity circular) were scarcely superior in the sense of being more simple to the forty epicycles of the refined Ptolemaic astronomy. See Burtt, *Foundations,* pp. 36–38, and Cecil J. Schneer, *The Evolution of Physical Science* (New York, 1960), pp. 46–52.

4. Frederick C. Copleston, *A History of Philosophy* (Garden City, 1963), 3: *Late Medieval and Renaissance Philosophy,* 93–94. For the text of the preface, *Three Copernican Treatises,* ed. Edward Rosen, 3rd ed. (New York, 1971), pp. 22–26.

5. In Galileo's "Letter to the Grand Duchess Christina," he reverses the primacy of reason versus revelation and enjoins "wise expositors" to seek out the "true senses of scriptural texts." This form of demythologizing "will unquestionably accord with the physical conclusions which manifest sense and necessary demonstrations have previously made certain to us."

6. *The Metamorphoses of the Circle,* trans. Carley Dawson and Elliott Coleman (Baltimore, 1966).

7. *Il saggiatore,* p. vi. See Copleston, p. 98.

8. Particularly true of Giordano Bruno. See Ernst Cassirer, *The Philosophy of the Enlightenment,* trans. F. Koelln and J. Pettegrove (Boston, 1955), pp. 40–41.

9. Norman Cohn, *The Pursuit of the Millennium: Revolutionary Messianism in Medieval and Reformation Europe and Its Bearing on Modern Totalitarian Movements,* 2nd ed. (New York, 1961), pp. 274–275. On chiliastic myths in Sweden at the beginning of the Great Power Era, see Henrik Sandblad, *De eskatologiska föreställningarna i Sverige under Reformation och Motreformation,* Lychnos-bibliotek, no. 5 (Uppsala, 1942).

10. Karl Mannheim, *Ideology and Utopia,* trans. Louis Wirth and Edward Shils (New York, 1936), p. 215. Mannheim sees Bakunin as being the closest inheritor to Thomas Münzer in seeing destruction as creative, but a closer parallel would be radical assaults on liberal institutions, particularly in view of Mannheim's distinction between the chiliastic atemporal ecstasy and the liberal apprehension of time as process (*Ideology and Utopia,* pp. 225–226).

11. If one defines "utopia," with Mannheim, as "that type of orientation which transcends reality and which at the same time breaks the bonds of the existing order" (*Ideology*, p. 192).

12. What Frank L. Borchardt calls "creative speculation" in his *German Antiquity in Renaissance Myth* (Baltimore, 1971), p. 10, was not seen as being that, but as scholarship. The Italian Renaissance, too, had its myths of origins, but what distinguishes these northern myths is the paucity of data supporting them.

13. *Ideology and Utopia*, p. 212.

14. Borchardt, *German Antiquity*, p. 303.

15. Josef Haslag, *"Gothic" im siebzehnten und achtzehnten Jahrhundert* (Cologne, 1963), pp. 37–43.

16. E. R. Curtius, *European Literature and the Latin Middle Ages*, trans. W. R. Trask (New York, 1953), pp. 28–30.

17. See J. Svennung, *Zur Geschichte des Goticismus*, Skrifter utgivna av K. Humanistiska Vetenskapssamfundet i Uppsala, 44, no. 2B (Uppsala, 1967), 13. Johannes Naucler, in his *Chronicon* (1516) states that the Germans, "due to their virtue and their efforts in the service of God, of the Church and the Senate and people of Rome, have been judged fit to rule the world" (p. 689).

18. See Richard Kuehnemund, *Arminius or the Rise of a National Symbol in Literature*, University of North Carolina Studies in the Germanic Languages and Literatures, vol. 8 (Chapel Hill, 1953).

19. Citations from *Tacitus on Britain and Germany*, trans. H. Mattingly (Baltimore, 1948). On the role of Tacitus, see the basic study by Paul Joachimsen, "Tacitus im deutschen Humanismus," *Neue Jahrbücher für das klassische Altertum*, 14 (1911), 695–717, and Hans Tiedemann, *Tacitus und das Nationalbewusstsein der deutschen Humanisten am Ende des 15. und Anfang des 16. Jahrhunderts* (Berlin, 1913).

20. On Erasmus, see Wallace Ferguson, *The Renaissance in Historical Thought* (Cambridge, 1948), p. 48.

21. *Characteristicks of Men, Manners, Opinions, Times* (London, 1727), 1:221–222.

22. R. G. Collingwood describes Tacitus' characterizations as "spectacles of virtue or vice" in *The Idea of History* (Oxford, 1946), p. 39. Lars Gustafsson, *Virtus politica*, Lychnos-Bibliotek, no. 15 (Uppsala, 1956), p. 231, notes that "for the Humanists, the concept of excellence and nobility was intimately connected with an ethical idealism, and their picture of their ancestors as virtue's warriors and the just punishers of Rome easily lent itself to an exaltation of their own nation's nobility."

23. Paul Joachimsen, *Geschichtsauffassung und Geschichtschreibung in Deutschland unter dem Einfluss des Humanismus*, Beiträge zur Kultruge-

schichte des Mittelalters und der Renaissance, 6, no. 1 (Leipzig, 1910), 157.

24. Joachimsen, *Geschichtsauffassung,* pp. 155–195; Friedrich Gotthelf, *Das deutsche Altertum in den Anschauungen des sechzehnten und siebzehnten Jahrhunderts,* Forschungen zur neueren Literaturgeschichte, ed. Muncker, 13 (Berlin, 1900), 1–47; 39–43 on Cluverius.

25. "Oratio in gymnasio in Ingelstadio publice recitata," in *Selections from Conrad Celtis,* ed. Leonard Forster (Cambridge, Eng., 1948), p. 47. Celtis is aware, however, that this *furor teutonicus* was cultural barbarism and suggests that the "ancient spirit" be revived by (somehow) synthesizing the indomitable strength with cultivation of classical learning. As will be shown, this dual view of the Nordic past was characteristic of the various myths. Celtis attempted to resolve the duality by discovering that even if it is implausible that the Germans originally spoke Greek, they knew Hellenic culture through refugee Druids (see Joachimsen, *Geschichtsauffassung,* pp. 111, 249).

26. *Epitoma germanicarum rerum,* Historicum opus, ed. S. Schardius (Basel, 1574), 1:398f. See Gustafsson, *Virtus politica,* p. 231.

27. *Germaniae exegeseos volumina XII* (1518), Book II: *Mores Germanorum.* See Svennung, *Goticismus,* p. 60, and Joachimsen, *Geschichtsauffassung,* pp. 169–181. Further, Borchardt, *German Antiquity,* pp. 144–148.

28. Borchardt, *German Antiquity,* pp. 89–91, and H. Dannenbauer, *Germanisches Altertum und deutsche Geschichtswissenschaft* (Tübingen, 1935).

29. An extreme (though symptomatic) illustration of this is Johannes Goropius Becanus, who applied the assumption that the first language must have been the most perfect to the German language, arguing that since German *is* the most perfect, it (or its ancestor) must have been the language of Adam; the "Cimbrians" were not present at the Tower of Babel. See R. F. Jones, *The Triumph of the English Language* (Stanford, 1953), pp. 214–218. Borchardt brings out the connection between myth and what Curtius called "Etymology as a Category of Thought" in his "Etymology and Tradition in the Northern Renaissance," *Journal of the History of Ideas,* vol. 29 (1968), saying that "the new was bound to the old by ultimate faith in the power of etymology. The obvious popularity of etymologizing in the Renaissance would be complete nonsense if the etymologers and their audience did not believe that the origin of the word revealed its power" (p. 429).

30. Borchardt, "Etymology and Tradition," 429, shows this true of Renaissance thought.

31. England's Classical (Trojan) origin had been disproved by Polydore Vergil (Jones, *Triumph,* p. 234).

32. Verstegen (*Restitution,* 1605) ties into the freedom myth by using the Saxons. On English liberty as social myth, see E. M. W. Tillyard, *Some Mythical Elements in English Literature* (London, 1961), pp. 108–138.

33. According to Cluverius, "Tuisto" is a misprint in Tacitus; the original was "Tuitso," an adjectival form of the god "Teuto," the supposed founder of the Germanic tribes. Teuto was the same as Mercury, who was worshiped by the Egyptians as Theut; Theut and Teuto are the same as the Greek Theos and Latin Deus. Thus Tuisto was really the one, true God of the Bible (Gotthelf, *Das deutsche Altertum*, p. 41).

34. Joachimsen, "Tacitus," p. 716.

35. Lohenstein, *Grossmüthiger Feldherr Arminius oder Hermann . . .* , 2 vols. (Leipzig, 1689–90). A plot summary can be found in Bernhard Asmuth, *Lohenstein und Tacitus* (Stuttgart, 1971), pp. 164–166. A detailed elaboration of the didactic aspects is in Dieter Kafitz, *Lohensteins "Arminius": Disputatorisches Verfahren und Lehrgehalt in einem Roman zwischen Barock und Aufklärung* (Stuttgart, 1970).

36. On Lohenstein's techniques for this, see Wilhelm Vosskamp, "Die Transparenz der Geschichtserzählung im *Arminius*-Roman," in his *Zeit- und Geschichtsauffassung im 17. Jahrhundert bei Gryphius und Lohenstein* (Bonn, 1967), pp. 214–220.

37. See Gotthelf, *Das deutsche Altertum*, pp. 60–68, and Luise Laporte, *Lohensteins "Arminius"*, Germanische Studien, 48 (Berlin, 1927), 5–30.

38. Laporte, for instance (*Arminius*, p. 96).

39. As an illustration, although Lohenstein contrasts the noble simplicity of the primitive Germans to the "Wollüste und Laster" of the Romans (1:923), he describes the Germanic heroine Thusnelda going to bed in this language: "Nach der um Mitternacht aufgehobenen Taffel ward die Fürstin Thussnelde von hundert edlen Jungfrauen in das Hertzogliche Schlaff-Gemach geleitet; sie aber vorher unter allerhand zierlichen Täntzen ihres Krantzes beraubet, und hernach gleichsam in die Hände der Cattischen Hertzogin und anderer anwesenden Fürstinnen überliefert; darauff in ein von lauter Eysvogel-Federn gefülletes, mit Gold und Seiden herrlich aufgeputztes Bette begleitet; und endlich dem über seinem Liebes-Siege nichts weniger als über dem erschlagene Varus freudigen Hermann Raum gemacht, der allervollkommensten Früchte zu genüssen; welche iemahls die Tugend von so reiner Keuschheit und unvergleichlichen Liebes- und Gemüths- Schönheit eingeerndet hat" (1:1184–1185).

40. Laporte, *Arminius*, p. 25.

41. 1:346; it is suggested that this came from Zoroaster (2:537).

42. This sensationalized description also has an historical source, probably Adam of Bremen, *Gesta Hamburgensis Ecclesiae pontificum*, 4:26–27.

43. Gotthelf, *Das deutsche Altertum*, pp. 65–66. The enigmatic character of the Druids soon established them as integral parts of the Nordic past, in that virtually any sublime mystery or monstrous rite could be ascribed to them. See A. L. Owen, *The Famous Druids* (Oxford, 1962).

44. For a survey of editions and translations, see F. E. Farley, *Scandinavian Influences in the English Romantic Movement,* Studies and Notes in Philology and Literature, 9 (Boston, 1903), 1–28; also E. V. Gordon, *An Introduction to Old Norse,* 2nd ed. (Oxford, 1957), pp. lxviii–lxxvii.

45. By 1770 the barbaric nature of the Scandinavian past had become so well established that an essayist in the *London Magazine* assumes his readers know Bartholin, or know of him, and begins his article on the "Extraordinary Heroism of the antient Scandinavians" by saying "The antient Scandinavians breathed nothing but war" *London Magazine,* 39 (1770), 501.

46. On Ragnar's history in English literature, see Farley, *Scandinavian Influences,* pp. 59–76.

47. Farley, *Scandinavian Influences,* pp. 190–203, and Thor J. Beck, *Northern Antiquities in French Learning and Literature (1755–1855)* (New York, 1935), 2:5–18.

48. *Works* (London, 1770), 3:352.

49. The stanzas are, of course, the skull-drinking and *ridens moriar* verses. Partly through these citations by Temple, these two items were incorporated into the Continental myth of the Nordic past; see Paul Van Tieghem, *Le préromantisme* (Paris, 1924), pp. 105–107, and Thor J. Beck, "Ragnar Lodbrok's Swan Song in the French Romantic Movement," *The Romanic Review,* 22 (1931), 218–223. Some travelers to Scandinavia found the custom of drinking from skulls confirmed by the toast "Skål."

50. "Of Ancient and Modern Learning," *Works,* 3:450–451.

51. Histories of this remarkable phase of Swedish history are available in English in the works of Michael Roberts: *The Early Vasas* (Cambridge, 1968), and *Gustavus Adolphus,* 2 vols. (London, 1953). See also Charles Fletcher, *Gustavus Adolfus and the Thirty Years War* (New York, 1963).

52. On this, see Svennung, *Goticismus,* pp. 1–10.

53. Johan Nordström, "Gotisk historieromantik och Stormaktstidens anda," in *De Yverbornes Ö* (Stockholm, 1934), pp. 60–63; also Roberts, *The Early Vasas,* p. 153, and Beata Losman, "Nikolaus Ragvaldis gotiska tal," *Lychnos* (1967–68), pp. 215–221.

54. Nordström, *Yverbornes Ö,* p. 64. "The Goths," says Johannes Magnus, "had as little, yes, even less knowledge of immorality than the renowned Philosophers had of how artfully and wisely to dispute about virtue" (*Historia de omnibus Gothorum Sveonumque regibus,* Rome, 1554, pp. 91–92, in Nordström, *Yverbornes Ö,* p. 99).

55. *Historia,* pp. 6–7, in Nordström, *Yverbornes Ö,* pp. 99–100.

56. Gustafsson, *Virtus politica,* p. 219.

57. See Nordström's essay, "Lejonet från norden," in *Yverbornes Ö,* pp. 9–51, and Roberts, *Gustavus Adolphus,* 1:522–527.

58. Ethel Seaton, *Literary Relations of England and Scandinavia in the*

Seventeenth Century (Oxford, 1935), pp. 75–90. As Haslag points out, it was this identification of the Scandinavians and the Goths that made the social myth possible (*"Gothic"*, p. 11).

59. *Alaric ou Rome vaincuë: poème heroique* (Brussels and Paris, 1656), pp. 14, 340; see Gustafsson, *Virtus politica,* pp. 211–212. On character-as-allegory, see N. Edelman, *Attitudes of Seventeenth-Century France toward the Middle Ages* (New York, 1946), p. 203, and René Bray, *La formation de la doctrine classique en France* (Paris, 1963), pp. 82–83.

60. This is Gustafsson's thesis in *Virtus politica;* see particularly the chapter "Virtus Gothica," pp. 172–239.

61. Gustafsson, *Virtus politica,* pp. 174–184.

62. Seaton, *Literary Relations,* p. 311. Giles Fletcher, certain that his metaphor has an empirical basis, asks in "Christ's Triumph after Death" (1611), "And you, dead Swallows, that so lively now / Through the flit aire your winged passage rowe, / How could new life into your frozen ashes flowe?"

63. See Ellen Jørgensen, *Historieforskning og historieskrivning i Danmark indtil aar 1800,* 2nd ed. (Copenhagen, 1960), pp. 85–160.

64. Dedication to *Herrauds och Bosa Saga* (Uppsala, 1666). The criterion for editing, says Nordström, was to make public those sagas which could document the growing idea that Sweden was the home of the fabled Hyperboreans (*Yverbornes Ö,* pp. 131–132).

65. This began with Bureus and his speculations upon the runes. See *Yverbornes Ö,* pp. 102–103, 111–121.

66. Stiernhielm was convinced that the "Scythians" best preserved mankind's original language, and that Swedish was the nearest derivative from Magogian Scythian; other languages and cultures (such as the Greek) were etymologically and historically derived from the mother tongue and tribe (*Yverbornes Ö,* pp. 121–130).

67. *Atland eller Manheim* (Uppsala, 1679–1702). Reprinted in 4 vols., ed. Axel Nelson, Lychnos Bibliotek, no. 2 (Uppsala, 1937–1950). Page references will be to the 1679 edition, but the older pagination is marked in the 1937 edition. For Rudbeck's proof that Atlantis and Sweden are one, see vol. 1, chaps. 7–8, and vol. 2, chap. 1; on Homer's trip to Sweden, where he was punished for revealing the sacred mysteries, see 1, chap. 22, 559–560; on Troy being built by Swedes, vol. 1, chap. 36, with Homer ("who better than any other Greek or Latin or other foreign writer has come close to our own sagas and wisdom") used to document this, 1:793–809. When classical writers (Herodotus, for example) appear to contradict Rudbeck, he is tolerant: "How beautifully our wise old forefathers deluded the learned Greeks through their mysteries and Skalds, they who thought themselves to be wiser than all

the others. Here Herodotus does not understand our Skalds at all" (1, chap. 10, 435).

68. "Leibnitz' bref till Sparfvenfelt. Med anmärkningar utg. af H. Wieselgren," *Antiqvarisk tidskrift för Sverige,* 8, no. 3 (1883), 40.

69. *Göttingsche gelehrte Anzeigen,* 33 (Zugabe, 1771), lxvi.

70. "Cold sweat, dear brother! breaks out on my brow, when I see how often Greek and Roman historians have disguised the names of Nordic places and persons . . . for example: Troilus is nothing other than Troels or Truels, Paris is Per Iversen," Epistle 194 in Holberg's *Epistler,* ed. F. J. Billeskov Jansen (Copenhagen, 1947), 3:32, 34.

71. Victor Hermanson, "Holberg og arkæologien," *Holberg-blandninger* (Copenhagen, 1941), 2:46.

72. Swift used the same parodistic method to deflate Richard Bentley in his "Discourse to prove the Antiquity of the English Tongue," saying that by etymology "Isaac is nothing else but Eyes Ake; because the Talmudists report that he had a pain in his eyes"; Dalin also ridiculed this aspect of validating the myth, suggesting that Eve was a Swedish name, "Eva": when Adam awoke, his first reaction to her was "Hey! hva?". Lessing, not given to parody, wrote to Mendelsohn, "Ich schätze das Studium der Alterthümer gerade so viel, als es werth ist: ein Steckenpferd mehr, sich die Reise des Lebens zu verkürzen."

73. See Martin Lamm, *Olof Dalin* (Uppsala, 1908), pp. 347–356, 431, and Bengt Hildebrand, *C. J. Thomsen och hans lärda förbindelser i Sverige, 1816–1837,* Kungliga Vitterhets Historie och Antikvitets Akademis Handlingar, 41, no. 1 (Stockholm, 1937), 19.

74. Voltaire, *Ancient and Modern History,* in *Works,* trans. William Fleming (New York, 1901), 24:137.

75. *Svea rikes historia* (Stockholm, 1747), 1:129–130. On Dalin's importance to "Gothicism" in formal literature, see Martin Lamm, *Upplysningstidens romantik* (Stockholm, 1918), 1:260–263, and Greta Hedin, *Manhemsförbundet,* Göteborgs Högskolas Årsskrift, 34 (Göteborg, 1928), no. 1, 78–82, 105–108.

CHAPTER 5

1. *The Disinherited Mind* (New York, 1959), p. 264.

2. "The Archetypes of Literature," in *Fables of Identity* (New York, 1963), pp. 12–13.

3. J. B. Bury, *The Idea of Progress* (New York, 1932), sees the idea of progress as moral doctrine first emerging clearly in the "Quarrel of the Ancients and the Moderns" (p. 79).

4. The development of behavioral psychology and social science stems from this apprehension of the world as a complex of forces. When Kepler describes elliptical orbits by saying, "my goal is to show that the heavenly machine is not a kind of divine being but similar to a clockwork" (Max Caspar, *Kepler,* trans. C. Doris Hellman Pepper, New York, 1959, p. 136), he is seeking laws of physical behavior much as B. F. Skinner advocates seeking the laws of human behavior.

5. In his "Letter to the Grand Duchess Christina," Galileo reconciles the story of Joshua with Copernican astronomy, but it is religious truth that must be brought into line with reason, not vice versa.

6. Ernst Cassirer, *The Philosophy of the Enlightenment,* trans. F. Koelln and J. Pettegrove (Boston, 1955), pp. 42–43.

7. See Basil Willey, "The Heroic Poem in a Scientific Age," in *The Seventeenth-Century Background* (London, 1934), pp. 205–219; on Sprat, pp. 206–216.

8. *Critical Essays of the Seventeenth Century,* ed. J. E. Spingarn (Bloomington, 1963), 2:62.

9. *Essays of John Dryden,* ed. W. P. Ker (Oxford, 1900), 1:153, 185.

10. Epistle 162, in *Epistler,* ed. F. J. Billeskov Jansen (Copenhagen, 1945), 2:267.

11. *Oeuvres* (Paris, 1827), 3:68.

12. This theme involves the myth of the noble savage; see for instance the descriptions by Thomasius in *De praejudiciis.*

13. *Oeuvres,* 3:80–81.

14. The *Monuments* was translated by Bishop Percy as *Northern Antiquities* (London, 1770), and citations will be from this translation.

15. *Five Pieces of Runic Poetry* (London, 1763), [p. xii].

16. *Northern Antiquities,* vol. 1, chap. 5. The simple Scythian religion was first altered by southerners, because of their climate-formed lively imaginations; the Scythians had fewer passions. Odin, however, ranks with Mahomet as an imposter, says Mallet, and though he was initially worshiped as a god of war, the ignorant masses came to mistake him for the Creator, which Odin did not discourage.

17. On Mallet and his influence, see Paul Van Tieghem, "Mythologie et poésie scandinaves," in *Le préromantisme* (Paris, 1924), 1:109–130; Anton Blanck, *Den nordiska Renässansen* (Stockholm, 1911), pp. 40–61; Thor Beck, *Northern Antiquities in French Learning and Literature (1755–1855)* (New York, 1935).

18. Jean Seznec, *The Survival of the Pagan Gods,* trans. Barbara Sessions (New York, 1953), pp. 319–323.

19. Lars Gustafsson, "Det 'underbara' och sannolikhetskravet i 1700-talets litteraturestetik," *Samlaren,* 82 (1961), 112.

20. Leopold, *Samlade skrifter* (Uppsala, 1873), 2:10–11.

21. *Christen Prams udvalgte digteriske arbeider,* ed. Rahbek (Copenhagen, 1828), p. 5.

22. Lionel Gossman, "Time and History in Rousseau," in *Studies on Voltaire and the Eighteenth Century,* 30 (Geneva, 1964), 311–349.

23. In his essay *On the Origin of Languages,* trans. John Moran (New York, 1961), Rousseau says that "feelings speak before reason," but reason, "while having perfected grammar, deprive[s] language of its vital, passionate qualities which made it so singable" (pp. 51, 69).

24. "Dialogue on the Golden Age of Queen Elizabeth," in *Hurd's Letters on Chivalry and Romance* (London, 1911), p. 71.

25. Lois Whitney, "English Primitivistic Theories of Epic Origins," *Modern Philology,* 21 (1924), 375.

26. John Brown, for example, elaborated in 1763 upon the "natural" unity of artistic expression in the primitive, and saw the inroads of reflective thought and civilization as the cause of the lamentable deterioration of this once spontaneous union. Sir William Jones put this question in the context of a fall from primitive monotheism, and described the singing primitive as "pouring his praises to the creator." For other illustrations of the naive perception, see Whitney, "Primitivistic Theories," 337–378.

27. Möser, *Sämmtliche Werke* (Berlin, 1843), 9:208.

28. See Martin Lamm, *Upplysningstidens romantik* (Stockholm, 1918), 1:263.

29. Cf. Lamm, *Upplysningstidens romantik,* 1:260–261; this was Rousseau's "amour-propre."

30. Dalin, *Svea rikes historia* (Stockholm, 1747), 1:129–130.

31. *Svea rikes historia,* 1:131–134, 140. Thor's visit to Útgarða-loki is interpreted as the God of Love, tempted, outwardly humiliated by evil, but in the end triumphant.

32. The effective inspiration, however, seems to have been Rousseau (Lamm, *Upplysningstidens romantik,* 1:472–479).

33. This from Fischerström, who continues that Ragnar Lodbrok, "who sang with laughing mouth" is proof of the heroic ferocity (Lamm, *Upplysningstidens romantik,* 1:310–312).

34. Suhm was as well versed in his knowledge of the Nordic past as any historian in Europe, and, as Lundgreen-Nielsen points out, is constantly attempting to give his stories a "realistic" base; see Flemming Lundgreen-Nielsen, *Den nordiske fortælling i det 18. århundrede,* Studier fra Sprog- og Oldtidsforskning, no. 268 (Copenhagen, 1968), p. 44. It is just that Suhm is writing out of a social myth, where it was taken as fact that in the Nordic past "modesty was then scarcely a virtue, at least not an advantage, since all women were modest." This from his prize-winning "Sigrid; Or, Love the

Reward of Bravery," in *Samlade skrifter* (Copenhagen, 1789), 2:241.
Lundgreen-Nielsen remarks that Suhm's characterizations in his "Nordic
tales" all show the dual nature of the Nordic hero, in that there is a conflict
between the concept of heroism and the characters' psychology (*Den nordiske
fortælling*, pp. 24–25).

35. Since primitive song was assumed to be everywhere the same, the
documents of "chronological primitivism" and "cultural primitivism"—
created as part of social-literary myth—showed the same characteristics; see
René Wellek, *The Rise of English Literary History*, (Chapel Hill, 1941), pp.
131–132.

36. Francis Bull, *Fra Holberg til Nordal Brun* (Christiania, 1916), p. 192.

37. See the discussion of the freedom myth in Bull, *Holberg til Nordal
Brun*, pp. 189–199.

38. Martin Lamm, *Johan Gabriel Oxenstierna* (Stockholm, 1911), p. 354.

39. *Skördarne* (Stockholm, 1796), pp. 13, 68–69; see also Lamm,
Oxenstierna, pp. 356–357. Oxenstierna as narrator sees himself as a link
between the Viking ancestors ("As a descendant, Swedish and free, I belong
to you," p. 79) and the contemporary *odalbonde*, who is addressed both as
character and audience.

40. Poem in Geijer's *Samlade skrifter* (Stockholm, 1875), 1:211–213.

CHAPTER 6

1. "Den nordiske mythologie synes at ville blive mode," rev. of Joh.
Erichsen, *Observationum ad antiquitates septentrionales* in *Kritisk journal*
(1769), 343.

2. Bengt Algot Sørensen, *Symbol und Symbolismus in den ästhetischen
Theorien des 18. Jahrhunderts und der deutschen Romantik* (Copenhagen,
1963). p. 17.

3. Rousseau, for example, in his polemic with Rameau on music, pointed
out that harmony is not a universal condition which structures music but is a
product of an individual's training within a cultural tradition. See Lionel
Gossman, "Time and History in Rousseau," in *Studies on Voltaire and the
Eighteenth Century*, 30 (Geneva, 1964), 319–327.

4. See Frank E. Manuel, *The Eighteenth Century Confronts the Gods*
(Cambridge, Mass., 1959), p. 132.

5. Ralph Cudworth, for instance, in his *Intellectual System of the Universe*
[1678] (London, 1820), concludes that the "pagans did distinguish, and put a
difference, betwixt the one supreme unmade Deity, and all their other inferior
gods" (1:524).

6. Manuel, *Eighteenth Century*, pp. 168–183, particularly p. 177, and Jan

de Vries, *Forschungsgeschichte der Mythologie* (Munich, 1961), pp. 104–107.

7. Ernst Cassirer, *The Philosophy of the Enlightenment,* trans. F. Koelln and J. Pettegrove (Boston, 1955), pp. 93–94, 301–302.

8. *Oeuvres* (Paris, 1792), 3:247.

9. Ibid., 3:272, 311.

10. *On the Origin of Language,* trans. Alexander Gode (New York, 1966), p. 133.

11. Cassirer, *Enlightenment,* p. 233.

12. Schiller, *Werke,* ed. B. von Wiese (Weimar, 1962), 20:413–503. On Schiller's concept of the "naive," see Gunnar Hansson, "Schillers bestämning av det naiva i Ueber naive und sentimentalische Dichtung," *Samlaren,* 85 (1964), 143–191 (with summary in German).

13. Cassirer, *Enlightenment,* pp. 297–304; M. H. Abrams, *The Mirror and the Lamp* (New York, 1958) pp. 265–275; Northrop Frye, "Towards Defining an Age of Sensibility," in *Fables of Identity* (New York, 1963), pp. 130–137.

14. Cassirer, *Enlightenment,* pp. 313–319, emphasizes the nonmechanistic basis of Shaftesbury's doctrine of the spontaneity of artistic creation. On Platonism and the creative process, see Albert Nilsson, *Svensk romantik: Den platoniska strömningen* (Stockholm, 1924), chap. 1; On Dubos, see his *Réflexions critiques* (1732), ii, xii, 178; also David Williams, *Voltaire: Literary Critic,* in *Studies on Voltaire and the Eighteenth Century,* 48 (Geneva, 1966), p. 65.

15. J. E. Spingarn, *Critical Essays of the Seventeenth Century* (Bloomington, 1957), 2:61–62.

16. Breitinger, *Critische Dichtkunst* (Zurich, 1740), 1:205–206. See Lars Gustafsson, "Det 'underbara' och sannolikhetskravet i 1700-talets litteraturestetik," *Samlaren,* 82 (1961), 121–124.

17. Gustafsson, "Det 'underbara,'" 112; Baumgarten's criterion for the employing of the "marvellous" was, according to notes from his lectures, "Wann die Vorstellungen so beschaffen sind, dass die Sinnlichkeit sogleich siehet, dass sie nicht möglich sind, so muss sie der schöne Geist zurücklassen" (cited in Gustafsson, "Det 'underbara,'" p. 114).

18. Ibid., p. 112.

19. Ibid., pp. 124–126; the interest in the mind and the creative process combined with the assumption that poetic truth is ultimately measured empirically led Breitinger, Hume and particularly Marmontel to observe that as long as "innocent peculiarities of manners" (Hume) were represented with historical fidelity, the modern reader through the imagination might experience them as probable.

20. Schönaich, *Hermann: Oder Das befreyte Deutschland* (Leipzig, 1751), p. xv.

21. Shaftesbury, *Characteristicks* (London, 1727), 2:195.

22. Hurd, "Dialogue on the Golden Age of Queen Elizabeth," in *Hurd's Letters on Chivalry and Romance,* ed. Morley (London, 1911), p. 56.

23. Alfred E. Longueil, "The Word 'Gothic' in Eighteenth-Century Criticism." *MLN,* 38 (1923), 456–457.

24. "Of the Origin of Romantic Fiction in Europe," in *The History of English Poetry* (London, 1774), 1:xxxi.

25. Beattie, *Works* (Philadelphia, 1809), 3:59–60.

26. This assumption produced its own problems, however. The discrepancies in the accounts of Odin, combined with the separation of "All-father" from Odin (a necessity if Nordic monotheism was to be a part of the myth) and the euhemeristic assumptions about mythology resulted in increasingly elaborate chronologies incorporating all the references in a rational sequence. A byproduct of this was that historians had to posit two or even three Odins in order to cover the time span. The definitive treatment was by P. F. Suhm, *Om Odin og den hedniske gudelære* (1771). Edward Gibbon remarked that the coupling of the migration with the myth of northern freedom might make a good epic poem, a suggestion adopted by the Swedish poet Pehr Henrik Ling in *Asarne* (1816–1833), one of his two colossal attempts to write the Swedish national epic. The confusion between the divine Æsir and the euhemerized Æsir became so great, however, that Ling had to put out a directory to the epic.

27. Duff, *An Essay on Original Genius, 1767,* ed. J. Mahoney (Gainesville, Fla., 1964), p. 267.

28. Blair, *Dissertation on the Poems of Ossian* (1763), p. 4. Blair too saw the earliest ages of society as the most "favorable to the poetical spirit," yet even in Percy and Herder the idea of the primitive poetry was undifferentiated, primitives assumed to be everywhere the same. See René Wellek, *The Rise of English Literary History* (Chapel Hill, 1941), p. 69.

29. Cf. Hansson, "Schillers bestämning av det naiva."

30. Schøning, *Norges riiges historie* (Sorö, 1771–1781), 2:96.

31. Martin Lamm, *Upplysningstidens romantik* (Stockholm, 1918), 1:466. Anton Blanck, *Den nordiska Renässansen* (Stockholm, 1911), pp. 368–378, discusses the relationship of Franzén's poem to Gray's "The Bard" and "The Progress of Poesy." On the history of the revision of "Creutz" see among others Paul V. Rubow, "Revision af det attende aarhundrede" in *Litterære studier* (Copenhagen, 1949), pp. 100–107. Text from Franzén's *Samlade dikter* (Örebro, 1867), 1:49–63.

32. Rubow, "Revision," p. 106.

33. W. K. Wimsatt, "The Structure of Romantic Nature Imagery," anthologized in *Romanticism and Consciousness*, ed. H. Bloom (New York, 1970), p. 79.

34. Lamm, *Upplysningstidens romantik*, 1:394.

35. Lessing, *Briefe, die neueste Literatur betreffend*, no. 48, in *Sämtliche Schriften*, ed. Lachmann (Stuttgart, 1882), 8:125–126.

36. Citations will be from *Johannes Ewalds samlede skrifter*, ed. Brix and Kuhr (Copenhagen, 1916), 3:19–84.

37. Balder has spared Hother's life, and Hother refuses to use the spear; Balder, beside himself, runs at Hother, but trips and falls on the spear. Even K. L. Rahbek, Ewald's most favorable critic, admitted that this was a blunder, but there was nothing else to do, since both characters were "exemplars of virtue."

38. Frye, "Myth, Fiction and Displacement," in *Fables of Identity* (New York, 1963), p. 35.

39. Cassirer, *An Essay on Man* (New Haven, 1944), p. 82.

40. Frye, *Fables*, pp. 130–137.

41. See Blanck, *Den nordiska Renässansen*, pp. 72, 368, on Gray's Bard as giving the definitive form to the character. Yet the Bard had had a long history prior to Gray in humanist social myth; see Frank L. Borchardt, *Germanic Antiquity in Renaissance Myth* (Baltimore, 1971), p. 170. Lohenstein had depicted the Bards as preservers of Teutonic monotheism, and English antiquarians also nationalized him in the attempt to establish their northern genesis. See Wellek, *Rise*, p. 126, and E. B. Howe, "The Idealised Bard of the Eighteenth Century," *Abstracts of Theses*, University of Chicago, Humanistic Series, VI (1927–1928), 367–371. That the death of the Bard signifies the passing of the Nordic golden age was made explicit by Victor Hugo in his "Les derniers bardes" (1819); "Vous ne reviendrez plus, beaux jours, siècles prospères!" (*Oeuvres poétiques*, ed. Albouy, I, 163).

42. "Towards Defining an Age of Sensibility," in *Fables*, p. 135.

43. Blanck, *Den nordiska Renässansen*, p. 72.

44. See Percy's "Essay on the Ancient Minstrels in England"; Percy, however, did not consider these primitive songs to be "true poetry" but interesting barbaric creations.

45. Scott, *Works* (Edinburgh, 1833), 6:37.

46. Ibid., 6:39.

CHAPTER 7

1. Citations from the Ossianic poems will be from the editions of *Fingal* (London, 1762) and *Temora* (London, 1763).

2. See Donald M. Foerster, *Homer in English Criticism*, Yale Studies in English, 105 (New Haven, 1947), 7, 59.

3. Percy, *Five Pieces of Runic Poetry* (London, 1763), pp.x–xi.

4. In Germany, the analogy was to the lost *Lieder* of Charlemagne (Denis); in Scandinavia, to the noble spirit of the sagas (Blicher).

5. See chapter 11 in *De la littérature*, "Literature of the North," in *Madame de Staël on Politics, Literature, and National Character*, trans. and ed. Monroe Berger (New York, 1964), pp. 191–192.

6. *Madame de Staël*, p. 193.

7. Cited in Anton Blanck, *Den nordiska Renässansen* (Stockholm, 1911), p. 260.

8. *Carl Gustaf af Leopolds samlade skrifter* (Stockholm, 1833), 5:14. Ironically, Leopold himself was assimilated into the Nordic muse (probably because of his tragedy *Oden*), and to indicate what strange bedfellows a mythic world can encompass, in 1821 the Swedish Academy gave its Grand Prize to a poem on "The World of Genius," which asked: "When your soul with painful exultation / Through the mist the Æolian harp does hear, / . . . Do you not sense then Ossian, . . . / Does your heart not sign for Leopold?" Cited in Theodor Hasselqvist, *"Ossian" i den svenska dikten och litteraturen* (Malmö, 1895), p. 101.

9. See Martin Lamm, *Upplysningstidens romantik* (Stockholm, 1918), 1:444

10. "The Passions" ("Passionerna"), 1st song. See also Hasselqvist, *"Ossian"*, pp. 79–80.

11. See Eugen Ehrmann, *Die bardische Lyrik im achtzehnten Jahrhundert* (Halle, 1892).

12. For a survey, R. Hamel, "Die Bardendichtung," in *Deutsche National-Literatur*, ed. Kürschner (Berlin and Stuttgart, n.d.), 48:i–xviii.

13. *Sämmtliche Werke*, ed. Suphan (Berlin, 1877), 1:173.

14. *SW*, 5:160.

15. Erwin Kircher, "Volkslied und Volkspoesie in der Sturm- und Drangzeit," *Zeitschrift für deutsche Wortforschung*, 4 (1903), 41, where he describes the "Einbürgerung des Volksliedbegriffs."

16. Percy, *Reliques*, p. 8. Herder's description of *Volkspoesie* as an expression of nature became an imperative: *Volkspoesie* should be an expression of nature; the literary conventions of nature descriptions, however, were antithetical to Herder's organic concept of poetry. See Kircher, "Volkslied," 34–42.

17. *Iris*, 5:129; for this, and other examples of the primitive as it appeared in "ladies' magazines," see Kircher, "Volkslied," p. 34.

18. Kircher, "Volkslied," p. 55.

19. Ibid., p. 6.

20. In 1772 Goethe said that the naive poets sang "like a bird in the air"; Jacobi picks up the simile in 1775, applying it to the German Minnesänger. The Bards, however, use the same image to describe their own poetry: Kretschmann, in the "Vorrede über das Bardiet" describes Bardic songs as "like the magnificent song of the bird in the forest" (Kircher, p. 33).

21. Denis, *Ossian und Sineds Lieder* (Vienna, 1784), 4:lxxxi.

22. Ibid., 4:lxxxv.

23. Text in *DNL*, 54:289–302.

24. Blanck, *Den nordiska Renässansen*, p. 141.

25. "So weit war der Skalde gekommen, und da der Leser nun mit einem gewissen Enthusiasmus für die kriegerischen Thaten der Alten und für ihre rauhe Sitten eingenommen ist, so weiss der Dichter, den Leser durch eine vortreffliche Wendung zu erinnern, dass die itzigen sanften Sitten und die itzige ruhigere Lebensart, weit vorzüglicher sey" *Allgemeine deutsche Bibliothek*, 5, no. 1 (1767), 213.

26. Blanck, *Den nordiska Renässansen*, pp. 158–159; Rudolf Tombo, *Ossian in Germany* (New York, 1901), pp. 99–101.

27. Text in *DNL*, 47:140.

28. Text in *DNL*, 47:4–5.

29. Blank, *Den nordiska Renässansen*, pp. 151–155, discusses this and other examples of Klopstock's inability to assimilate into his poems a subject matter distinctively "Nordic." It was to just this "plug-in" view of mythology's role in poetry that later poets and critics were to raise vehement objections.

30. Text in *DNL*, 48:53–146. This speech is from scene xi; Lessing's comment in a letter to Nicolai, 4 August 1767.

31. The "fictions" in the *Bardiet*, Klopstock states, "sich sehr genau auf die Sitten der gewählten Zeit beziehn" (p. 53). He assumes that the Bards must have been the composers of the historical *Bardieten,* since one manuscript of *Germania* reads that the Germans sang not *barriti* but *barditi*.

32. *DNL*, 48:65.

33. Denis, *Ossian und Sineds Lieder*, 4:lxxxix, xci.

34. Text in *DNL*, 48:325–369.

35.   So leben sie ein selig Leben.
      Der Wald, das Feld, die Quelle geben
      Genug für morgen und für heut.
      . . . .
      O Rom, hohnlächelnd niedersehen
      Auf unsre Hütten her:
      Hast du viel Glück? Wir haben mehr! (339–340)

36. Ehrmann, *Die bardische Lyrik,* pp. 36–38, gives other instances of the use of the echo effect by the Bards.

37. Ehrmann, *Die bardische Lyrik,* p. 50.

38. Hamel, "Die Bardendichtung," p. xvi.

39. *DNL,* 48:77.

40. *Allgemeine deutsche Bibliothek,* 17 (1779), 451.

41. Frye, "Towards Defining an Age of Sensibility," in *Fables of Identity* (New York, 1963), p. 137. Hamel touches upon the mythic aspect of the Bardic movement when he comments that their poetry "ob sie sich gleich mit Kostümen vergangener Tage drapierte, [wird] selbst ein Bild ihrer eigenen Zeit, und kann nichts anderes werden" (*DNL,* 48:xi).

42. *Allgemeine deutsche Bibliothek,* 17 (1779), 454.

43. See Cassirer's essay "Thorild und Herder," *Theoria,* 7 (1941), 75–92.

44. *Der neue teutsche Merkur* (Nov., 1800), 168–192.

45. Ibid. (Dec. 1800), 292–293.

46. Herder, in theory at least, was willing to let Ossian's merit be independent of Macpherson's role, but he never doubted the authenticity of the poems.

47. G. J. Adlerbeth, commenting upon the propriety of using Nordic subject matter in Swedish literature, said "I would like to support my idea by noting that Ossian's songs could be the object of our era's acclaim and admiration if it were decided whether Herr Macpherson were no more than a translator (*Adlerbeths poëtiska arbeten,* 1803, 2:134).

48. Pinkerton, *Inquiry,* 2:83–86.

49. Ibid., 2:85.

50. Ibid., 2:86.

51. Pinkerton, *Dissertation,* p. 184.

52. Geijer, "Betraktelser i afseende på de nordiska myternas användande i skön konst," *Samlade skrifter* (Stockholm, 1875), 1:176.

CHAPTER 8

1. Gräter dedicated his *Nordische Blumen* (Leipzig, 1789) to Suhm. In *Iduna und Hermode,* 1 (1812), his "Chöre der Barden vor der Hermannschlacht" is described as "an experiment" (18–19). Ling, in the Introduction to his *Gylfe* (1814), sees the essence of myth as being a consciously created allegory. See Erik Wallén, *Studier över romantisk mytologi i svensk litteratur* (Malmö, 1923), p. 97; in Ling's *Eddornas sinnebildslära* (*Samlade arbeten,* Stockholm, 1866, II, 323), he describes the Eddas as having been "thought out and developed."

2. Atterbom and Geijer both objected to the unpoetic abstraction in Ling. See Wallén, *Romantisk mytologi,* p. 101.

3. In the 1833 version of *Asarne,* Ling reworked the early parts to splice in romantic ideas of longing and synthesis, but the revision is quite superficial. See Hilma Borelius, *Lings Asarne* in *Till Per Henrik Lings minne.* Lunds Univ. Årsskrift, N.F. pt. 1, 9, no. 6 (Lund, 1913), 184ff.

4. Though we have confined ourselves here to the specific figure of the Nordic bard, M. H. Abrams sees "the persona of a bard who present, past, and future sees, and who undertakes the theme of mankind's journey back toward his spiritual home, which will be at once a paradise and golden age of peace after conflict, and of integration after severance" as a common Romantic device. See *Natural Supernaturalism* (New York, 1971), p. 225.

5. Text in Geijer's *Samlade skrifter* (Stockholm, 1875), 1:219–225.

6. Anton Blanck, *Geijers götiska diktning* (Uppsala, 1918), p. 170. Gray's Bard survived as myth, in that it was often cited as "realistic": in Sweden, Livijn writes to Hammarsköld in 1803, "I have never seen a more successful imitation of the old Goths than . . . "The Bard" . . . You can think you're hearing Ossian's harp sound" (Rudolf Hjärne, *Dagen före drabbningen eller nya skolan och dess män,* Stockholm, 1882, p. 59).

7. The five *Iduna* poems provide *in nuce* the spectrum of the Nordic past's mythic images. We have discussed "Odalbonden"; in addition to "The Last of the Skalds," Geijer wrote "The Last of the Warriors," "The Viking," and "Manhem." "Manhem" is a general praise of Sweden's primal greatness; the other four illustrate the dual nature of the myth: the warrior/skald, the Viking/*odalbonde.* See chap. 9.

8. Atterbom, in his review of *Iduna* (*Phosphoros,* 2:1811), says Geijer's poems are not just imitations but a "collective expression of an archetypal Nordic nature . . . form and essence are *one*" (p. 178). In the *Poetisk kalender* (1816), pp. 11f., Atterbom recalls Rudbeck (with a veneer of Schubart, *Ansichten von der Nachseite der Naturwissenschaft*) and asserts that the North was the historical site of the golden age.

9. In modern myth, Eliade notes, there is a conflict between the archaic apprehension of time and the modern, linear theory; reason demands linear, historical time; but "the desire to find a meaning and a transhistorical justification for historical events has its roots in myth." See *Cosmos and History,* trans. Willard R. Trask (New York, 1954), pp. 141, 146.

10. R. G. Collingwood, *The Idea of History* (New York, 1956), p. 79.

11. Cf. Voltaire, *Essai sur les moeurs,* chap. 197; *Oeuvres,* 18:425.

12. The faith in the symbol liberated the artist (and the scientist) from the bond to empirical nature, but, as Paul de Man shows, "The nostalgia for the object has become a nostalgia for an entity that could never, by its very nature, become a particularized presence." See "Intentional Structure of the Romantic Image," in *Romanticism and Consciousness,* ed. Harold Bloom (New York, 1970), p. 76. On Goethe's opposition to Newton, see Erich

Heller, "Goethe and the Scientific Truth," in *The Disinherited Mind* (New York, 1959), pp. 4–34.

13. "The Drunken Boat," anthologized in *Perspectives in Contemporary Criticism*, ed. S. N. Grebstein (New York, 1968), pp. 351–352.

14. Cf. Bengt Algot Sørensen, *Symbol und Symbolismus in den ästhetischen Theorien des 18. Jahrhunderts und der deutschen Romantik* (Copenhagen, 1963); it was with Kant that "symbolisch" was first contrasted to "diskursiv" (p. 16).

15. Alfred North Whitehead, *Science in the Modern World* (New York, 1925), p. 24.

16. John B. Bury, *The Idea of Progress* (New York, 1932), pp. 21–22. Bury points out, however, that these two elements, one based upon faith in human inquiry, the other in a mythic process, would later be combined.

17. Abrams, *Natural Supernaturalism*, p. 217; Paulus Svendsen, *Gullalderdrøm og utviklingstro* (Oslo, 1940), p. 146.

18. Svendsen, *Gullalderdrøm*, p. 149.

19. Collingwood, *Idea of History*, pp. 98–99.

20. Sørensen, *Symbol und Symbolismus*, pp. 58–59.

21. In the *Ideen zur Philosophie der Geschichte der Menschheit* (1784–1791), Herder sees history as a process of the development of reason (through Providence; cf. Bury, n. 16 above), but does not insist on a universal human nature; each culture develops differently (Collingwood, *Idea of History*, p. 91).

22. Elfriede Lämmerzahl, *Der Sündenfall in der Philosophie des deutschen Idealismus* (Berlin, 1934), p. 52.

23. See Frederik Böök, *Esaias Tegnér* (Stockholm, 1917), I, chap. 3, 6: "Den filosofiska bakgrunden til Svea. Fichte och det götiska," and Wallén, *Romantisk mytologi*, pp. 125, 128.

24. Lämmerzahl, *Der Sündenfall*, p. 66.

25. Schelling, *Sämmtliche Werke*, ed. K. F. A. Schelling (Stuttgart, 1856–1861), 1:8, 342, protests against the "world-as-a-dream" theme in Fichte; in the "Ideen zu einer Philosophie der Natur," Schelling insists on the identity of the system of nature and the system of our mind (ibid., 1:2, 39); by 1800, Schelling develops this into a full break with Fichte in the *System des transcendentalen Idealismus*.

26. It is just this interest in electricity, galvanism, and magnetism that distinguishes Schelling from Fichte. See Holger Frykenstedt, *Atterboms livs- och världsåskådning* (Lund, 1951), p. 171.

27. For Schelling, the development of the absolute synthesis in various sequences is history (*Sämmtliche Werke*, 1:3, 598).

28. Ibid., 1:5, 289–295.

29. The first spontaneous act began the fall from the Absolute, and history

will end with the "reign of Reason," the disappearance of spontaneity (ibid., 1:439, n.1 and 1:3, 589). The process of history is characterized as a fall away from the Absolute (man's Iliad) and a return (man's Odyssey) (ibid., 1:6, 57). Hence the importance of the past as a symbolic revelation of the future.

30. The intellectual aspect of Schelling's thought was distasteful to Schlegel, Schleiermacher, and Novalis, who characterized the Absolute as Love. In a sense Hegel's attempt to give the Absolute a moral character while keeping the commitment to a transcendental reason may be seen as a reaction to what he called the "hollow abyss of the Absolute."

31. See Burton Feldman and Robert D. Richardson, *The Rise of Modern Mythology* (Bloomington, 1972), p. 317.

32. Good and evil are not innately opposed, but became so in the process of the self-revelation of the Absolute (*Sämmtliche Werke,* 1:7, 407); evil is a product of profane time, not sacred time.

33. "In der obersten Wissenschaft ist alles eins und ursprünglich ver-knüpft, Natur und Gott, Wissenschaft und Kunst, Religion und Poesie, und wenn sie in sich alle Gegensätze aufhebt, steht sie auch mit nichts anderem nach aussen in wahrhafter oder anderer Entgegensetzung, als welche die Unwissenschaftlichkeit, der Empiricismus, oder eine oberflächliche Lieb-haberei, ohne Gestalt und Ernst, machen mögen" (ibid., 1:5, 279–280).

34. Paul Collins Hayner, *Reason and History, Schelling's Concept of His-tory* (Leiden, 1967), pp. 65–70.

35. Feldman and Richardson, *Rise of Modern Mythology,* p. 327.

36. *Om Odin og den hedniske gudelære og gudstieneste udi norden* (Copenhagen, 1771).

37. See Amos Leslie Willson, *A Mythical Image: The Ideal of India in German Romanticism* (Durham, N.C., 1964).

38. See for instance Görres, *Mythengeschichte der asiatischen Welt* (1810), where he considers the unity of all religions as proved.

39. See Sørensen, *Symbol und Symbolismus,* pp. 55–70: "Herders Theorie des 'Natursymbols.' "

40. In Geijer's review of Nyerup's Edda in *Iduna,* Norse mythology is interpreted in idealistic terms, and is on the same plane of truth as Christianity. In his essay "De nordiska myternas användande i skön konst," *Samlade skrifter* I, 175–199, Geijer says that the Nordic spirit cannot be imitated but must be expressed internally (pp. 198–199).

41. Fritz Strich, *Die Mythologie in der deutschen Literatur von Klopstock bis Wagner* (Halle, 1910), II, 353.

42. "Soll das höchste heilige immer namenlos und formlos bleiben, im Dunkel dem Zufall überlassen?" (*Prosaische Jugendschriften,* ed. Minor, II, 357–358).

43. Gräter, the Grimms and Fouqué were exceptions. Though Schelling

and Schlegel knew nothing of Norse mythology, some of those who did coupled the dynamic view of time-as-drama with the fact of Odin's migration; in Denmark, N. F. S. Grundtvig embodied the myth of history as drama in Nordic terms in *Scandinavia's Mythology*.

44. Wallén, *Romantisk mytologi*, p. 135.

45. Theodor Haering, *Novalis als Philosoph* (Stuttgart, 1954), chap. 11: "Der Begriff des 'Magischen' bei Novalis," pp. 364–381.

46. In *Philosophie und Religion* (1804), Schelling sees myth and religion expressing philosophy's deepest thoughts; through philosophy, feeling and faith can be elevated to systematic knowledge.

47. Sørensen, *Symbol und Symbolismus*, p. 260.

48. "Svar paa H. Capt. Abrahamsons Recension over mine nordiske Digte (1808)," in *Oehlenschlägers digterværker og prosaiske skrifter*, XXV (Copenhagen, 1854), 131, 147–148.

49. *Phosphoros* (Dec., 1810), 313.

50. Atterbom's main problem was to Schellingize Dalin, but since Ast in his *System der Kunstlehre* had already Schellingized the Trinity, Atterbom was able to use this triad to incorporate Dalin's earlier explication. See Wallén, *Romantisk mytologi*, p. 62.

51. *Phosphoros* (1811), 183.

52. For example, in Atterbom's essay "On Philosophy and Its Relation to Our Time" in *Svea*, 12 (1828), 230, where he declares that the "new philosophy" will not be the same as religion, but a synthesis of the sundering of knowledge stemming from the Fall, of Abraham and Plato.

53. *Svensk litteratur-tidning* (1817), particularly cols. 117–121.

54. Geijer's *Samlade skrifter*, I: 2, 55–56.

55. Greta Hedin, *Manhemsförbundet*, Göteborgs Högskolas Årsskrift, 34 (Göteborg, 1928), p. 206.

56. Abrams, *Natural Supernaturalism*, pp. 12, 190–191.

CHAPTER 9

1. Schelling, *Sämmtliche Werke*, ed. K. F. A. Schelling, (Stuttgart, 1856–1861), IV, 718. In the "Ideen zu einer Philosophie der Natur," Schelling insists on the identity of the system of nature and the system of our mind (ibid., I, 2, 39); by 1800, he developed this into a full break with Fichte's subjectivism in the *System des transcendentalen Idealismus*.

2. Eighth lecture; *Henrich Steffens indledning til philosophiske forelæsninger* (Copenhagen, 1968), p. 138.

3. See Carl Roos, "Ohlenschlæger og Ossian. til forklaring af et sted i Guldhornene," *Danske studier* (1951), 71–80.

4. Text in *Adam Øhlenslaeger Digte* 1803 (Copenhagen, 1966), pp. 69–74.

5. Steffens, following Schelling, sees that "the contrast between the old religiosity and the new can be characterized as Fate and Providence" (Eighth lecture, *Indledning*, p. 129).

6. Greta Hedin, *Manhemsförbundet*, Göteborgs Högskolas Årsskrift, 34 (Göteborg, 1928), 89. In his "Svar paa Hr. Capt. Abrahamsons Recension over mine nordiske Digte (1808)," in *Oehlenschlägers digterværker og prosaiske skrifter*, XXV (Copenhagen, 1854), he says, "A mythological fable stands *closer* to me than a historical act. The former is based in eternal nature, the latter in bygone time" (148).

7. "Svar paa Abrahamson," p. 130.

8. He would be following Herder in this (*Sämmtliche Werke*, ed. Suphan, XIV, 384–385), a couching of Goethe's contrast between paganism and Christianity in Gothic terms.

9. "Svar paa Abrahamson," pp. 147–148.

10. *Den dobbelte Eros* (Copenhagen, 1966), p. 70.

11. N. F. S. Grundtvig, *Værker i udvalg,* ed. Georg Christensen and Hal Koch (Copenhagen, 1940), I, 147.

12. As no other, Grundtvig broke away from classical models of the golden age as a time of peace and desirable tranquility. See Hans-Joachim Mähl, *Die Idee des goldenen Zeitalters im Werk des Novalis* (Heidelberg, 1965), pt. 1: Herkunft und Geschichte der Idee des Goldenen Zeitalters seit dem Altertum, pp. 11–252.

13. *Værker i udvalg,* I, 153. Atterbom thought the same; defending his "Skaldarmal," he wrote to Lorenzo Hammarsköld in 1811, "I do not start from a dead literalness; my goal is to restore Scandinavia's lost imagination" (letter in Erik Wallén, *Studier över romantisk mytologi i svensk litteratur,* Lund, 1923, p. 65).

14. *Udvalgte skrifter,* ed. Holger Begtrup (Copenhagen, 1904), I, 353.

15. *Grundtvig og romantiken* (Copenhagen, 1947), pp. 61–71.

16. Flemming Lundgreen-Nielsen, *N. F. S. Grundtvig: Skæbne og forsyn* (Copenhagen, 1964), p. 21.

17. Tangkiær says, "Look—you have Will, as every child of Earth. / Over *that* I have no control; do what you will" (*Yrsa,* lines 94–95).

18. Lundgreen-Nielsen, *Skæbne og forsyn,* p. 167.

19. Ibid., pp. 24–25.

20. Grundtvig later commented about the "Masked Ball," "I let the words stand to *my shame* and as a witness to what a man who, though he believed in Christ, could bring himself to say" (*Værker i udvalg,* I, 147).

21. Lundgreen-Nielsen, *Skæbne og forsyn,* p. 168.

22. Commentary to "Skaldarmal," *Phosphoros* (1811), p. 8.

23. Wallén, *Romantisk mytologi,* p. 147. More typical of Atterbom are his poems on "The Flowers."

24. Wallen, *Romantisk mytologi,* p. 174.

25. Anton Blanck, *Geijers götiska diktning* (Stockholm, 1918), p. 117.

26. Geijer, *Samlade skrifter* (Stockholm, 1875), I, 146ff.

27. Blanck, *Geijers götiska diktning,* p. 440.

28. Bengt Henningson, *Geijer som historiker* (Stockholm, 1968), p. 215.

29. Ibid., p. 214.

30. This contrast is borne out formally, for the more violent Viking speaks in a modified ballad-stanza, while the *odalbonde* speaks more in the gnomic style of "Hávamál."

31. Holger Frykenstedt, "Geijers Thorild och kritiken mot den tyska idealismen," *Geijerstudier* (Uppsala, 1958), p. 43.

32. Letter cited in Otto Sylwan, "Tegnérs Fritiofs Saga," *Edda,* 10 (1919), 218.

33. As in Geijer and Oehlenschläger, the theme is developed formally: the duality is emphasized in chap. 1 ("Fritiof and Ingeborg"), and told with ballad stanzas, as is the burning of Balder's Temple. "Reconciliation," however, is done in hexameters, with a connotation of the discipline and restraint the hero attains.

34. Though Oehlenschläger had relatively little religious commitment to the Nordic past, and used Nordic subject matter for many years, he too moved away from idealism as a background for his works. See his letter to H. C. Ørsted, 1807, cited in Frederik Böök, *Esaias Tegnér* (Stockholm, 1917), I, 286.

35. Robert Tucker, *Philosophy and Myth in Karl Marx* (Cambridge, England, 1971), p. 219.

CONCLUSION

1. Trans. Joseph Ward Swain (New York, 1965).

2. "The Hartford Heresies," *Time* (10 Feb. 1975), p. 47.

3. *Man in the Modern Age,* trans. E. and C. Paul (London, 1951), p. 183.

4. 2nd ed. (Chicago, 1900).

INDEX

Adam, 80
Adlerbeth, G. J., 214n47
"Allfather": as kenning for Odin, 89,
  210n26; as evidence for nordic
  monotheism, 106, 132; in Grundtvig,
  161, 162; in Tegnér, 167
Almquist, C. J. L., 155
Annius of Viterbo. *See* Pseudo-Berosus
Archetype: Jungian, 22; in social myth,
  61; duality in nordic, 71–76 *passim,*
  91, 92, 96–97, 100, 122–23, 137,
  143–44, 153, 157, 160–61, 164–65,
  166–68. *See also* Paradigms
Arminius (Hermann), 64, 69–70, 74,
  130–31, 132
Astronomy, 18, 44. *See also* Brahe,
  Copernicus, Galileo, Kepler
Atterbom, P. D. A.: and Aurora Society,
  154–55; "Skaldarmal" commentary,
  154, 163; and Fichte, 163; on Geijer,
  215n8; also 138, 144, 163–64, 166,
  168
Augustine, Saint: time in, 18, 35, 38;
  synthesis of myth and reason in, 44,
  47–48, 54; and paradox, 45; figural
  history in, 48; as source for conversion
  theology, 50; *translatio imperii* in, 64
Aurora Society, 144, 154, 156, 157, 163

Baden, Jacob, 99, 100
Balder, 78, 112–14, 153, 159, 160,
  211n37
Baptism, 50–51
Bard, 116–18, 126, 140, 211n41, 215n4.
  See also Naive experience
Bardic movement, 125–35, 140
Bartholin, Thomas, 71–77, 203n45
Basel, Council of, 74
Baumgarten, Alexander Gottlieb, 106,
  209n17
Beattie, James, 108
Becanus, Johannes Goropius, 201n29
Biörner, E. J., 80

Blair, Hugh, 109, 123
Bodmer, Johann Jakob, 105
Boulanger, Nicholas-Antoine, 102–3,
  108
Brahe, Tycho, 62
Breitinger, Johann Jakob, 105

Cædmon, story of, 34
Celtis, Conrad, 66, 201n25
Chiliastic myths, 63, 173–74, 199n9,n10
Christ, 46–47
Chronology, 68, 87
Clovis, 49
Cluverius, Phillippus, 69
Communal myth, 171
Concrescence, principle of, 11, 13,
  16–17, 26, 43–44
Condorcet, Marquis de, 104
Conversion, 26, 49–53, 53–55
Copernicus, Nicholas, 61, 62, 199n3
Council of Nicea, 47
Creation-myth: Babylonian, 12, 14;
  Norse, 27, 30, 38, 43, 55; Hebraic,
  189–90n25
Criticism, literary, 6–7, 21–22

Dalin, Olof, 80–82, 94, 95
Daniel, Bishop of Winchester, 53–54, 57
Demythologizing: of mythic symbol, 3;
  of communal myths, 8; and "terror of
  history," 14–15; latent in modern
  myth, 15, 42; conversion technique,
  42; and broken myth, 48–49; of
  Swedish Gothicism, 78–81; of Bardic
  movement, 134–38; also, 2, 6, 10, 25,
  171, 189n19, 190n28
Denis, Michael, 123, 127–28, 132,
  133–34
Diderot, Denis, 93
Displacement: in modern myth, 19;
  defined, 25; in "Völuspá," 29; in
  sagas, 29–41; and poetic imagery,
  83–84; parody as form of, 79–80, 84;